Foreword

>>>>>>>>

Here at last is comfort for the people who know in their souls that the cow is an essential part of our heritage, culture and ecology. Frank Jacobs has written *Cattle and Us, Frankly Speaking* (or, *Cattle Come in Five Sexes*) for people who hear the strident messages of the eco-warriors and doomsayers, particularly in relation to the beef industry, and wonder where the truth lies. This book eschews "political correctness" and tells it like it is – and it's fun to read.

Frank Jacobs has been around the Canadian beef cattle industry, as participant and observer, for a long time. His knowledge of the science and practice of agriculture and his standing in the community of cattlemen are widely recognized: he has been named Cattleman of the Year by the Canadian Cattlemen's Association, admitted to the Alberta Agriculture Hall of Fame and made a Fellow of the Agricultural Institute of Canada. Besides, he's an Agriculture graduate from the University of Alberta, so he must be good!

When Frank told me some years ago that one day he planned to write this book, I resolved to keep offering equal measure of encouragement and irritation until he did. He is uniquely qualified to write what really needed to be written. We hear so much bad news about the impact of science on agriculture, often exaggerated, sometimes maliciously.

The people most able to refute the bad news, when it would be appropriate to do so, are scientists. However, with their scientific training comes a thoughtful uncertainty ("Although it seems likely that the earth revolves around the sun, we cannot completely discount the possibility of a fundamental flaw in our calculations . . ."). This is too easily misinterpreted as prevarication. No wonder the public remains skeptical.

This book does not observe the niceties of scientific objectivity. You will be left in no doubt where Frank Jacobs stands on the issues, but it does explain what leads him to that position and does so with a clarity that should be envied by most practicing scientists.

Here we find him in his element, probing and analyzing, heaping scorn where it should be heaped, always softening it with humor. Frank Jacobs' love of cattle, familiarity with cattlemen's lore, skill and experience as a writer and knowledge of agriculture, blended with his own unique wit, make this book an excellent read. But watch out: its educational. Yur gonna learn stuff!

Mick Price, PAg, PhD
Professor of Livestock Growth and Meat Production
University of Alberta

Contents

≻≻≻≻≻≻

Financial support for Detselig Enterprises Ltd. 1993 publishing program is provided by the Department of Communications, Canada Council and the Alberta Foundation for the Arts, a beneficiary of the Lottery Fund of the Government of Alberta

Acknowledgments

A pathological procrastinator never gets anything done without some good-willed prodder/encouragers to goad him along his way. This book would never had got started without a regular and friendly question repeated over several years from Sherm Ewing, "How far along are you on your book?" This persistent query, along with the successful writing and publishing of Sherm's own book *The Range* – while I twiddled my thumbs – did the trick. I got at the job. Keeping me at it over three years was a regular prod/push/pull from Mick Price, the author of the introduction. I am indebted to both Sherm and Mick.

I also owe thanks to Mary Mahoney-Robson who gave me ego-building cheer and encouragement when the book was finished and needed a publisher.

I am especially grateful to Tom Eggertson who decided the book was important enough to publish, and saw that the job was done.

And to all the wonderful people in the cattle business who have been my teachers, mentors, companions, critics and good friends for three-quarters of a century, I say thank you. This book is dedicated to you, for without you – and your cattle – I would have had nothing to write about.

About the book Cattle and Us, Frankly Speaking . . .

This book, like a cow's stomach, has four parts. There is a sort of logic to the way the divisions follow each other, but they can be read in any order.

Part One. Everybody I know is interested in sex – some in a strictly clinical sense, others as a comparative-zoological phenomenon, many out of simple curiosity, most because it is one of the great mysteries of life and affects us all. The first four chapters are about the vital functions of bovines and sex – how, why and when the cows do (or do not) do it and why this is significant to mankind. No matter how much or how little you know about cattle, you will chuckle as you increase your understanding of not only cattle but of yourself, your friends and your acquaintances.

Part Two. This part is written for everyone who has eaten a hamburger, gone to a Western movie, supported 4H, sung a cowboy song, dressed western, or dreamed of owning a ranch. If you have been to a purebred cattle sale or show, you will be right at home. Like the rest of the book, Part Two draws on the Old Testament Bible, mythology, societal systems of organization – families, tribes, kingdoms, churches and man's "dominion over the beasts *and* the fields." It is about heroes and hero worship, tribal gods, Man as Horseman (from Attila to Ronald Reagan), the historic and modern ranch (and ranch family), how money is made and lost in the cattle business and how a remarkable new "religion," with beef cattle as "gods," developed in the Americas, Europe and Down Under. This sect has its own vestments (cowboy boots, shirts and hats), high priests (livestock auctioneers), money changers and scribes with their holy books.

This part also describes what happens on a ranch and what jobs have to be done during each month of the year. It reveals how, if you became a rancher, your talents and abilities will be challenged. You will discover how you may find fulfillment there, especially as you grow in expertise and competence and how the world beyond your fences will seek you out.

Part Three. These chapters describe dramatic changes in the cattle industry that occurred between 1954 and 1974. Science now has replaced a great deal of myth, and cattlemen are raising more efficient animals. Because of this revolution, you are eating leaner beef and paying less for it (adjusted for inflation, as the economists say). What startled traditional cattlemen and also city folk driving down country roads in the 1960s was the appearance of the huge European breeds –

Charolais, Simmental, Limousin and many others. As in other revolutions, there were great victories – and defeats. Much money was made and lost. For those in the business, it was an exciting time.

An important part of the continuing revolution results from "high-tech" advances in reproduction: artificial insemination, ova transplants, cloning and gene manipulation, now all grouped under the rubric "Genetic Engineering." The book describes how and when these techniques evolved, explains how they have changed beef production and suggests what may happen in the future because of them. When we start moving genes around, we have to consider morals and ethics, not just efficiency and profits.

Part Four. This is the very guts of the book – why it was written. If you are short of time, read these chapters first. The "eco-warriors" have spouted so much nonsense lately and preached so many convincing half truths that many people are confused.

In the book you will learn that the Amazon is not the "lungs of the world," that a meat-eater is a far better ecologist than a grain-eater, that without cattle (properly managed) grassland soils are changed to deserts by the plough, that soils lose fertility and structure under a tree cover and improve in fertility if covered by grass. You will come to understand that the combination of grain feeding and grass pasturage of cattle is a good use of resources – that in very few places on earth can grain be grown exclusively forever.

And you will be surprised to learn that a steer in a feedlot has entered a bovine "first world" of comfort, sanitation and health and is much better off than a "natural" beast which, without man's benevolent hand, would live in a "third world" of hunger, infection, infestation and predation. You likely don't believe that properly managed cattle herds on rangelands can improve the grass for elk and provide more game animals than would be the case if were "just wilderness." The last chapter tells how this can happen.

Does a cow's belching decrease the ozone layer? If she didn't eat that feed, it would rot on the ground or in a pond or be burned, or be eaten by another animal, even us. In any event, cow or no cow, it would decompose and in the process give off CO_2 and methane.

The cow does not, of course, provide all the answers to Planet Earth's problems, but she is a wonderful organism we can use to keep mankind living here for another thousand years.

PART ONE

Cattle and Their Sexes

Male and female He made them. So it is with almost all of us. It is with male and female terms we identify our friendly farm animals too, especially cattle.

But male and female tell only part of the story – either with ourselves or cattle. In cattle you will find that there are steers and oxen gomers and freemartins, spayed heifers and sweet-asses, proud-cuts and bullers (cows always in heat, usually because of ovarian cysts). Some sexes are produced "naturally," as our environmentalists would say, and others are a result of designing man working his way with them. Thus the subtitle on the cover of the book indicating five sexes may be an understatement.

As well as sexual *form* in cattle, we have created special *functions* for them – nurse cows, donor cows, recipient cows, milch cows, plow oxen, rodeo bulls, herd bulls, show cattle (three sexes), brood cows, boss cows, stockers and feeders. These can also be described according to reproductive condition – open, bred, dry (no milk), hot, barren, fertile, infertile, empty, pregnant. And by bodily condition: thin, fat, tired, sick, full, dry, thirsty, breedy, masculine, feminine, steery, stagy, humped-backed, dry-haired, patchy . . . the list could be much longer. You don't need a program to figure out many of these terms, but some, associated with cattlemen's peculiar beliefs, take time and instruction.

Cattle terminology is often untranslatable from English to any other language and even from one region of the world to another. A Texas rancher does not understand a Welsh hill farmer who says he favors "back-end calving." (The Welshman means his cows are bred to calve in the fall – the "back-end" of the year.) And some words just pass as is into other tongues with appropriate modification in pronunciation. For example, the Old Mexico *vaquero* (cowboy) becomes the New Mexico buckeroo (still a cowboy); in France, breeders keep their pedigrees in the Herd Book (pronounced "Aird Boook").

The story is told of the farmer who hitched his newly-bought prize bull to a plow and so condemned him to very hard labor. When a neighbor remonstrated at this abuse of such a valued animal, the farmer replied: "I'm teaching this cow-chaser that life isn't all romance!"

There is a great deal more than sex in the business of raising cattle, as shall be seen in the parts of this book following this part on sex. This part has four chapters – Cows; Bulls; The Neutral Zone; No Sex, Please!

Chapter One

Cows
>>>>>

So, let's look at the cow – the female among cattle. She may or may not be feminine but she is quintessentially female. Hers is a female life of getting pregnant, reproducing and lactating. Should she fail in any of these functions, her life is over and she goes to the packing plant. Of course she has to stay alive while performing her functions – any poor live cow is worth more than the best dead cow. We ask much of her: conceive, reproduce and lactate and she better do it efficiently, without wasting feed, getting sick or otherwise costing us money.

"Well . . . are ya' ready to start over?"

A good cow – big or little – is bred at 14 or 15 months of age. About 283 days later she calves.[1] If she's to keep her place in the herd, the cow has only 82 days to "clean" (shed all traces of the "afterbirth" or placenta, which usually "comes away" within hours but sometimes is retained for awhile), and get her ovaries, uterus and cervix back in working condition. She also has to reverse the flow of calcium from blood to bone, so that calcium can leave the bones and enter the bloodstream where it will travel to the udder to be incorporated into milk. She starts producing milk immediately, so this calcium reversal has to happen very quickly. If it doesn't, she will come down with milk fever, a deadly form of paralysis.

She also has to tell an ovary to crack out a follicle so she can begin "cycling" and thus have a ripe egg in a fallopian tube ready to be fertilized by sperm from a bull. Finally, she has to adjust her druthers to the point of accepting the rough and muscular attention and activities of the bull and she must be able to convey to him that, yes, she is ready, eager and waiting.

A vigorous and healthy cow may do all this in 40 or 50 (sometimes 30) days and so it is possible for her to "gain a month" if she is not too stressed. That is, she may calve a month earlier next year. If she's a two-year-old heifer, she's still growing and she is also milking, so she needs lots of good groceries. More than likely, a two-year-old will take her full 82 days, often longer, to get the rebreeding job done.

A mature cow of four years or older, in good condition and with lots of good feed, will cycle early. The cow's period is 21 days and is measured from standing heat to standing heat (the cow stands for the bull to mount.) If she is not in heat, she simply walks away – the classical turn-down common to all species, including ours. She stays in heat about 12 hours, during which she emits pheromones which attract all the bulls (including big husky calves) in the pasture and many of the steers as well as other cows that happen to be in heat, themselves. Some buller cows, who may cycle and get bred normally, respond to another cow in heat much like a bull, except that having mounted the victim, that's all there is to it. These are as close to lesbians as bovines get.

The cow in heat resembles Ulysses' wife Penelope, surrounded by avid and amoral suitors, or the young Scarlett O'Hara attended by her admirers. She will stand for all of them until the physical abuse gets to her and she decides she has had enough. Often as not, a bull will mount the cow several times. A large bull during a successful copulation may "put a hump in her back" and this painful situation usually tells her the game is well played and it's time to quit. From then on, she just keeps walking away from would-be paramours. Often as not, a bull will mount her several times, and the game is not over until his flagging flesh is unable to fulfill the demands of his eager spirit.

A friend of mine, who some years ago was a prominent politician as well as a successful rancher, was asked to speak to a group of bankers and economists. "You know what kinds of questions they asked," he said, as he described the meeting. "Not how I determined fixed costs, or my return on capital – nothing like that – but how many times a bull jumps a cow!"[2]

And now we must stop and say there are two kinds of cows – beef cows and dairy cows. They are so different in so many ways that they might as well be separate species. The friendly "all red and white" cow which a child loves with all his or her heart and which gives cream to eat with apple tart, is not the same kind of animal found in the herd of white-faced, cattle "lowing along the dusty trail." Not only are the cows different, but so are their owners and the "cattle religions" they embrace, the human social hierarchies which they support and the socio-economic philosophy which they engender.

Simply stated, dairy cows are kept primarily to produce milk, while beef cows raise calves which will eventually be sold as beef. We do eat dairy calves, too, usually when they are very young – that's what veal is. And all our milk cows (and bulls) end up as beef – often as hamburger. Our beef cows usually do produce milk, but usually just enough to raise a calf.

The dairy cow is bred aseptically and artificially: she almost never meets a bull, never suckles her calf and is milked twice a day by a cold, impersonal machine. The beef cow, on the other hand, is normally bred by a real live bull and raises her own calf, who comes to her warm side for refreshment and affection a dozen or more times a day. The dairy cow works much harder than her sister; every day she tucks into her capacious paunch 20 to 30 pounds (9 to 14 kilograms) of hay or grass, dry weight, and 100 to 130 lb. (45 to 60 kg) moist weight. And if she's spending her time down in the meadow where the grass is very lush and green, she may ingest up to 200 lb. (90 kg) of forage.

Meanwhile the dairyman has calculated how many additional calories his cow needs (both carbohydrates and protein) and he prepares up to 30 lb. (14 kg) of a grain-and-supplement mixture for her. In this feed are compounds of both calcium and phosphorus which are major components of both milk and bone. (Drink your milk; get your calcium.) She'll be on the milking string for about 10 months, during which time the machines will take from her udder up to six tons of milk, 10 or 12 tons in an especially productive cow. When she "freshens" she will produce between 60 and 120 or more pounds per day (28 to 55 kg) and just before she is "dried off[3]" she'll be down to 15 or 20 lb. per day (7 to 9 kg).

Then for about two months she will be dry, but will continue to eat a great deal of feed. So, by the time she freshens she will be carrying considerable fat on her back and mineral in her bones. It is in this condition – fat and sassy, her belly extended with a near-term calf, her udder engorged with yet-to-be-produced milk just before freshening – that the dairyman and the judges of dairy cattle consider her the most beautiful. If her owner is going to enter her in a show or fair, that's the best time for him to do it.

Her udder and teats are under great stress during lactation because of her tremendous workload, so they may get inflamed and infected. If they do, they will become the recipients of the most modern medical treatment. Veterinary medicine is always several years ahead of human medicine, for two reasons. First, it is dollar-driven – it pays to keep your cow producing, whereas many of us are quite cavalier in our approach to our own good health. Second, you can experiment with animals and prove a product useful and safe much faster than with humans. If the cow dies, it's a dollar loss, but if it's your loved one . . . ? The average dairy cow wears out quickly – after three to five years "on the line." She then augments the hamburger supply (though some go on to a ripe old age of 10 or 12).

Now let's look at the beef cow. She eats all the grass she can during the summer. But her milk output is only about one-fifth that of her dairy sister – 15, 20, perhaps 30 lb. (7 -14 kg) per day. And she nurses her calf only six or seven months. She attempts to adjust milk production to demand – a big aggressive calf will be constantly butting her udder for more milk, and she'll respond as best she can. But genetically she is programmed to limited milk production and many beef calves do not get as much milk as they would like. As long as the calf comes through the summer in a healthy and growthy condition, the cow has done her part.

It makes more sense for her to do something else with the available feed. All that beautiful, lush spring-and-summer grass provides more than enough nutrients to feed her, her nursing calf and the "new little stranger" in her womb. She's eating for three, but the feed is so abundant and her system so efficient, the extra calories have to go somewhere. They do – on her back. She'll gain back all the weight she lost during the previous cold winter, and in April and May when she was nursing her new calf and feed was still scarce.

In cattle country, fat is beautiful. What prettier sight than a field in October filled with fat cows trailing big, growthy calves!

The beef cow works the way nature intended, so she lasts twice as long as her dairy sister, usually staying in the herd for ten years. A very few last as long as twenty years.

The two types of cowmen gain different kinds of satisfaction: the dairyman is the operator, the man who manipulates nature and events to his advantage; the beefman works along with nature and gets his jollies from seeing everything happening in the way it is supposed to. It's much harder to be a good dairyman. Only a few share the temperament for it, but nearly everyone wants to be a cowboy and "run a few good Herefords" – or Angus or Charolais. Dairy cows are extremely demanding, while a beef herd will forgive quite a few mistakes. A dairyman goes broke fast if he doesn't meticulously cut the mustard, whereas a careless beef operator keeps on from year to year until he eventually runs out of grass or cattle or money, and often doesn't know how poorly he's doing. He still calls himself a rancher. Always there is someone with money or credit to buy him out, letting him retire with his pride intact.

The Mexicans have a little rhyme which explains this very nicely:

Con pasto, agua y dinero, quelquier bouey es ganadero.

It means that with plenty of grass, water and money, any ox can be a rancher. There is a double meaning here: As the *vaquero* recites this little poem under his breath, he will be thinking of the ineptitude of his *patron*. Why, even he, the unschooled *vaquero*, could run this *estancia* more efficiently than that ox of a patron. The second meaning hinges around the word *bouey* or ox. The implication here is that any of the steers on the range could do as good a job as the boss.

Racial background appears to influence the type of cattleman, for example, Dutchmen, Danes and Scots take to dairy cattle very well, Portuguese and Spaniards have century-old macho traditions of handling cattle.

In 1972, I visited a large *estancia* in southern Brazil, close to the Uruguayan and Argentinean borders. It was all pampas country. Great herds of beef cattle grazing on abundant grass, with skillful and colorful *gauchos* on beautiful horses in charge of them, as they had been for 300 years.

The owner ran three herds of beef cattle – Charolais, Brahman and Friesian (the North American Holstein-Friesian, commonly called Holstein). I was astounded to see the Holstein beef herd, because Holsteins are the super dairy breed. When I asked the owner why he was using dairy cattle as a beef herd, and if he was having any udder problems, he just shrugged his shoulders. He also ran a group of Friesians as a a a dairy herd, milking them morning and night and feeding the calves on milk replacer and calf meal.

Our group watched a late-afternoon episode with this herd. About five p.m., a group of gauchos gathered near the milking shed, which was open on all sides, with a tile roof, and steel stanchions running down the length of the shed. They prepared and drank their *maté*, a herbal tea which they consumed from special little gourds. Then they mounted their horses and galloped off across the pampas. Half an hour later they came back with a hundred Holstein cows running before them full-tilt, udders swinging from side to side, while the gauchos waved long rawhide ropes all around them. The cows rushed up to the stanchions, which closed on their necks in unison with a bang, and stood there trembling.

The cowboys dismounted from their horses and prepared a second round of *maté*. Meanwhile another group of men, probably the husbands of the milkers, approached the cows on foot and tied up their hind legs with rawhide ropes. They, too, then sat down and had their *maté*. Finally the milkers arrived: women, many of them with babies strapped to their backs, carrying pails. They were under the direction of a *major domo* who checked their work, measured the milk as it was carried to a large central tank and generally saw that things were done as they should be.

When the women were done, the rope-tying crew took off the rawhide ropes and the gauchos herded the cows back out onto the pampas.

Milk production was not impressive since cows handled in this manner just don't make or let down much milk. The owner was concerned about the low production. He had read about high milk yields in Canada and the U.S. and in an effort to emulate *quantos Americanos do Norte*, he was importing semen from Ontario with which to breed his cows artificially! Apparently he did not realize that improved genetics would not increase production one whit until the cows were gently handled as dairy cattle should be. Nor was that likely to happen because of macho personalities, social order and long-established custom.

Wonderful as the cow is at providing man with meat and milk and a host of marvelous by-products – everything from insulin to glue – we feel no kinship with her. As the poet said of the purple cow (which he had never seen) "I'd rather see than be one." More often than not, cow is a derogatory word when applied to humans. Call your girl friend cow-like, and, as the moderns say, you become history. All that bovine femaleness – conceiving, giving birth, lactating – is very biological but neither poetic nor romantic. Not so with the bull, as we shall see later.

In contemporary times, we may find amoral and insensitive men referring to not very lovely but eager and willing conquests as "heifers." It's not flattering. And if the young studs call them "cows," the suggestion is they're not worth seducing.

The Ancient Hebrew hero Samson said to his Philistine tormenters, "if ye had not plowed with my *heifer*, ye had not found my riddle."

The practice of using a beautiful woman to extract information from a besotted lover has since become a time-honored practice. The most recent victims (1987) were U.S. Marine Guards at the American Embassy in Moscow. But none of the great female lover-spies has even been referred to as a cow – Mata Hari, Christine Keeleter, and so on, have been anything but cow-like.[4]

The true role of the *cow* is economic – to produce milk and meat. Cattle as a whole, on the other hand, are part and parcel of a great mystique, as the following chapters reveal.

By the Way . . .

[1]The verb here is "to calve." She does not (grammatically) calve a calf; she simply calves. But for her owner or manager the operative verb is "to calve out." The object is not the calf but the cow; e.g., "This spring we calved out thirty cows." Sometimes the "out" part is only implied. Thus: "We're busy as hell, right in the middle of calving." Or, "We started calving last Wednesday." This is a verb that "comes" a lot. "How is your calving coming?" "Oh, we're coming pretty good." Or, "Oh, it's coming pretty good."

[2]The number of times a bull services a cow is a matter of supply and demand and individual proclivities. In a herd with several cows in heat at one time, a bull will "service" a cow only two or three times, perhaps only once. But if she is the only one in heat and his libido is keen, the game may be played longer and oftener. In AI studs, a bull may be "drawn" twice a week, with two ejaculations taken at each draw.

[3]A dairyman's dry cow has quit milking, her teats and udder are literally dry – no milk. A beef rancher's dry cow may also have quit milking, or she may be short of water. When he says, "Those cows are dry," he's worried. This condition usually happens on western ranges in the winter, when the open water is frozen and there is no snow.

[4]Horses are more sexy than cattle. The bed partners of one of our early King Georges were referred to by a member of the court as "Flanders Mares." To appreciate the analogy, think of the huge sorrel (blonde) Belgian draft horses, with massively muscled (and sweaty) hindquarters, which we see trotting around the show ring hitched to a beer wagon.

Chapter Two

Bulls

≻≻≻≻

The word is "bull." My mother, who was born in 1879 and was a young lady during the gay nineties, had difficultly saying it. In her day, nice people referred to "a gentleman cow" – just as some nice people today speak of "a lady dog," finding the mouthing of "bitch" too indelicate.

One can readily understand the reticence of nineteenth-century young ladies to discuss bulls. The good things that a cow did were obvious and were respectable – you put butter on your toast and milk on your porridge every morning. So it was genteel and proper for farmers to keep cows. And just as children had to have daddies (nice gentlemen), so those sweet little calves must have daddies, too: ergo, gentlemen cows.

Help! The . . . er . . . 'gentlemen cow' is out!"

And a bull is a true gentleman. If a cow shows no interest in his attentions, he quietly walks away.

Moreover, bulls are heroic. Nothing is more macho than a Spanish Fighting bull, except the matador who meets him in the arena of blood,

19

sand,[1] bravery and death. In 1972 I watched a bull fight in Madrid. Sitting two rows down from our group of Alberta ranchers were about 20 young women – 16 to 18 years old – from a girls' college in Kansas. Until that day they had never experienced the mystique of the bulls. Were they disgusted by the cruelty? Sickened by the blood? Not a whit. Their Mid-Western veneer of gentility was gone within minutes; *Los Toros* and their destroyers had completely bewitched them. With brazen voices, eyes transfixed, they cheered their raptors and tossed gloves, scarves, even notebooks into the ring.

But my rancher companions saw neither grace nor beauty in the spectacle. They became bored, left their seats and went down to see what happened to the bull carcasses which the mules (significantly sexless) hauled from the arena. They found the butchering of the expired Toro considerably less artful than his death and very unsanitary. Ranchers don't wince or flinch at an animal's pain; in fact, they inflict it routinely in branding, dehorning and castrating, but they see no point in making an animal suffer for no good purpose.

"And if you're going to kill the son of a bitch, for God's sake do it right," sums up a typical rancher's appraisal of a bullfight.

The young Mid-Western girls would have been offended by the rough handling, cutting and burning that takes place on a ranch in their own Big Bluestem country, but the sight, sounds and smells of the bullring touched primordial cords, which, since the time of Homer, have quickened and vibrated in woman as she beholds Man confronting Bull, or as Bull appears to her as Man, or Man as Bull. The ancient Greek legends have much to say about women and bulls. Consider the story of Europa and Zeus, and its sequel about Minos, Pasiphae, the Black Bull of Crete and the Minotaur. Once such legend goes like this.

One fine day, Zeus, (king of all the gods and father of many of them) looked out from Olympus and gazed upon the beautiful and earthly Europa, daughter of the King of Tyre. Now Zeus, who slept around profusely and prolifically with goddesses, nymphs, maidens, queens – whomever – decided that Europa was irresistible. He wooed her in the guise of a white bull. You may have seen the painting: there, clad in a diaphanous Greek gown, reclines Europa on the back of the great white bull as he carries her off to Crete. On her face is the transfixed gaze I saw three thousand years later on the face of a Kansas school girl at the bull fight in Madrid.

Zeus' fancies were fleeting; having had his way with Europa, he went on to other conquests. Meanwhile, Europa gave birth (nobody ever accused Zeus of being impotent) to Minos, who became King of Crete. He also assuumed the title of Judge of the Underworld (somewhat like Victoria proclaiming herself Empress of India).

Minos married Pasiphae, who was, of course, beautiful, amorous and vivacious. But Pasiphae loved another – not a man but the Black Bull of Crete. So great was her passion that she persuaded the marvelous craftsman and inventor Daedalus[2] to construct an artificial cow in which Pasiphae concealed herself.

After *that,* Pasiphae gave birth to the Minotaur, a horrible monster, half-bull and half-human who, among his other lusts, had a yen for eating young people. He devoured 20 virgins and 20 youths each year, sent over fresh from Athens. To keep some control over this awful creature, King Minos (husband of the unfaithful wife) had Daedalus construct the Labyrinth, where the Minotaur was imprisoned. (The great hero Perseus eventually slew the Minotaur, but that is another story.)

Centuries before King Minos was cuckolded by a bull, Egyptians had worshipped a bull god called Apis, a live bull. When an old Apis was reaching the end of his natural life span a search was instigated for his successor. This took some looking, for the new Apis had to have some special markings. david Attenborough, famed author and broadcaster, describes Apis in his book *The First Eden.* "He was black with a white inverted triangle on his brow. He had a pale patch shaped like a vulture with outstretched wings across his shoulders, a mark like a crescent moon on his flanks, and another the shape of a falcon which clasped his abdomen. His tail had double hairs, and beside his tongue was a black mark shaped like a scarab beetle." When found, the new Apis was led in Triumphant procession to his enthronement.

A contemporary of Apis was Nandi, a bull which was the pet or "familiar" of the Hindu god Vishnu. You will see statues of him, usually reclining and probably ruminating, in Hindu temples.[3]

To find the latest reincarnation of Apis, move several thousand years ahead, across the Atlantic to Austin, Texas. There he is in the football stadium, only now he is an ungainly steer called "Bevo." Complete with handlers ("priests"), he is paraded before fans ("worshippers"). They call him a mascot, but they have named their football gladiators after him: "The Longhorns."

So the ancient and outlandish can be brought up to date here and now in the strange world of cattle.

In modern times, however, the bull intrigues us as a sire rather than as a god. Let's take a look at his genes. In practical cattle genetics, the sexes are anything but equal. Every cow, if she is healthy and well-fed, has a calf every year.[4] Since she gives birth to only one calf per year, any one cow has little effect on the genetics of the species. In fact, her only significant contribution is through her sons – more about that later.

The bull, however, is at least half the herd in a genetic sense. Both in the wild state and under the control of man, a single bull may breed many cows and sire many calves. The head of a feral herd achieves and maintains a harem by fighting off rivals. So the most aggressive, powerful bull becomes husband and father of many. His genes shape the race.

On the domestic scene, man manipulates cattle genetics mainly through bulls. Parisien was the first Simmental bull (actually a Pie Rouge, the French version of the Swiss Simmenthaler) imported to North America. He left thousands of calves through the magic of AI (artificial insemination). Even naturally, a fertile bull could, through hand mating, leave 500 calves to claim his patrimony. Most range beef bulls, however, breed 20 to 40 cows a year, rarely for more than four years. This adds up to about 160 cows served. With a successful calf crop of 80 percent, that means a range bull may sire from 60 to 120 living calves (averaging perhaps 80) in his lifetime. A good fertile cow, meanwhile, will be lucky to drop[5] and raise ten calves; her average is eight.

Chances are that, among a bull's lifetime progeny, there will be a number of males that are even more aggressive and bigger and heavier than he is. In the wild state these become the natural herd-headers. So through the ages, bulls have become more aggressive, bigger and stronger until they reached physiological and morphological limits and the natural law of "regression towards the mean" took over. That means superlative members of any species, when mated together, will have some progeny as good as they are – perhaps a few even better. Although many will be somewhat above average, there will also be a large quota of ordinary Joes and Marys.

We see this with humans all the time: when the Agricultural Representative marries the District Nurse and they raise a family, many of their children (if it's a big family) will move up a few notches on the socio-economic scale. From the matings of this new-and-improved generation come Superior Court judges, MDs, senators and leaders of industry. And when these above-average people intermarry, they raise some super children (like themselves) but they also beget sons and daughters who just can't make it. Regression toward the mean – moving back to the average – thwarts them. Some alumni of Ivy League Universities contribute huge endowments to their alma maters with the hope that sons and daughters who aren't quite as bright as Mom and Dad will be given special consideration when admission lists are drawn up. This regression happens in all dynasties except perhaps those on TV.

Regression toward the mean – cattlemen call it "blood running out" – is the unseen enemy against which the cattle breeder must continually strive. It limits his success, particularly when his standards and selection procedures are based largely on myth rather than fact. For example, one early breeder believed it best to breed his oldest cows to his youngest bulls and vice versa. And until quite recently some serious breeders believed that a young (and therefore small) bull would sire smaller calves than a full-grown bull.

Thus the continual search by every cattle breeder for a new herd sire. He'll travel the continent, even the world, in his quest. He may buy a bull calf, a yearling, a two-year-old, perhaps a three-year-old or even an older bull. If he buys a young bull, he often dubs him his "junior herd sire" and will breed him experimentally to a fairly small group of females. If he likes the resultant calves, he'll call upon Junior for more activity next year. The second-string quarterback may soon replace the prime signal caller, or he may be quietly shipped off if he doesn't prove out. Sometimes one bull will appear to "nick" with certain cows but get only mediocre calves with others. He will be used on cows with which he nicks (A lot of myth in nicking, of course, it's part of Cattle Religion).

Running in pasture (as distinct from range), a bull may successfully serve (in bovlangia, to serve[8] is equivalent with the Biblical *know*) 20 to 50, even 60, cows in a two-month period, depending on his age, condition, sex drive – and eligible cows! If the bull has a natural tendency to love 'em and leave 'em – if he doesn't get emotionally bonded to each cow in succession – he'll be much more successful as a breeder and therefore in passing on his genes. Breed her and find another is the motto of the successful bull and as I pointed out earlier, this trait is enhanced by natural selection – modern novels and political scandals reveal the effects. The primitive polygamous male sired far more sons (like himself) than did the monogamous (in today's terms moral) man. Thus most men have inherited polygamous attitudes and capacities. In women this trait is neutral. Whether or not women had polyandrous inclinations, they always reproduced at the biological maximum. If there was an aggressive and dominant polygamist male about, he became the father of their sons and so the trait was reinforced.

If there are several bulls in a pasture, they quickly establish dominance – a lot of initial bellowing, pushing and shoving, tearing up of dirt, perhaps goring if the bulls have horns and sometimes a few injuries. After the pecking order has been established, they go about their business. If there's enough room, the bulls may establish their own harems – groups of cows they keep an eye on. More often, they'll move through the herd, the aggressive bulls pushing the others out of the way. But because of the shortness of the breeding season and the size of the task, there is usually work for all in the first three weeks when 70 percent or more of the cows will be bred.

For the next three weeks, one might expect the big boys to take over entirely. Often they don't: they're played out. The forced abstainers may now shine. Or they may have developed severe inferiority complexes, given up on the whole game and gathered in "bachelor clubs" down in a corner of the pasture. This, after all, is nature's way of handling excess males.[7] One rancher told me how he always turned out a few yearlings along with the older bulls. "They run around the outside and pick up quite a few," he said. (Sort of like the smooth-faced pages of a medieval court.) Some cattlemen keep back a number of bulls for two or three weeks and then turn them out as the main bull battery begins to flag. Fresh and roaring, they enter the fray after the major goals have been accomplished and make short work of still available opportunities. One cattleman, who has good control of his herd of 150 cows, changes his bulls every two days. He gets nearly all his cows bred in three weeks.

Two diseases, pink-eye and foot-rot, frequently play havoc with the bulls' effectiveness and then it's time for deploying fresh members of the team from the bench.

There are other hazards, like stifle-out (the upper leg joint, corresponding to our knee, which in cattle is near the flank, may become dislocated, or "out"). Or the hock may "break down." In either case, the bull cannot mount a cow. Occasionally, especially in rough country, a bull may "break his organ" and he's on his way to the packing house. Sometimes the penis may pick up a rose thorn or some other irritant. This is a special hazard with "polled" (naturally hornless) bulls. Why? Because associated with the gene which controls the polled factor is another gene which governs the retractor muscle of the penis. So, many polled bulls suffer from DP – even when the penis is not erect it protrudes – dangles – and becomes a target for thorny shrubbery. Infection, pain – all that bad stuff: No sex, no calves, no money for the rancher.

In the Northern Great Plains and in the Inter-Mountain country of North America, the natural time to breed is the fourth of July, or near to it. (Did you see the movie Picnic?) This is just after the summer solstice and both cow and bull have experienced the hormone-stimulating effects of increasing hours of sunlight. The cow has all the nutritional impact of fresh, green vitamin-laden spring grass, grass which is now maturing and so contains more carbohydrate and less water (the rancher says "less washy"). She has passed her flush of milk which occurs mid-May to mid-June. Moreover if she's bred now, she'll calve in mid-April, a good time weather-wise. And the calf will be well-grown and weaned before the snows of December.

Palmer Ranches of southern Alberta had no less than 4 000 cows and their fertility records computerized in the 1970s. They found the most fertile week for all their cows was the first week in July (the human clock appears to run two or three weeks earlier – June, moon, honeymoon). The bulls know this. Isolated from females since last September, they become increasingly restless during June – bellowing, pawing the dirt, "riding" each other, walking the fence line and bellowing some more. They'll find weaknesses in confining fences which they had ignored all winter. "I had to let the SOBs out before they tore the place down," said one rancher as he explained why his bulls were out a week earlier than usual.

Many ranchers "turn out" June 20 for April calves; some turn out as early as June 1 (for March calves), some on July 1 and some, (in areas where April is wet, muddy and often snowy)[9] in mid-to-late-July for May calves. (A quick way to figure the calving date is to go back three months from the breeding date and then add ten days.)

Where cattle are raised on relatively small pastures and not on the

`April`

open range, cows are often bred to calve as early as January. If you have some calving sheds, are prepared to put out extra feed and spend more time with the herd, this will make you money because the calves will be big and heavy by fall – and you sell them by pound. The worst month for a calf to be born is July – too light by fall to be sold for any amount of money, and if you decide to keep him over the winter, his mother will dry up when the cold weather hits, so he won't weigh much by next spring either.

Fall calving late August through October, on the other hand, often is a money maker. The cow calves in perfect weather – no scours (calf diarrhea) and she will suckle her calf most of the winter. All next summer, the now-weaned calf will eat grass and by fall will be big and heavy. Meanwhile the mother cow comes to spring grass in thin condition, but with no calf to "pull her down" she has all summer to lay on fat and she is in marvelous shape when she calves in the fall. Problem is you're working against Nature at time of breeding in November and December. Winter solstice coming, hormones turned off, no lush spring grass, all biological processes slowing down and cooling off – so bulls are less amorous and cows less fertile. But it can be made to work. In fact, dairymen breed many of their cows for fall calving so as to have abundant milk through the winter. And in much of the U.S. Southwest and Central Great Plains, fall calving is common and makes dollars and sense.

Good fertile bulls look like males. Females are attracted to muscular mesomorphs for a good reason – they tend to have great libido and to be fertile – sure breeders. Not always, of course, but the reason the football hero is able to get along with a beautiful girl is that he'll likely get the job done. Her instincts, going back thousands of years, tell her that this is her kind of guy.

In the world of bull buyers and bull sellers, this has created a real problem. Fat is pretty, so to sell his bull the breeder got him fat and the buyer paid top dollar. Result: disaster. Bull sales are generally held from January through March, and the breeding season as we've already stated is mainly June to July.

Problem: What to do with your recently-bought fat, pretty and expensive bull? In his condition he may not be able to mount a cow, let alone serve her. And he certainly can't go up and down hills and across the range in search of duties to perform. And even if he can do all these things, it's a toss-up whether his semen is any good. Will it contain enough vigorously motile sperm that will swarm through the twisted and tortuous path of the cow's cervix, cross the open sea of her uterus and finally into and up a fallopian tube? Probably not.

So the new owner – after having paid all that money for all that prettiness – has to take fat off. He calls it "letting the bull down" to get him in breeding shape. He cuts way back on feed – problem here is that fertility goes down with falling nutrition. The slimming bull is even less fertile than his former fat self. The object then, is to make him lose a great deal of weight till a month before the breeding season and then start feeding him again so that he will actually be gaining weight when he heads for the breeding field. Researchers will advise – and ranchers will confirm – that a rising plane of nutrition for both cows and bulls means enhanced fertility, more calves.

Scientists say it succinctly: "Mammals in an anabolic state conceive, those in a catabolic state are usually barren."

Why do knowledgeable and experienced men take their bulls through this crazy routine? If you asked that question in 1960, you simply revealed your ignorance of the purebred breeding business. And you certainly proclaimed that you were not an adherent to the cattle religion. (More about this later and of the revolution and reformation that changed all that.) Nowadays fewer bulls are fattened excessively, but far too many still are.

The buying and selling of a bull is much more than a mere commercial transaction. There is much socializing and fraternizing involved. In the late sixties I used to be invited regularly to a bull-sale luncheon in Calgary (the world's largest bull sale at that time) hosted by Canada's biggest bank for its customers who bought and sold bulls. I was a sort of "Poet Lower Yet" to the livestock industry. From me they expected a "poem" – earthy, relevant, glorifying the bank, and risqué enough to make the whiskey-inspired, all-male guests laugh and cheer. One of the most acceptable began like this:

> *O Royal Bank, in you we trust*
> *To buy our bulls and sate our lust.*
> *Fat bulls for profit, slim gals for pleasure,*
> *With a loan from the Royal, you will get full measure.*

It was a great all-boys-together time for the bank, for me and the "operators" in the purebred breeding business and faithful believers in the cattle religion. And as any reporter who interviews everyone from cowboys to cabinet ministers will indicate, these are the finest people on earth and have been ever since the days of Cain and Abel as we shall learn later.

It's a terrible bit of bad management to run out of bull power in the middle of the breeding season. Late calves and/or a short calf crop are extremely costly. If a rancher runs 300 cows, he'll need at least 15 bulls. That may not sound like much of a per-bull load, but remember the accidents that can befall a bull and the ones that lose hope and the ones that just don't have it, the "it" being viable semen. It's common now for a rancher to do fertility tests on his bulls before the breeding season. Almost always he pays a veterinarian to do it. The vet examines all the relevant parts for structure and function and usually does a semen test via an electro-ejaculator (shades of Daedalus!) which we won't describe here, except to say it involves a large electrode inserted into the bull's rectum and makes him groan a lot – sometimes on his knees!

Under a microscope, good semen reveals untold numbers of vigorous sperm, lashing their tails, charging hither and yon. Poor semen shows a lot of non-moving junk, with just a few motile sperm up and at it. The pros do what they call motility counts – so many moving sperm per millilitre.

Bulls which produce good semen usually have big, low-hanging testicles. The vet will measure with a tape the scrotum at its widest. He hopes to read something over 35 centimetres. Normal bovine blood is too hot for sperm – it cooks them. So the scrotum acts as a kind of radiator; the more it is exposed to the winds that blow, (the lower it "hangs") the more likely there'll be viable sperm. Small testicles held close to the belly are bad news, especially if they're surrounded by fat.

Sometimes as many as one out of four bulls won't pass his exam. He'll take his place in the breeding field, likely serve his allotted share of cows, all in vain. Meanwhile he has prevented a sure-fire bull from doing his part. Ergo: You should fertility test and dump the duds. Usually the infertile rate runs about one in ten, so in a large herd, with no fertility testing there will be quite a few free loaders.

In 1984 I visited a large community pasture in Alberta's Peace River Country, 400 miles (250 km) north of the Canada-U.S. border. Some 400 cows owned by 20 or so patrons ran together as a breeding herd. Each owner of 20 cows was required to supply a bull. If a bull failed his test, he was sold for beef and the owner had to buy another bull. This put some patrons to considerable expense. I asked the pasture manager how the association had resolved this problem. Did they have a kind of insurance fund so the cost of a dud replacement would be pooled? "Oh, no," he said. "We just stopped testing the bulls!"

Wonderful people, these cattlemen, but as you have now discovered, they're not really into rationality.

Before we leave the bulls, a parting question: why is the Jersey bull the most vicious and dangerous of our domestic breeds, while the Jersey cow is the sweetest and gentlest? Answer: Because they're ectomorphs and because in dairy cattle the sexes are truly opposite. More about that when we talk about breeds.

We must now turn to the would-be and once-were bulls – steers, oxen, gomers, proud-cuts, et al.

| By the Way . . . |

[1]The Spanish word for sand is arena.

[2]Daedalus also built the first airplanes, with gauze-like wings, for himself and his son Icarus, who flew too close to the sun, and had his wings singed, etc., etc., but not much about cattle in that story.

[3] An avatar or incarnation of Vishnu was Krishna, and Krishnagar was the name of a Hereford bull imported to Canada from England by the late Roy Bond of Calgary in the 1960s during the North American battle against dwarfism.

[4] Al Beatty of Calgary, who worked for a number of years as an agricultural extension officer in Lesotho, an African Homeland where wealth is measured in cattle numbers, said that he never saw a cow being bred all the time he was there. They just didn't get enough to eat.

[5] If she *drops* a calf, that's good – a normal birth. But if she *slips* a calf, that's bad – she has aborted it. It's dead. And for any number of reasons the cow may be sent to a packing plant.

[6] In Britain and down under the verb "to join" is used to describe what happens when male and female are brought together. Whereas service is an act performed by the bull, joining is reciprocal. The bull does not join the cow but is joined with her, or she with him. Social gaffe in Australian cattle circles: "Will you join me at lunch?"

[7] In human society, which by nature is polygamous but by civilized custom monogamous, many females, who in a feral state would become part of a dominant male's harem, are forced by tradition and propriety to seek mates from among non-agressive males – the guys who have found peace and contentment in "bachelor clubs." This has given rise to great industries in fashion, cosmetics, high couture and publishing.

[8] Joke. Victorian music hall M.C. says: Let us drink a toast to her Britannic Majesty, Queen Victoria. Long may she continue to reign over us! Andd to her First Minister, William Ewart Gladstone. Long may he continue to *serve* her Majesty – and Mrs. Gladstone! (To non-livestock audiences, this joke has to be explained.)

[9] In Alberta more snow falls in April than in any other month.

Chapter Three

The Neutral Zone
>>>>>>>>>>>>>>

Among the earthy sallies and repartees of teenage farm boys, nothing is funnier than a steer joke. Like them, the steer is unfulfilled sexually but whereas they have hopes and expectations, the steer's present and future is hopeless.

But he can try.

And that's one of the jokes. If a farm boy justifies his failure of a difficult task by saying, "Anyway I tried," his companion will jeer, "So did the steer!"

He is referring to the steer in the pasture near a cow in heat. Some steers simply ignore the suppliant female, but sometimes a steer will still have enough testosterone floating around in his blood to respond to the feminine pheromones wafting his way. He approaches her, mounts her – and not much else. Rarely a steer, especially if "proud-cut" (part of a testicle not completely removed at castration) may get a small erection – 2 or 3 inches (about 7 cm) compared to the bull's 12 to 20 inches (30 to 50 cm) but he can't complete the act. All he can do is try. He looks bewildered: is this all there is to life? After a few seconds he backs down, having accomplished nothing.

The castration act produces profound changes, both physical and psychological, in the young bull. The farm boys say with a chortle, "We've sure changed his attitude."

The fact that steers can only try is the reason for making them steers. They can be run together with cows and heifers, even bulls, with very little fuss. Steers don't fight bulls or each other. Ranchers, who have enough steers and heifers to justify separate pastures for them, run one field with heifers and another with steers. They do this because there will always be some steers who do a lot of riding[1] and in a heifer field there is always something in heat. Same thing in feedlots – steers and heifers are penned separately. But steers don't rant and roar, paw the ground, walk fence lines nor breed cows.

From time immemorial, steers have been used to pull plows and wagons as oxen. They played an enormous role during America's settlement, dragging Conestoga wagons across the plains and breaking the new sod at the end of the trail. On the old Santa Fe trail, from Franklin Missouri a thousand miles (1 600 km) to Santa Fe, New

Mexico, the wheel ruts of freight wagons which passed that way from 1821 to 1880 are well preserved in many places and the trail may be seen for miles from the air. The famed "bull teams," which Montana artist Charles Russell has so graphically depicted, hauled freight from the steamboat landing at Fort Benton on the Missouri River in Montana Territory two hundred miles (320 km) north to Fort Macleod in Canada. These were not bulls but oxen – even though they were universally referred to as "them bulls." Canada's Red River carts, made entirely of wood and rawhide – never greased, and therefore screechingly noisy – made great circles west from the Red River in Manitoba to Wood Mountain and the Cypress Hills in what is now southern Saskatchewan during the annual migration of the Metis buffalo hunters in the nineteenth century. Each cart was pulled by a single ox.

And in far-away South Africa, the Boer Voortrekkers, fed up with the impositions of the British Empire (which in 1832 abolished slave labor upon which the Booer economy depended), travelled hundreds of miles north and east to establish the Orange Free State. Their wagons were pulled by oxen and at night they were drawn into a circle – a *laager* – for protection not just against lions, but against the legions (*Impis*) of

Zulus who were advancing from the North to occupy what till then had been an empty land.

In Eastern North America, settlers used oxen to clear the great hardwood forests they had pre-empted from the Iroquois and Hurons. Oxen are great for pulling stumps, much better than horses; they'll lean into the yoke or harness, gradually increasing the heave till the stump comes out. Horses, on the other hand, are much more nervous; they tend to "hit their collars" and then, if the stump doesn't move, rear back and hit again. It takes a very good teamster to make his impatient horses pull in the steady, sustained way that is natural for the ox.

Australians still use bullocks (the team is driven by a "bullocky") to jerk timber out of the forests on the eastern slopes.

The digestive system of a mature ox holds almost twice as much as that of a horse, so he can go longer and stronger than a horse when there is heavy work to do. But you are not going to mount an ox to make a gallant but futile charge into the mouths of canon at Balaclava, or to rally your countrymen by crying "The British are coming!" These are no places for oxen; for gallantry, the horse wins hands down.

Though the ox, generally a plodder – a patient dumb beast – who will accept all kinds of abuse[3] the ox sometimes rebels. Often he just quits and no amount of beating will convince him to get on with it. But flies and mosquitoes can conquer him: Almost every account of pioneer settlement has a story of how the oxen, tormented on a hot, sticky day by mosquitoes and flies, left the furrow/trail with plow/wagon/hay rack (or buggy containing wife and baby) and bolted for a nearby stream/lake/slough pulling whatever (whomever) was hitched to them into the water.

Ben and Brake were the oxen's names in the school readers of 100 years ago. The activities of this pair introduced children with slates in log schools to the written word, just as Dick and Jane did 50 or 60 years later to their grandchildren.

In American mythology, Paul Bunyan and his Blue Ox flourished in the nineteenth century in North American forests. His domain was from the Great Lakes to the Pacific Northwest and he was especially revered by Scandinavian immigrants. Bunyan and his Ox are very much part of our heritage. Carved wooden images of these tribal gods are still extant in the areas of their influence. Prodigious size and strength joined with miraculous powers to enable this partnership to overcome all odds in the performance of great deeds.

Castration is generally done with a knife or a scalpel. Old-timers favor a "stockman's jackknife," but the scalpel has a number of advantages, chief of which is the disposable blade, which when dull can be immediately replaced by a new and a very sharp one. The operator may frequently dip his hands and the knife or scalpel in a pail of disinfectant. Often the scrotum is washed with the same germ-killing solution before and after the operation. Thousands of calves, however, are castrated without benefit of disinfectant. It doesn't seem to make much difference. There is some bleeding, and this is considered good because the blood will wash away infectious material from the wound; the rancher likes to see the scrotum "drain."

With young calves, problems are few and the calves recover in a few days, appearing "just a little stiff" the day after the operation. With bigger calves, there is more bleeding and a few more complications. Often there will be some swelling of the scrotum but this usually reverts back to normal size after a few days.

If the calf is beginning to show some sexual maturity and the testicles are quite large, the preferred way to castrate is to hold the standing young bull in a squeeze with a head-gate and, while the animal is thus more or less immobilized, stand behind him and perform the operation from the rear. You won't believe it till you see it, but he stands still.

Some people are turned off by knives and blood; they just can't or don't want to cut into living flesh. Two bloodless options are available for these squeamish ones. There's the Burdizzo (invented by an Italian of the same name) a set of flat pincers with precision-ground jaws. These are clamped on the spermatic cord above the testicle, one side at a time. The operation is quick and since the skin is not broken, bloodless. Apparently it causes little pain. The clamping act severs the spermatic cord and the artery accompanying it. In due course, with the blood supply cut off, the testicles atrophy and are eventually absorbed via the remaining blood vessels. The main disadvantage of this method is that you may not have got the clamp positioned just right and so missed crushing the cord – therefore he's still a bull.

If you don't like the Burdizzo you can use "rings." A strong elastic ring is slipped up the scrotum above the testicles (but below the teats) and is released. You need a special tool to do this because the ring is so tough. The ring effectively shuts off all blood circulation below it, so everything down there dies and drops off.

Most stockmen like to use the knife. They can carry it in a pocket, so it's always handy when they run across a calf missed at the spring branding. The rancher takes pride in the edge he puts on the blade and uses it for nothing else. (Woe betide the kid who uses Dad's "cutting" blade to do some whittling!) But a growing number prefer the scalpel; at a branding, where several men will be castrating, both are used. If you talk to stockmen and stockwomen who perform their own procedures on livestock (including artificial insemination, delivering calves, dehorning, drenching) you'll discover that they "love to operate." There's the challenge of doing the job with skill and deftness. They get satisfaction from having done it right – no botching – the members of this fraternity quickly recognize each other.

As well as robbing him of his prime purpose in life, castration changes the animal's growth pattern, muscular development and the way he lays down fat. He'll not be as heavily muscled as a bull,[4] nor will his muscle be as coarsely grained but he will put on more fat. With respect to muscle and fat, he is midway between cows and bulls – more muscle than the cow but less fat and almost as finely grained. That's why we prize steer beef. The flavor is also not as "beefy," as intense, as bull beef.

Animal rightists haven't hit us squarely yet about desexing of animals before eating them. No doubt they will come up with potent slogans and perhaps boycotts of the butcher.

Steers grow slower than bulls and use their feed less efficiently. (It takes two and a half times as much feed to put on a pound of fat as is required to increase muscle weight by the same amount.) So a cattleman has an economic saw-off to contend with: if he castrates bull calves when they're very young, the shock of the operation is minimal – they'll hardly know what happened to them and the calves recover quickly. They are small and easily handled when operated on and they won't be "tailing" the cows in heat in the pasture. The bigger the calf the more likely he is to suffer from shock or blood loss and the more likely the danger of infection. These are all good reasons for early castration. Most ranchers "cut" their April-dropped calves in June at the time of the spring branding.

Calves intended for show steers are usually castrated late, since this makes them look beefier and "breedier" – but if the delay is too long, the calf will take on a "stagy" appearance.

If the calves are not cut at the spring branding, they'll be quite a bit heavier than steers when they're weaned in the fall. If the rancher is going to feed them himself this may be an advantage; however, if he offers them for sale as bulls they'll be heavily discounted in price. And if he is going to "background them over" for several months (enabling them to grow for awhile before going to heavy feed) he's got management problems, because these young bulls have all the bull instincts – they're like 16-year-old boys.

So much for no castration. Why not let them grow as bull calves all summer while they're sucking their dams and thus get extra weight and size, then cut them? Many ranchers do this, but the calves don't recover as quickly and, as they now weigh 500 lb. (227 kg), they are considerably harder to "flat ass."

Flat ass? Two men (often teenage boys or girls) wrestle a calf. One flops the calf to the ground by lifting it at front and rear flanks. Then he grabs and twists a front leg while kneeling on its head and neck. His partner grabs the top-side rear leg and draws it towards his chest and sits (flat-ass) directly behind the calf. He pushes one foot against the bottom hind leg just above the hock, and this effectively controls both hind legs and exposes the scrotum for surgery. The calf's thigh, rib (side) and shoulder are also exposed for the brander and his iron. Loose folds of skin are also available for *sub-cue* vaccination in the neck, dewlap or front flank. If intra-muscular injection

is required, the hip is fully exposed. If dehorning is part of the program, the front "wrestler" kneels on the neck and adjusts the calf's head using its nose as a handle.

When handling big calves in the fall, some cattlemen use a calf table, a squeeze affair that can be rolled on its side after the calf is in it. This is not nearly as much fun as flat-assing but it's fairly easy and doesn't take as big a crew. Two people, even one, can do the branding with a table but at a much slower pace.

The traditional way, which is still carried out on many ranches, is for a mounted roper to "heel" a calf – dropping a lariat loop in front of the calf's hind legs so that as the calf steps – or jumps – forward he is caught neatly by both hind legs. The rider then takes a "dally" around the horn of his saddle and drags the calf close to the branding crew.

With the calf's hind legs held taut, straight behind, only one wrestler is needed. He holds the calf's front leg. Usually, however, the rope will be slipped off (enabling the heeler to go back and get another calf immediately) and a flat-asser will assume his position. Heelers are a unique breed of cowman with special horses. They love what they do and will travel (with their horses in trailers) wherever they're invited to help out. A good heeler, who may be a teenager or in his seventies, takes great pride in his skill and his horses – he's a true Marlboro Man and is much admired.

As we will learn in a few pages ahead, there are not many good reasons for "spaying" (de-sexing) heifers, but making steers out of bulls is a general practice. Englishmen favor the meat of heifers, but almost all Australians, New Zealanders, South Africans and both North and South Americans prefer steers beef. In Europe, however, steers are a rarity and young bull beef is considered supreme. There they eat the bulls entire (including the testicles!). On this continent many of us have been eating bull beef unknowingly. In the U.S., the old, lean bulls are made into hamburger. Waste fat trimmed from choice grade steers and heifers is added for flavor and appearance – and to reduce the cost of the product!

And have you heard of "virgin" bulls? Nothing to do with bovine morals, just a kind of market beef. Young bull calves are put on heavy feed and fattened as quickly as possible in an entirely male environment. As a result, they really don't get a chance to read the book of knowledge – just grow and fatten. But because male hormones are secreting away, they are more muscular (meaty) than steers. The steaks are bigger and the roasts need less trimming.

As for taste, it's a matter of taste. Some can't tell the difference; others note that the bull beef is "richer in flavor." In research taste-panels, the meat has always been acceptable. It does not have the high flavor and toughness of an older bull who has lived a full and active co-ed life.

Problems arise not from the meat but from the special handling necessary to get a bull fat fast and still maintain the "virgin" condition. If a bull is rough-handled just before slaughter, the stress may cause his meat to take on a dark, unattractive color. Such carcasses are called "dark cutters" and sell for less money. The younger the bull, the more his meat is like that of the steer.

Spring-born calves become "short yearlings" the next spring. Common practice is to summer them on grass, the cheapest way to put on weight and then sell them in the fall as "long yearlings" ready for grain finishing. Yearling steers are generally summered by themselves, apart from cows and heifers. This prevents them from riding the females, thus avoiding weight loss in both. Whereas cows with calves usually follow a pattern of grazing a known summer range, steers tend to wander. They need good fences or natural barriers to control their adventuresome spirits.

While bulls, especially dairy bulls, can be dangerous to humans, and cows with young calves (especially Angus or anything with Brahman blood) may charge a good-intentioned intruder, steers are usually non-aggressive. Exception: if they're "on the prod" or "riled" – a form of temporary insanity usually occurring after rough or strenuous handling – they can be dangerous. All kinds of cattle can get on the prod, but dairy cows rarely do. That's why there are posts in auction-sale rings; the handlers and ringmen have some place to duck behind when charged by a riled critter.

"Watch out!"

Some breeds are more easily riled than others. The red, white-faced Herefords are one of the most docile of beef breeds, a factor in their long-time supremacy on western ranches, but they, too, can go on the prod on occasion. Range-raised cattle are semi-wild and may pose a threat to people on foot. Eastern or European cattlemen, when visiting a western ranch, invariably have to be cautioned about this, as they, more foolhardy than fearless, "bravely" approach a group of range cattle.

Such cattle are usually handled on horseback. If you go to a cattle sale at the big Buenos Aires market in Argentina, you'll find everybody on horseback – including the auctioneer and the buyers. Or go 6 000 miles (3 750 km) north to the fall sale at Williams Lake in British Columbia's Cariboo country and again mounted horsemen are moving the cattle in and out of the sales ring.

The steer's lack of aggression toward man, makes him the animal of choice for several rodeo events: steer wrestling, team roping and boys' steer riding. When a bull rider dismounts or is thrown from a bull, he has to make quick moves to evade the charging bull. Bull fighters who double as rodeo clowns intervene to draw the bull away before he takes his revenge.

Young boys routinely ride steers which just keep on going once they've lost their mounts. Steer wrestling, in the rodeo arena at least, is an unequal contest – the man usually wins. Bull wrestling also would be unequal – the bull would win – just look at the muscles on his neck! And he wouldn't be a good sport about leaving the game once he had won. If he got you down – very bad news!

Since steers never achieve sexual maturity, rarely do they reach full growth – they keep getting bigger year after year. In 1970 the Earl of Egmont, who owns the Two Dot Ranch near Nanton, Alberta, showed me a pair of steers which were then seven and nine years old and weighed about 3 000 lb. (1 364 kg) each. He was keeping them as a sort of lark. Nobody in the commercial cattle business keeps steers beyond three years of age, and most of them are ready for market by (or before) they are two years old.

"Delicious!
What are 'prairie oysters' anyway?"

In the old range days, the practice was to sell four-year-old steers to slaughter. The price increased ten dollars for each year of age: weaned calves sold for ten dollars, yearlings for twenty, twos for thirty and three-year-olds for forty dollars. Running steers was the easiest and best way for ranchers to make money in the 1880s and 1890s and into the twentieth century. The Matador Ranch, with headquarters in Dundee, Scotland, had vast holdings in Texas, Colorado and Saskatchewan. The Saskatchewan ranch summered three- and four-year-old steers "in bond." The cattle were shipped in from the U.S. ranches in the spring – paying no duty as they crossed the Canadian border. They gained 250 to 300 lb. (113 to 136 kg) each on the Saskatchewan grass before being shipped to Chicago on the SOO Line in the fall. When they crossed the border at Portal, N.D., the bond was released and they paid no duty there either. It was a very profitable operation.

Pat Burns, Canada's best known old-time rancher and meat packer, ran thousands of cattle in Alberta for many years, but he didn't own a cow herd till 1918, after three decades as a rancher. He bought steers, ran them from one to three years and then killed them in his packing plant. Burns was the main cattle buyer in western Canada at that time and he took everything from weaned calves up.

Most traditional cattlemen are fussy about their meat. They like to eat beef, thus making a statement about themselves and their business. Usually they do not like offals[5] – heart, liver tongue, sweetbread, and tripe – but a few of them take a special pleasure in preparing and serving "prairie oysters." These are the testicles of bull calves, saved in a bucket at a branding and then washed and prepared (slitting away the mesentery) for cooking. Sometimes they go into a freezer to be used later as *hors d'oeuvres* at a party. This is an acquired taste and more readily acquired if you don't know the source!

There are many anecdotes told by cattlemen concerning the eating of prairie oysters by friends and other visitors to their ranches. It's a good subject for jokes. Calgary's former mayor Ralph Klein, who later became premier of Alberta, told a group of old-time rangemen at a large banquet about an American gourmet attending the bullfights in a Spanish city:

> The gourmet determined where the bull carcasses were processed and also which restaurant made a specialty of serving the testicles from the vanquished toros. For two evenings he went for dinner at this restaurant and each evening was presented with the specialty of the house, served in large longitudinally sliced portions. On the third evening, however, the portions were miniscule. On asking the waiter what had happened, he was told, "Señor, the matador does not always win!"

By the Way . . .

[1] Among both male and female bovines, homosexual non-copulatory "riding" occurs when females (either *riders* or *ridees*) are in estrus, and when bulls are "randy," which is most of the time.

[2] From 1821, when the trail opened following Mexican independence from Spain, till 1848, after the United States had defeated Mexico and annexed many of its northern territories (California, Colorado, Nevada, New Mexico, Arizona), Santa Fe was in Mexico, often called Old Mexico by the cowboys.

[3] When American and Canadian buyers went to Italy in the late 1960s and early 70s to select cattle for importation to North America, they

noted the Italian farmers were particularly cruel in the treatment of their cattle, using great clubs to beat them into submission.

[4]The presence of sex hormones increases the rate of muscle growth and size of the muscle – that's why weightlifters, wrestlers, rock musicians, boys on the beach and football players take hormones. Extra testosterone also increases aggression and so can be useful to wheeler-dealers during difficult negotiations. Hormone-induced aggression probably explains why a professional football player bit a stewardess on the thigh on a flight returning from a game. The additional hormone – the antithesis of castration – had "adjusted" his attitude.

[5]Pampas gauchos, in contrast, relish these special meats.

Chapter Four

No Sex Please!
We're Bovines
>>>>>>>>>>

I don't know *why* they call her a freemartin but I know *what* she is. It's like this. Your cow has twins. One is a bull and the other is a heifer – a freemartin. Because her twin brother is a bull, something happened to her in utero that made her different from all her other playmates. Like so many other strange things that affect us, as well as cattle, let's blame it on hormones.

As the two little calves grew inside their mother, there came a time when the boy calf became quite different from his sister – he began to develop testicles while she began to form ovaries. And as these organs grew, they began to secrete hormones – sex hormones.

She grew up fine and healthy and in her owner's eye, was one of the prettiest heifers in the field – if beef was what he was looking for. That's because female hormones tend to make any mammalian *she* look lithe and slender, whereas a lack of these cause her to be thicker in her muscles and muscle is meat. Just look at the "female" athletes from behind the former Iron Curtain to see how sex hormones change muscle development!

The world's most famous freemartin was dropped in 1806 on the farm of Robert Colling of Darlington in Durham County in the north of England. Pure white, she was known as "The White Heifer that Travelled" because she was exhibited throughout the country in full fit to publicize the Shorthorn breed. She was a fine-boned, pretty heifer and, at a weight of 2300 lb. (1 045 kg) very big and fat – over twice the weight of heifers being slaughtered in North America today.

The freemartin will grow a little slower than her brothers and sisters because she doesn't have hormones to push her along; but she will fatten rapidly and dress out a fine carcass in due course. All her life she will be virgin-pure and will cause no scandal or trouble with any of the herd. She could make a pretty good 4H calf, but she is such a rarity that very few 4H club members have seen a freemartin, let alone fattened one.

This may change. With high-tech procedures there is an interesting way to produce lots of twins from very valuable breeding stock. Multi-ovulation is induced by hormones in the "donor" cow; then her many eggs are fertilized and transplanted in pairs into "recipient" cows. According to simple Mendelian distribution, half the heifer twins will be freemartins, but the others will have their sexual parts in order, as will all the bulls.

The freemartin is a natural thing; a spayed heifer is man-made. She shares with the steer the indignity of an embarrassing operation and like him, is positioned mid-way between the sexes. Her operation, spaying, involves removing the ovaries through an incision in her side. Since this requires an invasion of the body cavity, the operation is more difficult and more life-threatening than castration. Every rancher can and does castrate bulls, but those who spay heifers are rare and getting rarer. The operation requires skill and is easily botched. But times are a-changing. A new spaying procedure called the "drop technique" involves the insertion of a small knife through the vaginal wall in the area of the ovaries. These are then snipped off and allowed to "drop" into the abdominal cavity where they are eventually resorbed. This is, of course, a veterinarian's task and so an added cost for the rancher but it is gaining in popularity because it is so much easier on the heifer and losses are minimal.

Spayed heifers can run by themselves or with any other cattle with ascetic non-involvement – never a lustful moo. But if left entire, a group of heifers, in either a pasture or a feedlot, will always have about five percent of their number in standing heat – to ride the others or be ridden by them. Estrus heifers are quite indiscriminate sex-wise, they'll swing either way, sometimes *hetero* and sometimes *homo*. If no bulls are around, they mount each other.

Hormone-driven stimulation in cases like this is all wasted excitement and effort, so in terms of efficient weight gain in cattle, spaying has an obvious advantage. And if, for any reason, the rancher does not want his heifers bred, then spaying is fool-proof. The disadvantage comes from lack of growth enhancement; just like the freemartin, the spayed heifer grows more slowly and takes more feed to put on a pound of gain.

The slower growth of freemartins, spayed heifers – and steers too, of course – can be partially overcome by implanting hormone pellets in their ears. The pellets are absorbed very slowly over time and so give a continuous boost to muscle growth and feed efficiency. An extra bonus comes from bigger and leaner cuts of meat resulting from the hormone stimulation. This is the same physiological effect that rock singers, football players, Olympic athletes and beach boys get from hormones – more muscle, less flab.

Aha! they say. I knew it; they're putting all those terrible artificial things in the meat. Truth is the hormones are used up in the metabolic process – how else could they do their job? Still, it's worth looking at how much you can find in the beef from a hormone-treated animal – much better than getting all hot and fuzzy about those "awful additives".

Suppose you are supping on beef and cabbage, 100 grams of each. If the beef is from a hormone-treated steer, you will consume only 1.9 nanograms of estrogen (a nanogram is one billionth of a gram). But from the cabbage you will get 2 400 nanograms, over 1200 times as much. And if you are a normal, healthy woman, you will be manufacturing in your own body an average of 480 000 nanograms of estrogen every day – the amount varies with the menstrual cycle. Even your cute ten-year-old Little Leaguer will be turning out 41 000 a day – despite the fact he's a boy! (Alberta Cattle Commission, *Just Facts*. Calgary, Alberta: 1990).

There's a specified time period after implantation before the beast may be slaughtered. This assures the hormones have done their thing and are long gone. Dining on hormone-stimulated beef, a woman would have to eat *eight full-grown cattle every day* before she would reach a hormone-in-food level exceeding government standards.

Compare this with what Henry VIII ordered for the lovely Lady Lucy:

Every morning for breakfast, one whole fillet of beef. At dinner, a piece of salt beef, a slice of roast beef. At supper, a joint of mutton.

In addition, she was allowed:

a gallon of strong beer [with each meal], a four-pound loaf and divers poultry, tarts and delicacies.

And (anticipating Henry's evening visit):

a half-gallon of wine for late supper! (Graham Reynolds, collator, Gastronomic Pleasures. London W1: Art and Technics Ltd., 1950)

Since these victuals were sent to Lucy's own room, we can suppose that Good King Hal would be visiting her and so satisfying several fleshly desires. But even their combined appetites coultn't come close to the beef Ms. North America would have to consume in 1993 before overloading with hormones. However, in response to the concerns of concerned consumers, some cattlemen are selling "natural" beef without hormones or antibiotics. You can buy such beef at specialty stores if you are willing to pay through the nose for it.

Before leaving the "neutral zone," let's take a look at those cows which have been desexed by age, disease or accident. Age is easy to understand – one cow-year roughly equals five woman-years, though the "equals" skews away at both ends of a lifetime. For his banker's benefit, when that worthy asks for a projection on next year's finances, the rancher figures his cows to last eight years in the breeding herd, that is till they are 10 years old. Sure, he'll have some cows going to fourteen, even eighteen years, and many are just in their prime as ten-year-olds. But it's a matter of averages. If he doesn't replace at least a tenth of his herd each year, he soon will be out of cows.

All the non-producers of both sexes and all ages are called "culls" and the more severe the culling, the faster the herd improves. But there's no free lunch. It is very costly to raise a heifer to breeding age without getting anything in return. So the good manager attempts to balance off the costs and benefits but he always culls the "empty" (not pregnant) cows and also the "drys" (those which had no calf to nurse them and so quit milking).

Twenty-five years ago, before a vaccine for vibriosis had been developed, the late Charles S. McKinnon, a prominent and much-respected Alberta rancher, was told that to eliminate this contagious and sexually-transmitted disease, his cows should be provided with sexual rest.

McKinnon replied: "The only sexual rest my cows are going to get is in the packing house."

He was right, of course. The only sexual rest any beef animal should have, if not in a field growing or breeding or gestating or in a feed-yard growing or putting on beef, is in that great pasture in the sky.

PART TWO

Cattlemen and Their Cattle

⋗⋗⋗⋗⋗⋗⋗⋗⋗⋗⋗⋗⋗⋗⋗⋗⋗⋗⋗⋗⋗

It happened on Day Six.

If you read the first chapter of Genesis, you discover that God made all the animals, including cattle, *before* He made Man. Then He looked at this menagerie "and saw that it was good." But the animals needed someone to watch over them; so God made man and gave him dominion over the whole ball of wax: "the cattle, and over all the earth, and every creeping thing that creepeth upon the earth."

Thus, by the beginning of the Seventh Day, the stage was set for man to become a hunter-gatherer, a herdsman, a farmer, a fisherman, an irrigationist, a lumberman, a miner, an oil driller . . . in short, ours is "the world and all that is in it." It is only in my lifetime that this "dominion over" idea has been challenged by the "new wave" people who think that bears and wild horses and lice and mice and tubercle bacilli have "equal rights" with us and we are wicked to have our way with them. The history of mankind tells of our dependence on and control of animals and also of the lands and forests, and the air and seas in which they have dwelt.

Until recently, the only way morality got involved was in the nature of our stewardship and in our dealings with other people as we executed this stewardship. Thus buffalo hunting was all right but wanton slaughter of the big beasts was immoral. Horse ownership is a noble activity but cruelty to horses is despicable. Similarly, the tilling of the soil so as to maintain and enhance its fertility has been much lauded (as has been the yeoman farmer) but the strip-mining of Appalachia is often called a "raping of the earth."

The next six chapters tell how man has exercised his dominion over cattle and the lands where they have grazed and how this relationship is a reciprocal thing – cattle (and the horses needed to manage them) have had profound effects on us. There are ranches and rangelands, and cows and cowboys – they all need each other.

Since everybody wants to be one, let's start with the cowboy. Let's discover who he is, what he does, why he dresses the way he does, what songs he sings and why he is heroic.

Chapter Five

The Cowboy
(as Hero, Warrior, Trial God, Entertainer and Real Man)

You've likely heard of the old-time song "The Cowboy and the Farmer Should be Friends."

Why aren't they friends? And did their enmity begin only a hundred years ago, as the film industry has taught us? For answers look in the book of Genesis. Read about Cain and Abel in the fourth chapter. Abel was the cowboy and Cain the farmer: "Cain brought forth of the fruit of the ground an offering unto the Lord. And Abel, he also brought of the firstlings of his flock and of the fat thereof. And the Lord had respect unto Abel and to his offering. But unto Cain and to his offering, he had not respect."

Later on, Cain, who just couldn't stand his inferior position, slew Abel. This hardly-fraternal foul deed aroused the wrath of Yaweh – but Cain also gained Yaweh's protection. Such a schlemiel! He is needing help already!

Thus was set the comparative roles of earth-tillers and herd-followers: the one group despised, but protected by the mark of Cain; the other exalted by his god, but destroyed by the farmer. And so it has been ever since. It's not a perfect division, of course, since some of Cain's descendents[1] became herdsmen – followed herds and lived in tents – but the spiritual ancestor of all stockmen is Abel.

After some time stockmen acquired horses and so climbed further in the socio-spiritual hierarchy. The horse enabled our ancestral cowboy to move his herds farther and faster and to defend them against marauders. Since the horse was also a war animal, mounted herdsmen doubled as cavalry.[2] Attila[3] the Hun and Ghengis Khan swept out of Asia having amassed huge armies of mounted soldiers from among the horsemen who followed herds across the harsh and untillable steppe.

The mounted soldier is a superior soldier, not only in battle, but socially in the bar room and in the drawing room – as a man among men, and particularly as a man among women. The words *chevalier*, *cavalier* and *caballero* became synonymous with the word "gentleman." A maiden's heart beat faster when wooed by a cavalier and he who would lead troops in battle could best do so on a horse. The innumerable statues of Simon Bolivar, the liberator of most of South America, depict him, sword in hand, astride a superb mount. And among the

many items of delicious humor in Al Capp's "L'il Abner" comic strip was his drawing of pot-bellied general Jubilation T. Cornpone, uneasily riding a decrepit and aging plug.

The herdsman, if he rode a horse, came to be identified with the mounted warrior, though the kinship was lost for a thousand years in medieval Europe. Lost, in fact, until the spiritual successors to Attila, *the gauchos* of the South American pampas re-established the concept of cowboy-as-hero in the eighteenth century. General Juan de Rosas, who became the governor-dictator of the province of Buenos Aires in 1828 after Spain had been defeated, was chosen as leader by his gaucho followers because he had successfully passed the ultimate test of pampas horsemanship. A band of wild horses was herded through a gate, above which Rosas hung from a crossbar. He dropped to the back of one of the wild ones and, after several hours, returned riding the now completely tamed horse, without benefit of saddle or bridle.

To the *gaucho*, the *vaquero* and the cowboy a horse is essential. All the cowboy's elements of nobility – his way of life, his dress, his dealings with bad hombres, his gallantry toward women – would be farcical without the horse as his alter ego. Can you picture a Marlboro man without spurs, boots, hat and vest? Would he sell any cigarettes? C'est a rire!

True enough, social prominence can be achieved or enhanced just by owning and breeding cattle, *sans* horse. Consider Ike Eisenhower and Queen Elizabeth. Already occupying society's zenith, they, by breeding and raising cattle, further ennobled their own positions and also conferred this nobility on fellow breeders of pedigreed cattle.

But put either of these larger-than-life figures on a horse and the majesty becomes awesome. How great the adulation when British subjects see their queen uniformed and mounted albeit side-saddle in a parade before Buckingham Palace. And let's not forget another queen, also named Elizabeth, who won her spurs, as it were, and a great victory on horseback – surely you remember the lovely adolescent Elizabeth Taylor in the film *National Velvet*.

Nor should we forget Theodore Roosevelt who "converted" himself into a cowboy – wore the outfits, rode the horses and shot the guns – and then reinforced this macho image by a second conversion – into a cavalry officer who led a victorious charge into battle and soon afterwards he was elected President of the United States of America.

Then there is the Great Communicator himself. In downtown Santa Barbara, California, an area has been restored to the days of Spanish settlement, a time when all the land in California was owned either by church missions or by *rancheros*, the descendants of grandees who had received royal grants from the Spanish crown. It is a delightful place where tourists can spend their money surrounded by an ancient ambience. The local reverence of and connection to Spanish colonial times is evident everywhere – in restaurants, shops, street decor and the names of places and buildings. One building, small, low-set and anything but pretentious, stands near the edge of the re-development. Above its door is written "Los Rancheros Visitadores," and if you are up on such things, you know that an honorary member of this most exclusive club is Ronald Reagan.

"Los Rancheros Visitadores" is an organization going back to the days when the Spanish *colones* visited each other, going from one *estancia* to another as they brought news from the Old World, from the colonial government in Mexico City and from other *ranchero*s and their families. The visits were great social affairs. One of their functions was to introduce young men and women to each other. A very exclusive club, of course, then – and now.

In Hollywood, or in Santa Barbara, a few hours drive from L.A., the cowboys aren't "real," everybody knows that this is just a pretend world. To experience the real thing – cowboys, ranches, with the range stretching for hundreds of miles with no big cities to pollute or corrupt, where it's easy to *connect* with the heroic past – go to Montana.

I love Montana. When I first came to know its ranchers and their picturesque and historic spreads in the early fifties, what struck me was that every place, big and little, had a bar. We in pious Canada were still limited to a drink in our homes or hotel rooms. So, to stand up and order a drink at a bar, then savor it as I talked about cows to whoever was also leaning there gave me a marvelous sense of being a free man in the best of all worlds.

I had grown up with cattle in southern Alberta, close to ranch country; but our place was really a farm not a ranch, and this was the first time I'd ever been right in the heart of cow country. And at a bar, with silver dollars[4] jingling across it. Cowmen all around me, Charlie Russell prints on the wall, everyone wearing riding boots and jeans (in those times, only cowmen and those who aped them wore jeans) and Stetson hats, and everyone talking cows and grass and hay and rainfall and phosphorus deficiency and steer prices . . . I had discovered a new heaven and a new earth – the domain of the real cowboy. Here the myth, glorified by Will James, Zane Grey and all the other *western* writers, and, of course, by the movies, was alive and wonderfully well.

Can such a heaven on earth exist without gods? Hardly. As always, man here created the god(s) he needed. Chief of the pantheon is Charles M. Russell – the greatest of all western artists – the cowboy whose work is displayed everywhere in cow country, who was himself a working cowhand. Next in line (in 1954) was native Montanan Gary Cooper, who displayed on the silver screen all that was good and admirable in the person of the cowboy. Then there were (and still are) a host of ranchers, wagon bosses, artists, bronc riders, authors, gun fighters and explorers (the names of Lewis and Clark appear all over the state). And, of course cavalrymen: on the Little Bighorn in Montana Territory, George Custer made his last stand against Sitting Bull, Crazy Horse and their Sioux and Cheyenne warriors.

And while we're talking about Indians, let's recall that it was across Montana, from southwest to northeast, that the great Chief Joseph of the Nez Percé led his entire tribe, replete with hundreds of horses and cattle, pursued by two armies. He was seeking sanctuary in the land of the Great White Mother, where the Longknives could no longer slaughter his people. But winter, starvation and General Miles caught up to him in the Bear Paw mountains just two days short of the Medicine Line and freedom in Canada.

Montana, the Magazine of Western History tells and retells the wonderful tales. And who among its readers would ever doubt the two great tenets of the faith: to be a cowboy is to be the noblest of men, and to raise beef cattle on the range is the noblest duty of man. And he who was a part of all this a hundred years ago, may enter into the revered pantheon.

The deity of Gary Cooper is in trouble. He is still fondly remembered from time to time, but he is being replaced by more ancient – and younger – gods, just as Baal superseded Yahweh. But because art on the wall is a more lasting and dollar-appreciating medium than the flickering – and fickle – screen, Charlie Russell's immortality is assured.

In 1987 I attended a memorial service for George Renner, a man whose avocation was the compilation and study of Russell's works and relevant memorabilia. It was a big event, held in the Russell Museum in Great Falls. The faithful from all America west of the Mississippi were there, including (from southern California) Jack Russell, the adopted son of Charles. Since Russell's works now sell for great sums[5] and as the Russell myths become more hallowed, the worship of him as tribal god is certain to continue for a long time.

Mere men can act like gods if properly motivated. And the motivation here is revealed by "everybody wants to be a cowboy." John Wayne, Lorne Greene[6] and Ronald Reagan won fame by pretending they were cowboys and in Reagan's case, so great was the adulation that his people made him "king" as well as god.

Lesser mortals – also "pretend" cowboys but not famous – are content to wear any or all of the vestments to show they are at least part of the congregation. Texas oil men wear the hats and boots. Dairymen, who work with cows but aren't really cowboys, often "fake it" with cowboy gear. And just beyond suburbia are small acreages which their owners call "ranches." Denizens of these places drive pick-up trucks, often with a bale or two of hay or straw and an Australian Blue Heeler in the back. They may even own stock racks on which traces of manure bear proud evidence of contact with cattle or horses. Often as not a gun rack across the rear window obscures the driver's vision, and he's likely to have a rifle there with telescopic sights during hunting season.

The heroic Marlboro Man is all macho image – powerful and masculine, master of the horse – usually a whole herd of them. Can leather-jacketed motor cyclist compete with him? Macho and masculine? Yes. But heroic? No. The dispossessed losers outside respectable social fabric may aspire to ride the big bikes, but the real men – of position and power, the recipients of monetary perks and adulation, these heroes of the establishment and idols of the upwardly mobile – find their altar image in the Marlboro Man. And smoke his cigarettes.

At least Americans do. Europeans, on the other hand, speak derogatorily of cowboys. They saw "cowboy" Ronald Reagan as a sort of loose canon unrestrained by a sense of history of the real world or by the rules it runs by. But his American subjects, enraptured by and with the most powerful of all American myths, let him do anything he liked as long as he did it heroically – in a grand cause, with the noblest of purpose, firm and steadfast against the enemy and kind and loving to his people. In spite of controversy surrounding the mystifying Iran Arms sales, the adoring people of his pasture forgave him – or refused to concede he had done anything wrong.

While cowboys and ranchers can be romantic figures, there isn't much romance in milking cows. No status. On the big ranches, nobody wanted to be the milker. The typical cowboy disdained the chore and despised anyone who would think of making a living "pulling tits." No macho man here, with a milk bucket in one hand and a cigarette in the other! An old-time southern Alberta rancher used to refer to Edmonton as "the pail bunting [dairy] capital of Alberta," the implication being that anyone living there wasn't much of a person. (A pail bunter is a calf fed from a pail, which is how dairy calves are raised.)

In South America, this social distinction does not exist, mainly because it is women who do the milking and accept their inferior lot; any man rich enough to have a substantial dairy herd also owns a great deal of land. In much of the world, cow milking is women's work, not a proper task for a he-man. On Hutterite colonies in western Canada,[7] there are two cow herds – the men's herd (beef cattle) and the women's herd (dairy cattle). In the Scottish Hebrides the women look after the cattle and do the milking because the men "will be away to the fishing." The concept of milking as low-status women's work was taught to me by an old first-generation Ukrainian farmer. "No, I'm nod likink kedle," he insisted, "Vhen I come in to supper after a hard day, I vant-it my supper. But vhere is the old lady? She's oud feedink the cowss!" Some dairymen dress "western," but when the cowboy sees such a one he asks himself, "Who does he think he's kidding?"

During most of the twentieth century all boys played Cowboys and Indians. Cowboys were the good guys and, of course, the ultimate victors. Though Indians were killed, they often died noble as well as fearful deaths. Costumes, weapons and make-belief horses all played important roles in these games. Language, too, was important – the Indians speaking in guttural monosyllables, while the Cowboys spoke a tongue learned from the movies or radio and later from TV dramas.

The historian Arnold Toynbee has pointed out that heroes and heroic sagas and great literature are engendered by a "time of troubles" when there is no established order and heroic men are struggling against not only evil forces but against each other for supremacy. When order is established by powerful empires, *Pax Romana, Pax Britanica,*

Pax America, great deeds are few. The minstrels must sing of the matchless deeds of previous times of troubles – all the novels and films of both World Wars, the Westerns, the Vietnam revelations or even of a troubled time to come: *Star Wars*. And now, with the new Arabian time of troubles, can the troubadours of every ilk be saved? They can sing of the great war in Iraq. Or can they? We sacrificed too little – the song cannot be sweet if it is not also sad . . .

The history of the American West, before law, order and government tamed its multifarious peoples, tells of great deeds, evil and good constantly at war – a true heroic age. Contrast this with the development of the Canadian West: here The Hudson's Bay Company, the Anglican and Roman churches and the Mounted Police established stability, control and order long before the settlers came.

So there was no time of troubles in Western Canada (except in British Columbia during the mid-century gold rush and during the Riel Rebellion on the plains – both before the settlers came) and therefore no great heroes or legends. Thus the Canadian cowboy had to derive most of his traditions from the United States, despite the fact that the American cowboy played a relatively small part in the development of Canadian ranching. In Western Canada the North West Mounted Police achieved heroic stature. Robert W. Service in *Clancy of the Mounted*, said:

> In the little crimson manual, 'tis written plain and clear
> That he who wears the scarlet coat must say good bye to fear.

and then discarded their pill-box caps to wear, guess what? – a Stetson much like the American cowboy's.

The golden age of the cowboy was about 30 years, from the end of the Civil War to the nineties. And at both the beginning and end of this period, ranching was under extreme pressures. In the 1860s the Indians had not yet been "pacified" nor had the buffalo been removed from what were to become cattle ranges; by the eighties most of the "free range" had been grazed into the ground.

Land that had not been abused into non-productivity was being quickly filed on by homesteaders, and sheepmen had corralled the water holes. In the 1870s great trail herds moved north into Montana (Blackfoot country[8]) from Texas, searching for greener pastures – the *Lonesome Dove* saga. Other herds came east over the mountains from the Oregon territory. In the eighties these herds continued north into Canada to stock the new 100 000-acre leases[9] like that of Matthew Cochrane.

Early ranches in Western Canada were mainly owned/managed by well-to-do business men from Eastern Canada and by the English gentry. *Ranching with Lords and Commons* by John Craig is an interesting chronicle of this period. The homesteaders or "squatters" on the leases held by these upper-class operators were mainly from Ontario and the American Mid-West and were the natural "enemies" of the ranchers – classical Cains versus Abels. The North West Mounted Police patrolled the leases, evicting squatters and arresting marauding Indians[10] who had developed a taste for beef. A number of the police, on completion of their term of service, also became ranchers, sometimes in partnership with wealthy Easterners.

But the mark of Cain could not be denied: pioneer farmers Sam Livingston and John Glenn set up successful farms right on the Cochrane lease. Over a period of 20 years the ranchers gradually gave way to the homesteaders and were pushed back either into the hills or out onto the driest part of the plains where farming wasn't feasible. Most of them went broke and were succeeded by homesteaders who had gradually added to their first quarter or half section until they were big enough to call themselves ranchers. Cain had won the land, but the cream of Southern Alberta's society is still the rancher.

But nature abhors a vacuum. As the real cowboys declined in number, they were succeeded by two strains of pseudo-cowboys, entertainers and rodeo hands. The creator of both was William F. Cody – Buffalo Bill. Cody presented his first Wild West Show in 1883, just two years after the first big trail-herd was driven from Montana to the Cochrane lease in Alberta. He travelled all over the States and then took his show to Europe. Audiences acclaimed him everywhere. The show reenacted the great deeds of the frontiersman: pistol shooting (both as duels with blank ammunition and sharp-shooting with live bullets), trick roping, Indian Wars, trick riding, bronco-busting, buffalo hunting, and range wars, all in costume and with a great deal of realism.

It was but a short step to add cowboy songs.

The songs were first sung by night herders on the trail drives. The long, drawn-out notes of the mournful ballads – many of which were derived from old English and Irish[11] folk songs – encouraged the cattle to lie down peacefully and chew their cuds rather than breaking into a wild stampede. "The Old Chisholm Trail," on the other hand, was a good brisk tune to get the cattle up and going in the morning.

The popularity of cowboy music was mainly due to role-playing. The singer or the listener projected himself into the *persona* of the cowboy and so vicariously became brave and heroic. This explains how some cowboy singers without much talent still became popular among those who felt kinship with the historic cowboy. Twangy, nasal vowels, reached by slow glissading up to the top and then sliding mournfully down, sounded like finger nails on a blackboard if you didn't appreciate cowboy music. On the other hand, where good musicianship was the rule, the songs could be enjoyed by huge audiences. I well remember tuning into KSL Salt Lake City to listen to the Utah Buckaroos on a winter's night in 1931, but I never did appreciate Wilf Carter (Montana Slim in the U.S.) who added yodeling to the cowboys' repertoire.

In the Big Time, young America learned to adulate Roy Rogers and his wife Dale Evans, a pair in which all virtue was embodied. Gene Autry sang of true love as did a host of others. What is now known as Country and Western has a number of parents: the cowboy songs of course, but even more dominant in the lineage are the lovin'-cheatin'-hurtin' ballads right out of the Ozarks, with some old-country songs of the people added for good measure.

Ferde Grofe's "Grand Canyon Suite" is as western as you can get, but the era of the American cowboy was too short for the development of a world-class folkloric music such as we may hear on the Argentine pampas. The great bulk of Western music we hear today was composed after the true cowboy era. Radio, the movies and T.V. have revived the old themes and carried them to a world-wide audience Nor are there cowboy "dances" to compare with those of the *gaucho*. The cowboys had only 30 to 40 years, compared with the *gauchos'* 300, in which to create great art forms. What they did achieve in that short period is quite truly remarkable.

The greatest artistic impact of the cowboy theme has been in film. Right from the days of Tom Mix and Hoot Gibson, "Westerns" have had huge, if cyclic, appeal. That's where Montana's tribal god Gary Cooper acquired his divinity, and in this medium "The Duke," big John Wayne, achieved world-wide fame.

On printed pages, "western" writers have told their own stories (Will James), written romantic fictional action-adventures (Zane Gray), churned out violent pot boilers (Harold Robbins) and created vast libraries covering everything from children's books to "serious" literature. While cowboy singers don't have to be *real* men, bronco busters do.

The successful rodeo cowboy has to be in top shape to take the pounding he receives from the animals he masters – or which master him! In the contest between man and beast there is no place for "sissies." The Spanish words tell us that the sport is older than U.S. and Canadian ranching. There were *vaqueros* before there were buckaroos and contests among them long before the days of Bill Cody.

In Mexico, gentlemen cowboys, called *charros*, hold *charriadas*. The contests here are easier on the man and tougher on the beast. In a favorite event, the mounted *charro* chases a cow, grabs her tail, takes a dally around his saddle horn with the tail and then throws her on her back. After a few such throws, the cow becomes very evasive as our hero chases her. Cows are used rather than steers, probably because steers shortly will be beef and it would be a waste to use it up in the arena. For spectators *charriadas* are not as much fun as rodeos but they are easier on the contestants. And, therefore, not very heroic! It is significant that the Americans adopted the *rodeo* and the *vaquero* rather than the *charriada* and the *charro*.

In Canada *the* rodeo is the Calgary Stampede, which for decades has proclaimed itself The Greatest Outdoor Show on Earth. The first Stampede took place in 1912 under the direction (and assisted by the promotion) of an American named Guy Weadick. He was backed by four prominent ranchers, two of whom were also businessmen. They guaranteed Weadick $50 000 for his show.

It was a great success but was not re-staged till after the Great War, when a Victory Stampede was held. Shortly after that it was melded into the Calgary Exhibition and ever since the double-barrelled event has been known as the Calgary Exhibition and Stampede. The names of the four backers have been enshrined in the Big Four Building on the Stampede grounds. Their names (and brands) are prominently displayed there – Pat Burns, A.E Cross, Archie MacLean and George Lane.

Part of the appeal of rodeo is that the odds are so bad for the cowboy. Not only does he have to best the animal, he has to do it faster/better than all the other "hands" competing against him. And he pays for the privilege!

Buffalo Bill paid his hands by the day or show, but today's rodeo cowboy pays his entry fee before he can enter a contest.

Often the prize money totalled only the entrants' fees pooled and divided among the winners – a real deal for the management! Such a sweet deal that the cowboys organized themselves into a protective (later professional) association in order to bargain with the rodeo managers. The latter then formed their own association. There are no malingerers in rodeo – the money you may be losing is your own.

Pro rodeo can be a stepping stone to other, steadier occupations. Stock contractor, supplying animals for rodeos for a fee, is a prized calling. Often a cowboy has fantasies about "owning a nice piece of grass and a few good cattle" and sometimes the dream becomes reality. Occasionally a contestant shows talent as an entertainer. Instead of competing against his *confreres*, he is now paid by them as he sings/plays. Most just wear out and return (with their gimpy knees and uncertain backs) to the farms, trucks, barber shops, or wherever they took off from.

When anybody in rodeo says "cowboy," he's referring to a rodeo contestant. When a rancher says "cowboy," he's talking of a cowhand. The two may be the same man, but likely they're not.

Not many rodeo cowboys come from ranches anymore, partly because there are not many true ranches left and the remaining ones do not employ many hands. More important is the fact that contestants have to be athletes with innate ability who follow rigorous training.

Clothing and gear may be similar but often the rodeo cowboy's will be more flamboyant in color and design. Both, however, follow certain codes of proper dress. Considerable prestige goes with working for a big outfit; the cowboys of the Douglas Lake Ranch in British Columbia (Canada's largest) can be readily identified in the Nicola valley by their hats, vests and chaps. A neighboring rancher said to me of one we met on the road, "There's a Douglas Lake cowboy in his uniform!" Since to be a Douglas Lake cowboy is to be on top of the heap, he wants the world to recognize his status.

And to many in this world the cowboys' clothes are not simply to be admired but to be treasured. Judith MacFarlane of Manhattan, Montana, collects worn jeans from local cowhands and *registers* them – writes the story of the cowboy, his work, the name of his ranch (or its brand) and attaches the "papers" to the jeans. Then she ships them to a boutique in San Francisco where they are sold – with rips and holes – at $40 to $50 a pair as "Montana Broke Cowboy Jeans." She shares her profits 50/50 with the co-operating cowboys.

What a cowboy wears and what he puts on his horse make bold statements. The clothing and tack at world-class riding and jumping events such as The Masters', held at Calgary's Spruce Meadows, just don't seem right to the cowhand. The silly little saddles, the funny caps, the breeches – ugh! They're not for him. He calls this funny stuff Eastern or English and his own outfit Western.

The genesis of his Western gear lies beyond England, in southern Spain and the Camargue marshes of southern France. Even today, the cowboys of the Camargue dress something like our cowboys but they carry long-handled tridents to poke the cows and bulls with, an element of equipment that survives this side of the Atlantic as an electric prod.

The hats, boots, saddles, bridles and bits, ropes, stirrups – all these came our way from Mexico, together with words to describe them: lariat, from *la riata*; sombrero unchanged from the Spanish *sombrero* (makes a shade or a shadow); chaps from *chaparejos*, the leather trouser worn by the *vaqueros* in the spiny and tangled *chaparral*. *Arena* is the Spanish word for sand, which was spread in the rings where the contests (often bloody) took place between man and beast.

The essence of the working cowboy, what sets him apart from other men is his belief in the two tenets of faith: if the highest duty of man is the raising of beef cattle, then the noblest of men do just that. If you put it to him in words, he would tell you were crazy and full of BS and you sure were ignorant of the cow business. But what he does during emergencies proves it is not nonsense. Wallace Stegner's *Wolf Willow*, an exposition and descriptive narrative about ranching in the Cypress Hills of Saskatchewan, tells how the ranch foreman suffers tremendous privation in saving the herd during a winter storm. He comes near death but stays with his cattle till all are safe. It is part of an unwritten code or creed which all cattlemen – and cattle women – understand, but rarely talk about, except to say, "That was sure a helluva storm!"

In the same vein, old-time cowman, the late Joe Gilchrist of Medicine Hat, writes of moving a herd from southern Saskatchewan 100 miles (160 km) west into Alberta. After they got the cattle located, the three cowboys made for an old shack where they thought they might find some grub. All there was to eat was some oatmeal that the mice had got into. That was just about enough for one of the hands, who swore he would leave the blankety-blank outfit. But, Joe goes on, the fellow not only stayed the night – and the morning for breakfast! – but continued to work for the outfit for years and was one of their most dependable hands.

"I wouldn't do that for any man," my hired foreman's wife said to no one in particular, as the three of us reviewed a two-day ordeal after a late-spring blizzard knocked out the power,[12] buried the calving sheds in snow, smothered some of the calves and even some cows, made hauling feed impossible . . . but the cows giving birth and their new calves had to be attended to and they were. She was right, her husband hadn't done it for me, the owner, but for himself. He had saved all those calves against impossible odds and won.

That's what it's all about.

By the Way . . .

[1]"And Adah bare Jabal; he was the father of such as dwell in tents, and of such as have cattle."

[2]Philip II of Macedonia was the first leader to use mounted warriors in battle. He defeated a much larger force in 338 B.C. at Chaeronia

with a well-timed charge of 2 000 cavalry. His son, Alexander the Great, conquered most of the known world astride (without stirrups) his famous horse Bucephalus, which means "bull-headed."

[3]The nomads rode mares, whose milk they fermented and used as an on-going food supply. The stallions of the Christian knights went bananas at the proximity of so much she-stuff, and their actions, more amorous than martial, greatly embarrassed their noble riders.

[4]In those years, Montana used actual silver cartwheels in place of dollar bills in order to support its silver mined.

[5]Russell painted two water-color posters, at $10 a piece, for rancher-inventor William Heydlauff of Wild Horse, Alberta to promote a safety seat-lock for wagons. Both pictures show a young couple with a baby riding in a wagon as danger draws nigh: the horses shy wildly as a motor car approaches and the wife and child are thrown from the wagon without the safety lock; but with the safety lock in place, all is serene aboard the wagon despite the threatening auto which has run the team off the road. Russell was then (1910) a cowboy who painted pictures now and then for some extra cash. Elizabeth Dear, Curator of the C.M. Russell Museum in Great Falls, which owns the originals, says: "Both paintings have been reproduced as prints (which are no longer available) and are also reproduced in our collection catalog which can be purchased for $10 through our shop."

[6]Greene was originally a Canadian newscaster whose rich mellifluous voice brought us comfort and assurance during the terrible days of the World War Two blitz. At the height of his T.V. fame, a quarter of a century later, as patriarchal Ben Cartwright of the Ponderosa Ranch, he appeared at the Edmonton Spring Rodeo as a special guest. His "act" was to gallop around the arena to the ringing cheers of thousands. The kids loved him, but what any horseman saw was a very large and overly-heavy middle-aged man flopping about without skill or grace on a horse big enough and powerful enough to submit to this indignity.

[7]An Anabaptist German-speaking sect somewhat similar to the Amish who live in communal groups on large farms.

[8]The Blackfoot (now the Siksika and which were called Blackfeet in the U.S.) were the most warlike of all the Northern Plains tribes. Both explorers and settlers by-passed their territory, going north or south of their hunting grounds, on their way to the Pacific coast.

[9]John A. Macdonald, the Canadian prime minister, hoped to avoid the major problems encountered by early U.S. ranching: over-grazing and range wars. He conferred with his friend, Matthew Cochrane of Compton County, Quebec. They devised a scheme whereby leases (of

100 000 acres) would be granted only to those who could stock them – essentially, the wealthy. No one but the lease holder could run cattle on the lease. Cochrane was granted the first such lease in 1881; he stocked it with cattle driven up from Montana.

[10]There are too few Mounties and too many Indians; a group of ranchers from the Fort Macleod area moved down to Montana to escape Indian depredations. A Mrs. Armstrong, her two daughters and her foreman, named Williams, turn up in western legends. They had been running a dairy near Calgary and later at Macleod and they too moved down to Montana, along with the ranchers. They escaped the Indians but Mrs. Armstrong and her foreman were murdered by outlaws. The daughters witnessed the foul deeds from a hiding place. They reported the murders to the sheriff who promptly rounded up all newcomers. The girls identified the culprits who were summarily strung up.

[11]*The Streets of Laredo* is sung to a tune derived from an Irish ballad in which an old man gazes at the illegitimate baby son of his adulterous young wife.

[12]On a ranch when the power goes off, the water pumps stop – no water for either man or beast. There is no heat or light in the house, no heat-lamps to warm and dry weak calves, no hot food – not even hot coffee. As the cowboys say, "It's a helluva time."

Chapter Six

Blue Bloods, White-Faces
and Half Castes

>>>>>>>>>>>>>>>>>>>>>

Royalty is older than history. Anybody who feels important is very proud of his or her heritage. The late Shah of Iran could trace his royal line back only one generation – to his opportunistic father – so he spent millions of dollars telling the world how right was *his* claim to the ancient Peacock Throne. But he lacked the real criterion – *blood.*

Can you trace your blood back a long way to some great historic figure? Two writers of the New Testament take considerable trouble to trace Jesus' descent from King David. That the accounts don't agree exactly doesn't seem to bother many people, nor does the pursuing of the line to Joseph, who was not, after all, Jesus' corporeal father. But still, they believed it worthwhile to set it all down. If the Israelites were going to have a Messiah, it was important that he be of the Royal Line.

When Bonny Prince Charles revealed himself to Scottish crofters as their "lawful king," they knelt before him in fear and trembling and near adoration. They swore undying fealty – and died at Culloden. Even today, royal lines can make otherwise rational people do very strange things. But a prince without a pedigree is a poor thing, indeed.

This business of hereditary chieftainship is firmly rooted in all cultures. Look at the Nehru-Ghandi-Ghandi dynasty in recent India, or just next door where Bhuto-pere was followed by Bhuto-fille. And was it not proper that Oliver Cromwell's son follow his illustrious father as Protector of the British realm? The U.S. is by no means immune; just add up the high-position Adamses in the early years of the Republic. In business, dynasty-building is accepted, but here power and wealth also contribute to successorship. In the ranching business, feudalism is readily apparent. Old friends of prominent families watch with pleasure as a new generation takes over. In meeting a young rancher, a member of the old guard will, if he recognizes the surname, ask "Now, who is your dad?"

Not only is royal lineage important, but the VIP likes to assign certain royal attributes to his possessions. Of what value is a fake Reubens? Or a car that just looks like a Rolls? So a long time ago, Man began to trace the bloodlines of those of his possessions which reproduced.

It began with the Arabs and their horses at least a thousand years ago, and was brought to England in the bodies of three stallions which became the founders of the Thoroughbred breed: the Byerly Turk, the Darley Arabian and the Godolphin Arabian. All Thoroughbreds trace to these horses, generally to all three many times over, if their pedigrees are traced far enough back (pedigree is derived from Old French, meaning the foot of a crane; early pedigrees were drawn like a bird's foot).

In the same way, people are proud of the animals they own with impeccable bloodlines. Breeders have formed associations to keep their animals' *blood pure* and have written in a book the names of all ancestors back to the founders of the particular breed.

All animals with pedigrees (and often also performance and/or appearance) acceptable to an association may be registered in their book. The animal is then called "registered" or "purebred." (Thoroughbred, spelled with a capital "T," applies as a breed name only to a certain breed of horse. Saying you have a "thoroughbred bull" will brand you as a charlatan or ignoramus.)

Horses are registered in stud books and most other farm livestock in herd books. Farms that raise pedigreed animals are called purebred farms in North America and stud farms everywhere else. The owners of these establishments are called registered breeders in North America and stud breeders elsewhere but are also known as purebred breeders everywhere. The word stud is not used much in North America except to refer to a stallion, where its use is considered somewhat indelicate, about the same shock value as the word bitch. In Britain and Down Under, however, stud is a perfectly acceptable word.

A breed is made up of the animals in the herd book. But also recognized as being part of the breed are those animals of similar characteristics and breeding but are not registered in the herd book. These animals are "grades." Most animals raised commercially are grades and the breeders of them are called commercial breeders. It is common in North America to refer to a breeder as a "man" instead of a "breeder." Thus: "LBJ was a purebred man, had a bunch of pretty little Herefords." Or: "Hell, no! I don't want nothin' to do with them purebreds. I'm a commercial man."

Nowadays many commercial cattle are "crossbreds," animals whose parents were of different breeds. The very common crossbred on the western ranges is the "black baldy," a cross between Hereford and Angus parents. The baldy is black and hornless with a white or mottled face. Most commer-

cial herds have a considerable number of crossbred cattle but there are still quite a few "straight" commercial herds made up of grades of one breed. A common sight is a herd made up of straight cows and crossbred calves, for example Hereford cows with Charolais-cross calves.

If a cattleman consistently uses bulls of one breed on commercial cows over several generations, he is said to be "grading up." This tactic was used by western ranchers in the early part of this century as they graded up the original Longhorn cattle to the white-faced Herefords. Similarly it was used by the importers of European cattle (Exotics) in the sixties and seventies to increase the numbers of the new breeds.

Whereas the ranchers weren't too concerned about blood percentages, the Exotic breeders were very anxious to reach some level of near-purity as fast as possible. Their first crosses were called half-bloods, the second three-quarter bloods and so on. Some herd books accepted 7/8 as "purebred," while others asked for 15/16 or even 31/32. In these herd books, cattle going through the up-grading process were *recorded* in the herd book, not *were not registered*.

In the case of the Charolais breed, the matter was further complicated by the fact that there was already a Canadian herd book in operation when the first French cattle were imported to Canada in 1966. In this book domestic cattle had already been registered (or recorded). The owners of domestic Charolais attempted to trace their stock's ancestry to French cattle that had been imported into Mexico years earlier and then exported (illegally) to the U.S. From these early importations, grading up had produced a number of domestic purebreds (at least 15/16 pure). A lot of guessing went into picking appropriate blood percentages because early records were scanty. At the same time (and in the same book), there were a number of Charolais cattle from Mexico that had no admixture of domestic blood; these were called "full bloods."

Thus there were no less than three categories of purebreds. You might have in the same pen a domestic purebred alongside a full-blood purebred and beside them a full-French purebred, all registered in the same book. The law of supply and demand soon sorted them out in order of dollar[1] worthiness: first the full French, then the full bloods, and finally the domestic purebreds.

The situation was even more complicated than that because in the U.S. there were already several Charolais associations with their separate herd books before the Canadian[2] imports arrived and there was some controversy about registering an animal from a competing book. (Chapter 14, "The Exotics" will have more to say about the Charolais as well as other European breeds which revolutionized the beef industry in Canada and made a lesser but still important impact in the United States.)

The first "improvement" of domestic cattle began in Northern England in the valley of the Tees river in the eighteenth century. These Teeswater cattle were called Shorthorns to distinguish them from a competing breed[3] with longer horns. William Bates and the Brothers Colling noticed that some cattle were vastly superior to others in their rate of growth and particularly in how they "fleshed out." They began to breed these animals together so as to produce a superior "breed." Much of this breeding was very "close," that is, the animals were closely related. One of Bates' favorite bulls, "Champion of England,"

was mated to daughters, sisters, the bull's own mother and numerous other close relatives. This "incestuous" activity scandalized many of his neighbors and other members of society who might be equated with our modern animal-rights activists. Moreover it flew in the face of practical experience – every breeder knew that close matings usually resulted in poor beasts and sometimes produced monsters.

No one knew anything about genetics at that time, except that "like begets like" and of course there was all this nonsense floating around about "blood." But the early Shorthorn breeders had hit upon Darwin's principle of genetic science, something they didn't understand but nonetheless used to advantage. It goes like this: Every animal inherits half its characteristics from each parent. Some characteristics are "hidden" and some are "expressed." Some are "dominant" and some "recessive," a few are "blended." Some are generally "good" for the animal's welfare but some are "bad." Many of the bad characteristics are recessive and are expressed most readily when close matings occur. These generalizations are also evident in "closed" human populations, such as the Hutterites in western Canada, isolated northern Indian bands and the peoples of Pitcairns and Easter Islands. Most of the good characteristics are dominant and are expressed most positively when the mating animals are not related.

However, if close breeding is followed and all the poor-doing animals are eliminated, the ones that are left may perform well. What is most important, they will "breed true." So, after the initial culling of these bad individuals, what is left can make you money. And there is another tremendous advantage that follows after some generations of close breeding: the hybrid vigor that occurs in the offspring when unrelated inbred lines are crossed.

Let's look how the wolves do it, entirely naturally. They run in packs. In each pack is an alpha male and an alpha female. They are easily recognized because they carry their tails high; the slinking or skulking wolf with his tail between his legs does not breed. The breeders are the superior animals and the rest of the pack know it. (In fact, to leave "with your tail between your legs" implies that you have been taught quite severely just how inferior your status is.) But to get back to the wolves. As long as food is scarce, the pack remains static, the February matings of the alphas resulting in a small litter each spring, with perhaps one from the litter surviving the first year. In a static pack, the alpha bitch will jealously prevent the other females from breeding or will kill their pups. The alphas are replaced as they grow old by their most aggressive son and daughter. Thus, over a few generations the wolf pack becomes very inbred; recessive bad genes

are revealed and their bearers can't keep up and so die. The gene pool decreases in number but increases in quality because only the strongest and most aggressive animals are surviving and breeding.

But when there is food in abundance, watch out! Other females get bred and soon there is a raft of new pups of six to eight in each litter. The population explodes, the pack becomes too big for one boss and the young aggressive males challenge the alpha king. If the king wins, the challenger leaves the pack and goes to find a mate from another pack. If the upstart bests his father, the old Lothario will look for a new love with new and different genes.

The alpha queen is also challenged; if she is dethroned, she may find a boyfriend over the hill. Some of the remaining daughters, who still aren't quite equal to mother (or her successor), leave home and find fulfillment with the lusty new kids on the block. And so out-crossing rather than inbreeding becomes the mode.

Thus there is an explosive joining of unrelated good genes – the offspring are wonderfully swift and powerful and fertile and suddenly there are wolves everywhere and all the stockmen are calling for the reinstatement of bounties. Nature's scheme is to alternate periods of inbreeding (to eliminate bad genes) with periods of wide crossing (to produce stronger more aggressive animals).

Whether we are proud of it or not, we instinctively follow Nature's mandates. Our instincts are animal instincts that developed over thousands of years. Understanding ourselves enables us to better understand animals and vice versa.

A reading of the Old Testament reveals how man has two conflicting – to some, unnatural – urges: to inbreed and to outcross. The ancient Hebrews were always berating their young men for "lusting after strange women," while King David had a real problem with one of his sons who lusted after his sister. The theme recurs several times, sometimes in most dramatic context. We recall how Jacob was all for finding a strange woman, so his father Isaac sent him to another village to find his cousin Rachel.

But to go back to the Shorthorn cattle beside the Tees river. The first Shorthorn herd book was published in 1822. Breeders were so successful with their cattle and breeding methods that they were imitated across Britain and eventually around the world. The French adopted this philosophy entire, even using the Anglo term herd book-While the early improvers were not long on genetics, they were no slouches when it came to business. So they devised a theory about purebred livestock that has carried down even until this day. The idea was to make money today and tomorrow and forever.

Here's the thesis. The best stock are raised by the founders of the breed and a few of their associates who have acquired some of the best of the original breed. These are called "elite" breeders and their stock are supposed to sell for the highest prices. The elite breeders make the progeny of their cattle available to the next level in the hierarchy, whose main job is to increase numbers for distribution to the ordinary pure-bred breeder. He in turn supplies the commercial farmer or rancher with bulls to breed grade cows. It was generally assumed that, as you proceeded down the ladder, both quality and price would be lower.

It doesn't always work out that way by any means. There is a continual shifting and juggling for position and every year a new breeder with either high-priced or championship cattle appears, while some of the old faithfuls fade into the shadows. Competition for elite status is fierce, for not only are there monetary rewards, but great advancement in status for those who make it to the top.

If a dear-departed were a successful purebred breeder in his life-time, this condition will always be favorably extolled during the eulogy at his funeral. And while living, the breeder is paid respect by his neighbors, other breeders and frequently governments. He is often a leader in community affairs and his advice is sought by young men, ministers of the church, new settlers and even bankers. The more show winnings his cattle have garnered and the more money they have sold for, the more is he respected. But with this esteem comes responsibility. The successful breeder is expected to be honest in all his dealings and to be "fair" to his customers. No *caveat emptor* here. Instead, it's, "If she don't get in calf, bring her back and you can pick another one." With few exceptions, top breeders are exemplary[4] citizens.

The theory of breeder hierarchy is dependent on another interesting creed, that of "blood running out." It goes like this: the more generations removed from the primal source (the elite breeder) the weaker the blood.[5] After a few generations it runs out and you have to return to the source to renew the blood.

Argentinean cattle breeders swallowed this myth hook, line and sinker and year after year they would return to the big Shorthorn sale in Perth, Scotland to renew the blood. It was a wonderful system for all concerned. The Argentinean could boast among his wealthy *ranchero* friends how he had bought the Grand Champion at Perth. And, of course, these same *rancheros* would line up to buy the progeny of this great bull. Meanwhile the breeders in Britain went to the bank happy.

The doctrine was particularly useful if the potential buyer were wealthy; if he were also titled, it was a great victory, indeed. In the 1920s, the then Prince of Wales owned a ranch in Southern Alberta about 60 miles (96 km) from Calgary. He had stocked this ranch with purebred Shorthorn cattle with the beneficent ambition to sell progeny of this elite stock in Canada and so carry out a princely function. To head his herd, he bought a magnificent white bull, "King of the Fairies," which had been Grand Champion at the Chicago International Exposition. Things went along as they should and in due course my father bought a grandson of the King (from a multiplier breeder) to head our herd of some- purebred and some-commercial cows. My father, who was a graduate of the Guelph Agricultural College and so held a degree granted by the University of Toronto, took great pride in the bull and in a non-boastful way would tell anyone who was interested that "His grandsire was King of the Fairies." I didn't think much of him as a bull and figured that the blood had certainly run out.

Note that I speak of "creeds and tenets and faith." Have you begun to wonder if is was a religious subject? Indeed it is but not as religion is viewed on earth. The next chapter describes the Cattle Religion. You can't understand the purebred cattle business if you don't have the faith!

$$\boxed{\text{By the Way}\ldots}$$

[1]The first importations in 1966 cost their Canadian owners less than $7 000. Some of these were shortly resold to American buyers for from $30 000 to $60 000. The boom was on!

[2]European cattle were not imported directly into the United States but came via Canada, which had set up a very comprehensive testing and quarantine program. (Read the chapter on the Exotics.)

[3]The first improvement of cattle in England was actually done with the ancient Longhorn breed – at one time the most popular in the country. These are the massive multi-colored cattle you see in seventeenth and eighteenth century paintings of rural England. The in-

spired breeder, Robert Bakewell, lost out to the Shorthorn breeders and the Longhorns became almost extinct. I saw a remnant herd grazing the "meadow" of Christ Church College in Oxford in April, 1992. The college porters (the chaps you'll find at the college gates wearing bowler hats and black coats) assured me (quite erroneously, of course) that this breed had been used in developing the American Longhorn. Elizabeth Henson, the secretary of the Longhorn breed association, who, with her fatther, operates a rare-breeds farm, told me the porters were wrong and that she would write the college, putting them straight.

[4]Colin Thatcher, who was found guilty of murdering his wife, was sometime President of the Saskatchewan Hereford Association and a Director of the Canadian Hereford Association. Many of his neighbors and fellow breeders still hold him in high regard.

[5]The strange tenet of faith – that the further removed a generation is from the purebred breeder, the weaker the blood – is incorporated into the laws governing the production and sale of registered seed grains. Intelligent people still believe that seed does "run out."

Tumultuous Worship

Silent Worship

Chapter Seven

Cattle Religions
>>>>>>>>>>>>

In September, 1969, residents of the little village of Priddis, which is thirty miles (48 km) southwest of Calgary, were wakened at two a.m. by what sounded like the bang of a supersonic jet. The noise continued for several seconds, accompanied by the roaring and whistling of a great wind. Then all was quiet. The "big bang" made good conversation in the village post office and general store, but it was not until two days later that a probable cause for the strange event was revealed.

A local cowboy on a routine stock check found a newly-made quarter-acre clearing in an aspen grove in a remote corner of the ranch's fall-calving pasture. There were no trails, other than those made by game, leading from the pasture to the clearing. And just a few yards away was the boundary fence of the Sarcee Indian Reserve, beyond which was a black-spruce bog. The cowboy, who was part Indian, knew that nobody from the reserve had been near the bog in years. The aspen poplar appeared to have been blown out and away from the centre of the clearing, at which point there was an elliptical crater about 30' (9 metres) wide. Some of the bushes and leaves around the crater were partially burned.

The cowboy reported his find to the ranch owner who promptly called the RCMP in Calgary. The arrival of the police and their subsequent investigation set the rural community buzzing. The general impression left in the neighborhood was that there had been an extraterrestrial visitation. A month earlier a similar inexplicable clearing, also with evidence of fire, had been discovered 180 miles (288 km) further north, near Alder Flats. Thus there was considerable expectation of another visit – perhaps even an invasion.

But what the police had found at the scene and about which they said nothing the police determined that was a canister filled with computer tapes. With the help of code experts these tapes, apparently left here by the extraterrestrials, revealed a whimsical view of social life in North America. Finally, the police decided the tapes were simply the work of a crank and hushed the whole thing up for fear of looking foolish. Some years later I was able (I won't reveal how for fear of compromising some members of the police force) able to "read" one of the tapes. It was entitled, "The Cattle Religions."

The first part of the tape gave a detailed account of the sacred cows of India and how this peculiar worship affected – mostly adversely – the social and economic life of the people there. The second section dealt with the cattle religion of the Americas, Western Erurope and Australasia. A somewhat abridged form of this section follows:

"The Great Cattle Religions" can be compared with other great religions of the western world. It has a priesthood, holy books, sacred cities[1] articles of faith, priestly and lay vestments, meetings of congregations and formal organizations. It also has a number of sects which vie with each other for followers – in fact here may be seen most of the trappings of the other religions, with two specific differences: first, whereas all the major religions are monotheistic, that is they worship one god, the followers of the cattle religion worship a large number of a special kind of cattle which they call "pedigreed" or "purebred." There are thousands of such cattle, but followers of the faith seem to limit their adulation and worship to a limited number and kind which they call their breed. The second difference is that, whereas the other religions give promise of a hereafter, cattle people deal entirely with life on earth, a life which they promise will be made happier and richer to those who join their faith and buy their cattle.

Vestments and trappings are most evident in North America. All male members of the faith wear a stylized "cowboy" costume, though many of them rarely, if ever, ride a horse. The hat, made of felt or straw, is wide-brimmed and usually high-crowned. The fashion is derived from the *vaqueros* of Mexico and traces back in origin to Andalusia in Spain and the Camargue marshes in southern France. The neck piece is usually of silk and can be worn loose or knotted. If a suit jacket is worn, it can be identified as being "of the flock" by a unique cutting and stitching across the back and shoulders. Shirts are colorful and may be form-fitting for those who have lithesome figures or wide and billowy.

The trousers, which also are derived from southern Europe, fit the hips and legs closely and are supported by a belt, usually with an enormous buckle. A silver buckle is sometimes significant of a strange cult activity involving wrestling and other contests with male or neutered cattle. These wretched beasts are obviously not sacred but are perhaps part of the sect's demon world.

When affluence and middle age strike the believer, he finds his belly, now inappropriately large, prevents him from pulling the trousers up to the waist. Common practice is to shorten the trouser leg, pull the trousers about half-way up the belly, and secure them with a belt just a few inches above the genitals. It is obvious that faith is stronger than the believer's sense of form and of propriety.

The boots – again with Mediterranean origins – fit the legs closely. They are frequently hidden by the pant leg for "dress" occasions and sometimes for work. For most work situations, the trouser is often put inside the boot, especially for rough work. The boots can be either mass-produced quite cheaply or be hand-made and expensive. Both types have pointed toes but the hand-made boots are more rounded in the toe. They can be of any kind of leather, from cowhide to snake skin and alligator skin. For people who do not raise cattle, the boot is a medium of conspicuous consumption among both the wealthy and the pretentious.

The clothing just described applies to men. Women frequently wear a feminized version, including hat, boots, shirt and trousers, but they often wear what is referred to as a "squaw" dress – a highly colored article with a flaring skirt and a tight waist. The reference to costumes of aboriginal females seems most inappropriate. Children, for festive occasions, are frequently dressed in garb similar to that of their parents.

As among other religions, there are many false prophets and insincere worshippers. These non-believers, known as "Urban Cowboys," are not entitled to wear the religious vestments, but they wear them anyway, often without consideration for religious significance, much to the annoyance of the truly faithful.

In this religion there are two major methods of public worship – silent and tumultuous – the latter not unlike the exuberant gatherings of some Christian sects in the southern United States. The two forms are held sequentially: first silent worship and then tumultuous worship. The latter, as is the case in many churches, attracts much larger congregations, including not only the faithful and their business and family associates; also a number of heathen who are merely curious and looking for an interesting spectacle. Members of competing sects frequently appear at services of their rivals but, as is often the case with other churches, only as spectators – they do not usually join in the prayers and affirmations of faith.

Silent worship is held in an enclosed arena, usually covered. The service begins with some oratory by a senior priest. He welcomes the congregation and then takes some time to extol the holy cattle which will soon be led before them. This somewhat resembles what is called the "Gloria" in traditional churches. Next to the orator, are a number of scribes, lesser priests and high-ranking laymen and a much-respected person who might correspond to a bishop – the judge. All these people wear holy raiment, spotlessly clean in spite of the environment.

The scribes are representatives of holy books called breed publications. Owners of sacred cattle pay tithes to them, and, in turn, the scribes extoll the virtues of the owners' cattle not only during tumultuous worship, which is to follow, but also in the sacred book. They regularly publish pictures of the sacred cattle if the owner is a generous contributor. In addition, since the scribe is considered an expert in the various degrees of merit and holiness of the sacred cattle, he will advise other members of the faith to buy the cattle he writes and talks about. He promotes in accordance with the degree of tithing. The moral tenet of this faith seems to be: much can be expected if much is given. During silent prayer these scribes look very wise, smile upon occasion, but say very little.

From time to time they may be called to assist the bishop [judge] and his altar boy [ringmaster]. The altar boy carries a cane which he uses to direct proceedings in the church. Some scribes also carry canes which gives them a special air of dignity, if not authority.

After some announcements, the main service begins by attractive young women, the spiritual successors to the vestal virgins of antiquity, carrying banners which name and extol the faith. This procession resembles closely the entrance procession which initiates tumultuous prayer in the Roman Catholic, Orthodox and Anglican communities, but differs from these in that there is no singing by either the congregation or persons in the procession. Instead, members of the congregation greet their appearance with applause and then turn to their prayer books as a group of young cattle are led into the arena in single file.

These sacred cattle have been washed, combed and perfumed, their hair has been cut here and there, their hooves polished and their tails (in some instances) rolled into balls. They present a pleasing sight. Most of the persons leading the cattle are adolescent, about equally divided between the sexes. Among them are, however, a number of middle-aged men, known as "old pros," who have been showing cattle for years and are reputed to be able to overcome a beast's sins by various artifices. The younger members of this group are sometimes called "steer jockeys."

The bishop walks among the cattle gods, obviously assessing them for degrees of holiness. After some minutes, he confers with the ring- master who then directs the young men and women to line the cattle up at one end of the arena in accordance with their holy rank.

At this juncture there frequently is some applause, but also some groans may be heard; apparently some members of the congregation are repenting their sins. When the cattle have been placed in a lateral line, the bishop nods towards the desk where some other scribes have been arranging small banners and ribbons of various colors. A young woman gives each of the persons holding the cattle a ribbon of a different color, each color representing a different level of holiness. The cattle are then led out.

This part of the service is repeated again and again, each time with different and bigger cattle. Eventually a holy-of-holies [the Grand Champion] is determined to much applause (and a little repentant groaning) and several altar boys hold graven wooden images and brass vessels over the most sacred cattle as the scribes photograph them and their caretakers [owners]. Both sexes of cattle go through this performance. It is a tedious, drawn-out affair and thus not surprising to see some members of the congregation leave the church to take refreshment in the form of food and drink.

Rarely is there a recessional march by the high and low priests but the holiest cattle [the champions] may be led around the ring, at which time the congregation applauds. During this recession a barely audible prayer from one of the previous groaners may be heard: "Gehu, that guy has to be blind!"

Tumultuous worship is more exciting. Celebrated when purebred cattle are sold at public auction, it may follow silent worship either by a few hours or by a day, or may be held with no previous silent worship. Just as with the other religions, where worship may be held in very humble "mission" churches or in extremely large and ornate cathedrals and all manner of places in between, so cattle auctions are held everywhere, from modest farm corrals to the grandest and most palatial ballrooms of the continent's poshest hotels.

The object of the ritual of tumultuous worship is to gain new converts, enable believers to reaffirm their faith, publicize the sect [breed], renew friendships among believers, generally have a good time, and make money – for the cattle owners, scribes, church and for a remarkable evangelic high priest called "auctioneer." The money comes from a number of sources. Believers tend to buy each others' cattle. They put a "floor" under the market, for no breeder wants to see the average price for the breed cheapened.

A few cattle may be sold to commercial breeders – people who believe only some of the tenets of faith – or none of them – but want to use the cattle in their herds, the progeny of which will be sold for beef for humans. This group is much larger than that of the proclaimed adherents to the faith but provide only a small portion of the buying power at a sale, except for bulls, of which they buy the major share. They somewhat resemble the general members of a conventional church who don't have much faith in its doctrines and don't give it much support but use it on rare occasions for such necessary rites as baptisms, weddings and funerals.

The most avidly sought-after members of the congregation are rich business and professional men, industrialists[2], movie stars and prominent politicians[3]. If they can be converted to the faith, they will provide a magnificent market and pay prices to fit their superior standing. Moreover, they will be around for years as buyers but will probably not offer much selling competition to breeders of reputation cattle – cattle which have sold for high prices and have also received recognition at the silent worship services in major (and holy) cattle cities. After conversion, such prominent people often become avid evangelists themselves.

At any tumultuous service, however, it is absolutely essential that breeders attend to support their fellow breeders. They do this by encouraging the non-faithful to bid, and by bidding themselves on many animals, while buying only a few. This is called "helping the sale along" as the breeder supports his friends. Some breeders are tempted to support their own sale but this activity is frowned on by everyone and is prohibited at most sales. The owner is usually given the right of one bid or a reserve bid so as not to sacrifice his cattle. In this religion, sacrifices are avoided as much as possible, but they do occur upon occasion. The effect of such sacrifice is not to strengthen the faith but to weaken it. Sometimes an owner will have a close friend support his sale, assuring the helper that he will buy back any animals that the friend gets left with, or caught with. This practice is frowned upon, but appears to be fairly common.

From time to time, those running the tumultuous service are advised beforehand that a recent convert, with money, will attend and affirm his faith often and even with abandon. They will say privately of such a person that they "saw him coming." Under such circumstances the event is considered to be a great success and is colloquially referred to as a "helluva sale."

The service begins after a number of faith affirmations have been made by the scribes, owners and others. The priest starts his chant as a sacred animal, in finest fit, is led before him into a small ring. The priest cries from an elevated platform or pulpit, using an audio-magnifying device of great power. Beneath him, surrounding the sacred beast, the scribes gyrate feverishly, waving and pointing with their prayer books [catalogs] at the congregation, repeating in loud voices a few words and numbers from the auctioneer's chant. This chant is in a strange and difficult tongue which the auctioneer has learned at a special school. Apparently the only part of the chant which the congregation understands and has to be concerned with are the numbers which are repeated at the end of each sentence.

The noise level is very high. The faithful sit immobile. If they move a hand or nod a head, the priest may accept this as an affirmation of faith and declare the sacred animal given to their care. The congregation study their prayer books dutifully every minute or so, stare at the cattle-god in the ring and occasionally whisper a word or two to a neighbor. Meanwhile the auctioneer's voice and tempo of speech are increasing, as is tension throughout the church. Repeatedly, a few worshippers will wave their prayer books, thus affirming their faith and indicating they will pay even more for the prize. With each affirmation, a scribe [ringman] calls "Ho" in a loud voice and points his prayer book directly at the high priest and so conveys the prayer directly to him.

Surely this will be the climax! But no. The high priest suddenly drops his voice to a low tone and says some lovely and intimate things about the animal in the ring, its parentage, close relations and the man who raised him and perhaps the man who raised his grandsire. Then either a scribe or a companion high priest will take the microphone and extol the virtues of the bull or cow and advise the world that the price bid is ridiculous, that surely there is someone there who realizes the value, the potential of this great animal; what a marvelous opportunity is presented at this moment, tomorrow will be too late. Then the auctioneer has another turn. After a few minutes, everyone senses the moment of truth is nigh and the auctioneer then says the holiest of holy words: "sold."

It is irrevocable. No confession of a contrite heart can stop the moving finger that has writ. Someone has bought the god-beast and the money changer beside the high priest writes numbers and names in his book.

The animal is led out and another brought in and the performance repeated.

There does not appear to be any relationship between the contemporary cattle religion and the bull worship that occurred in what is known as the Ancient World. Egyptians, Mesopotamians and the many enemies of the Israelites along the River Jordan, all bowed down before cattle or images of cattle but there is no continuum between these ancient faiths and the worship of purebred cattle in the twentieth century.

Here we will leave our alien friends and I will take up the narrative again, adding perhaps a few earthly insights.

As the extraterrestrials noted, the auctioneer is the "high priest of the service." Usually a man of national and sometimes international stature, he travels extensively, often by air. His reputation assures the sale will be as successful as possible under the circumstances. He has many friends in the faith and frequently solicits their assistance in a sale, some time before the sale takes place. The friend agrees to buy certain animals at a specified price or range of prices. It is very comforting to the vendors to know that the auctioneer has some orders in his pocket.

Such a circumstance enables the auctioneer to take some bids "off the rafters," using the bid in his pocket as assurance he "won't get stuck with some son of a bitch."

This colloquial euphemism means that he has taken a non-existent bid and so he now owns the animal himself. He will explain that he has bought the animal "on order" for a non-present buyer. Sometimes he extricates himself from such a position by pretending to have mistaken a sign given him by a member of the congregation as a bid. He asks the surprised victim to reconfirm his bid.

"You were in at three thousand and twenty? Right?"

The victim denies everything and the auctioneer starts the sale again, at a bid or two below his rafters bid. This can be and often is an honest mistake. If it does not happen often, nothing is said.

If the auctioneer "has seen coming" a wealthy and eager prospective buyer, he may alternate bids made by the rafter and bids made by the prospect. The art is to run the prospect to close to his limit and then sell him the animal at that figure. This takes much skill and a gambling instinct on the part of the auctioneer. This is risky. If the congregation suspects the high priest is "running the sale" with rafter bids, no one will bid, the sale will be a disaster and the reputation of the auctioneer will be seriously impaired, even destroyed. On the other hand, the sale can become deadly boring and slow if the auctioneer sees not the rafters.

Usually the Grand Champions are sold first to set the tone of the sale and establish a good average. At other times, they may be sold somewhat later when more buyers have assembled in the church. When it is over, there is often a sort of victory feast sponsored by the sellers. Often as not there is what is called a pre-sale party, at which prospective buyers drink wine and spirits proffered by the sellers and the scribes.

Most services of tumultuous worship are positive and relatively happy events, whereas silent worship is satisfying only to a few because "we all can't be winners."

Some observation of tumultuous worship leads one to the conclusion that it no place for babes in the woods, either as buyer or seller. A good businessman may soon learn the art and science of buying purebred cattle but selling them involves so many unspoken imponderables that the wise among them retain a sales management company to handle the whole business.

For a percentage of the proceeds the sales company rents the church, pays the auctioneer and clerk, advertises the event via not only the holy books but in other media (including radio and television in some instances), encourages prospective buyers, seeks firm pre-sale bids, gains as much free publicity as possible from all media, arranges for trucks, often arranges for hotel and local transportation needs of some buyers, takes charge of the pre-sale party and the post-sale celebration if these are held, prepares and prints the catalogs (holy books) and distributes these in advance to prospective buyers, prepares and mails news releases and sale reports and most important, visits the owner's farm or ranch and helps select cattle, checks pedigrees . . . whatever it takes to make a good sale. His fee is usually 10 to 15 percent of the gross. Sometimes the sale manager is the auctioneer, sometimes there is only arms-length relationship with the auctioneer and sometimes the manager and the auctioneer work hand-in-glove. The auctioneer will get between five and 10 percent of the gross in small specialty sales; the fee will be less in large sales.

The whole business is very much "free enterprise" with all kinds of deals possible. The active men in the tumultuous service, particularly the auctioneers, have aggressive, outgoing personalities, very friendly and optimistic and have a fantastic amount of energy and stamina. Nearly all are muscular mesomorphs. With time they may develop substantial bellies, but this is rare. They appear to savor life immensely, especially that part of it dealing with cattle. They often enjoy drinking alcoholic beverages but are aware that drunkenness means their careers are finished. It is essential that people like and trust them and have faith that they will do the best they can for their clients. They often enjoy and participate in practical jokes. The take their jobs seriously, however. Part of their business credo is "Don't try to b.s. me!"

The major sacred books, the breed publications, will receive advertising either directly from the vendor or from the sales agency. The scribe will write up the sale after it is over and may give it pre-sale publicity, depending on its importance and how much space has been bought in the paper.[4] If adequate space has been bought, he will appear at the sale to act as a ringman, the auctioneer's assistant. As the sale is taking place, he identifies the active bidders and encourages them in every way to bid again. If the bidder is near the ring, he may talk to him in an intimate and friendly manner, telling him good things about the animal in the ring. Generally, he stands inside the ring[5] shouting, gesticulating and pointing with his catalog at the penultimate bidder.

He often assists at the parties and may go to the farm with the sales manager to help identify the sale cattle. At times he places some of the advertising with other books at the request of either the sale manager or the owner.

The auctioneer, the sales manager and breed publication editor all have great knowledge of the breed being sold. In this respect they somewhat resemble Moslem and Jewish scholars who are known and respected for their knowledge of holy writ. They can recite pedigrees, show winnings and prices of hundreds of animals over many years. They also remember photographs and advertisements in the books. This knowledge is used during the tumultuous service: two of the trio often assuring each other, by reference to the great events of the past, that opportunity for buyers is here and now.

"Remember, Jock, when we sold the full brother of this bull last year at Regina? Bred the same way as this bull here from the same breeder. And we've only got half the money for him!"

"That's right, Ken, and I think this could be an even better bull. Now, what am I bid? I have thirty three hundred, thirty three hundred . . . ."

Before leaving a discussion on the cattle religion, it is appropriate to say a few words about the tenets of faith which somewhat parallel the Nicene Creed in other faiths. This creed is in two parts: the first describes the holiness of the ideal type and in theory, at least, can apply to all breeds or sects; the second part names specific attributes of the favored breed which make it unique[6] and by implication better – than all other breeds. These tenets baffle the novice at a silent worship service because all the animals in the ring seem to fit the requirements. How can the judge measure their comparative holiness? Quickly he learns that it's "how the judge sees it" that is important; that different judges might place the animals differently, it's a matter of opinion. But the judge must agree with a goodly number of the congregation, or he won't be asked to judge again. Otherwise there will be too many prayers about Gehu and the blind.

Often a judge is a prominent breeder from some distance, a prophet in a foreign land. The sponsors hope he will approve of what he sees and will be encouraged to buy some cattle from the area and will then advise his constituents of the superior stock available from the show contributors.

This movement of judges also helps to standardize the ideal type and at the same time enables leadership among prominent breeders to occur as type evolves to meet new demands.

So much for the tape. I think it is useful to add a few words on the subject of beef type.

From the late 1920s through the 1940s and into the fifties, the ideal beef type was a short-legged, short-backed animal, very broad, very thick-fleshed, very deep in the body. Through those years the type also got smaller to adapt to the myth of the "small-roast" family. From the sixties to the nineties, the trend has been to a "long, tall" type, almost the antithesis of its predecessor, even though families are now smaller than ever! This change was in response to a perceived demand for less fat and more lean (muscle) in cuts of meat.

Considerable artificiality and myth is associated with beef type. And where artificiality and myth exist, some thinking people are eventually going to challenge them, even when the myth is garnering millions of dollars. This happened in the beef breeding business over a 30-year period, beginning shortly after World War II. Part III, "Revolution," describes these exciting times.

By the Way ...

[1] Some sacred cities with prominent temples: Denver, Calgary, Chicago, Houston, Perth (Scotland), Kansas City, Buenos Aires (Palermo), Sydney, Regina, Fort Worth, Toronto, San Francisco (and its Cow Palace).

[2] Bunker Hunt who, with his brothers, almost cornered the silver market in the late seventies, was a prominent breeder and buyer of Charolais cattle in the sixties.

[3] Ex-presidents Ike Eisenhauer raised purebred Angus, Lyndon Banes Johnson purebred Herefords.

[4] The breed publication may become very powerful. In the 1960s the American Hereford Association arranged to have the American Hereford Journal purchased from its owners to bring power back into the hands of the breeders.

[5] If the holy cattle are of the British breeds, the ringmen stand *inside* the ring but when selling the European breeds, the ringmen usually position themselves *outside* the ring because of the fractious dispositions of some of these cattle.

[6] Everyone knows that Herefords have white faces and red bodies, and that Charolais are white. In addition there are many differences between these breeds that are not superficially recognized.

Chapter Eight

Dat Ol' Time Religion

>>>>>>>>>>>>>>>>>>

The cattle religion reached its zenith at about 1951. It was taught by father to son, at schools, colleges and even universities. Some "cow colleges" had judging teams which competed with other teams from other colleges, just like debating teams, but without the glamor and hype of the football squads. Teenagers were a prime target: the 4H clubs,[1] with strong community support, were used to inculcate the creed into receptive minds. "Showmanship" was both a skill and an art. Mastery of it was an achievement to be rewarded with prizes and trophies secondary only to those given for the fatted calf.

Master Science degrees were granted in animal breeding to students who did substantial research in pedigrees, somewhat akin to the holiness accorded Arab students who memorize great portions of the Koran. Governments had programs which subsidized the purchase of purebred bulls by farmers and ranchers. Most Canadian provinces were "purebred sire areas," where it was against the law to breed a cow with anything but a purebred bull. And for many years the western provinces funded the "Toronto Royal" train, a trainload of livestock cars carrying the finest of the West's livestock to Canada's premier fair. Government officials helped breed reps pick the stock, and a prized perk for somebody in the Livestock Branch was the privilege of accompanying the train to Toronto. Winners at the Royal show received wide publicity and were honored back home for so convincingly "putting us on the map."

And on the ranches back home, young people were "in training" so that one day they too would be going to the Royal. Everybody in the community got behind the 4H youngsters, helping them in every way possible. Especially at sale time, when local merchants vied with packer buyers and purebred breeders to pay top dollar – usually much higher than the current market – for the champions, with a nice premium for the rest of the calves. The objects of this benevolence were then resold to a packer at the going price, with the sponsor bearing the loss and gaining the publicity. Supermarkets, particularly, liked to buy the champions, giving a message to consumers that yes indeed we are offering you the very best beef and we are also giving support to those fine young people in the 4H clubs.

4H sales were great for breed promotion – the major breeds gave prizes such as show halters to every winner if the winner was of their breed. Sometimes an association would buy a champion to be used as the beef for a special breed association function.[2] And frequently a neighbor who had taken a special interest in a boy or girl would buy the calf in a sort of godfatherly way.

This still goes on, in some places more than ever. And much of it is essentially on the side of the angels. The training we give to 4H club members benefits them in many ways. They learn a great deal about the practical side of raising a calf; they experience group activity in a common cause; they learn to speak effectively in public, to conduct meetings, to argue a point, and to meet other young people with the same interests who may come from a considerable distance. They learn to compete fiercely and then to accept either victory or defeat and keep on playing; to associate with knowledgeable elders and to help train their juniors. They are introduced to the arithmetic of cattle raising (admittedly in a somewhat artificial context) so that they see how the dollar sign moves the business.

It's excellent training, especially in a social and business context and in the practical aspects of animal nutrition and health. Much of what we teach these bright young people is as close to being scientific fact as we can get. But some of what we're teaching is the "old-time cattle religion." Some is the "new religion." In the 1940s when I was a club leader, the old-time religion was what it was all about.

It's really old-time. Goes back, like so many other things that affect us, to the Book of Genesis. There we can read how Jacob worked two seven-year stints for a pair of wives – actually he wanted only the beautiful one, Rachel (which then meant "ewe") – but he had to work an additional seven years because his father-in-law Laban did a bait and switch on him with Rachel's older and plainer sister, Leah, (which then meant "cow" in ancient Hebrew). During the 14 years Jacob did not waste his time. He undoubtedly was the first to follow what is now an old adage: Don't get mad, get even. Actually, he did much more than get even. He laid down the fundamentals of breeding purebred livestock.

The old man agreed to give him, in addition to the two women, a share of the herds and flocks, the kind of deal which is carried on to this day as young men strive to get a start in the cow business. Jacob was to get all the spotted and ring-straked cattle and Laban would keep the solid-colored ones. This should have been a straight-forward deal.

But Jacob did not win his reputation as king of the flim-flams unworthily. His challenge was to make sure that the multi-colored cattle became the best. How he did this suggests that the writers of the Old Testament hadn't studied the science of genetics, but it makes a good story.

First, consider that it was a hot and dusty country with few water holes. During most of the day, the herds would be out grazing but periodically they would come to the water holes to drink. The bulls, being experienced lotharios, would hang around the wells, happy in the conviction that they would be able to breed all the cows in the outfit by just waiting for them to come to water. This, for a bull, was much simpler and more labor-efficient than wandering all over the range checking each cow to see if she was in heat. Bulls today often behave in the same manner. In fact if you are running an AI (artificial insemination) program on dry-land range, it's a good plan to build your inseminating chutes close to a water hole.

So, now that Jacob had all the cows getting bred as they stood drinking at the water troughs he

Took him rods of green poplar and of the hazel and chestnut tree; and pilled white strakes in them, and made the white appear which was in the rods. And he set the rods which he had pilled before the flocks in the

> *gutters in the watering troughs when the flocks came to drink, that they should conceive when they came to drink. And the flocks conceived before the rods, and brought forth cattle ring-straked, speckled and spotted.*

That was the first step. He had found a way to increase the number of the off-colors in the herd. The next task was to make sure that these were also the best cattle. Jacob was smart:

> *Whensoever the stronger cattle did conceive, Jacob laid the rods before the eyes of the cattle in the gutters, that they might conceive among the rods.*

So, now that he was getting the best of the herd, what do you think he did for Laban?

> *But when the cattle were feeble, he put them not in: so the feebler were Laban's and the stronger Jacob's.*

After that it was all downhill for Laban. He didn't have many cattle left and those he did have were pretty well all culls. As for Jacob

> *He increased exceedingly and had much cattle, and maidservants, and menservants, and camels, and asses.*

So what, you may ask, has this to do with the Canadian Hereford Association or 4H clubs or the studious perusal of pedigrees by earnest and intelligent people? Let's analyze what Jacob did.

He selected a distinct population, discernible by obvious physical characteristics, particularly color. He also selected, for good performance, the stronger cattle. He then incorporated the desirable performance characteristics into the cattle selected for color. Finally he bred these cattle together. It worked. He produced superior cattle, all marked the same.

That's what every purebred breeder does, or at least sets out to do. It's crucial to him that the colors are right – red with a white face if he is a Hereford[3] breeder; solid black if he is an Angus breeder (or solid red if he is breeding Red Angus); creamy white if his breed is Charolais. Of course there are other breed characteristics that are not revealed by the beasts' hair color but are also critical to the breeder: the Hereford's ability to "thrive on grief and grass"; the easy calving of the Angus cow and the marbling quality of the Angus carcass; the great growth rate and large rib-eye muscle of the Charolais.

And many others, not all of them desirable. For instance, some cattlemen will tell you the Hereford is subject to "cancer eye" because there is no pigment around the eye to protect it in the bright sun[4] or they'll say you have to be a "little better cowboy" to run Angus because of their temperament. And you may have to buy a calf puller the year after you buy your first Charolais bull. Breeders of these breeds hotly deny such derogatory allusions but commercial cattlemen expect them to "come with the territory." There are, of course, many Hereford cowherds with no record of cancer eye, a great many docile and even-tempered Angus and a goodly number of "easy-calving" Charolais bulls.

It's these not-readily-seen factors that make for great discussions among cattlemen and determine the economics of raising cattle of any particular breed. In addition, there are many hidden characteristics, both good and bad, not specific to a breed. You'll frequently hear, "There's more difference between animals of the same breed than there is between animals of different breeds." Not always true, but definitely more than a kernel of verity is in there somewhere. Occasionally you'll run into a "Laban" (though I have never heard him called that – not much Old Testament reading among breeders) who has cattle well-marked for the breed but which are the pits when it comes to performance.

The late Harry Hays, who developed his own breed which he called the "Hays Converter," had a marvelous sense of humor and a propensity for pulling off a good practical joke, even at some cost to himself. When he was developing his new breed, he used to go to the annual sales of the major Hereford breeders and buy cows or heifers which had been named grand champions at some of the shows. He then would turn these females (a common livestock term to include both cows and heifers) out with his Converters and let them rough it for a year. To make his point in the joke, he then invited the original breeder to come and see how his "champion" was doing. The latter had been gently nurtured and overfed. These "kindnesses" had destroyed her liver with abscesses. As the hard life of the Hays Ranch shocked her system, she invariably began to "look like hell." Also, the Converters, with both Holstein and Brown Swiss in their ancestry, were much larger than the once-pretty champions.

"I'd tell him," Harry would say as he laughed in his great auctioneer's voice at the discomfiture of the embarrassed breeder, "I'd tell him that what he should be doing is crossing his Herefords with Holsteins, like I do!"

Holstein is a bad word among Hereford breeders and Harry's joke did not amuse them.

Why did the champion cow do so badly on Hays's ranch? Herefords, after all, are good cattle and still the dominant breed in ranch country. Actually she lost out in the battle between nature and nurture, between heredity and environment. No matter what good genes she may have had in her DNA, her treatment by man – overfeeding, which damaged both her liver and her rumen – had made her unsurpassingly beautiful for a time and then condemned her forever to shoals and shallows, and the jeers of the likes of Harry Hays.

Heredity and environment. In the world of the cattle breeder, these become "pedigree" and "fitting-for-show." Let's first take a look at fitting-for-show, the manipulation of an animal by man to make it look prettier and sell for more money.

If you are a breeder and have a beast favored by nature, why not make it look even better if you can? You would be foolish not to. That's where nurture comes in. One of the early breeders of Aberdeen-Angus cattle said: "I doubled, yea tripled, my meal" in order to make his cattle look more attractive. The great increase of grain in the ration meant that the beasts grew faster and bigger and fatter. If you are around purebred cattle much you soon learn that fat is a pretty color. It covers the rough bumps, fills in the hollows, makes the animal look broader, deeper and "meatier." The skin over a fat rib feels loose and soft and pliable – all indicators of a "good-doing" animal and also of "mellow fleshing."

If the breeder is not skilled in the art of enabling the animal to "show what she can do," or has not the time for it, he hires a herdsman. This is an honored and skilled profession (The Scots are noted for their abilities as herdsmen) and in many instances a well-paid one. In addition to the general tasks of getting the cows bred and calved out and fed and watered, plus keeping the herd healthy and thrifty, the herdsman's major task is to lead out champions in the show ring. If these cattle are also sale-toppers, then the herdsman is indeed a jewel.

He devises rations which will make his charges look bigger and better than the competition. He uses additives which will make the hair coat thick and rich and glossy. At show time he trims and brushes the hair to hide faults and accentuate strong points. He either trims the feet himself or hires a professional to do the job so the best stance can be achieved. Of course, he must be a master of showmanship in the ring, so that the judge sees the animal always to the exhibitor's best advantage.

For many years, his best friend was a Holstein "nurse" cow. From day one, the nurse cow provided vast amounts of milk to make the calf grow fast and fat. The natural mother may not have had much milk – first, because she was a beef cow, not a dairy cow, and second, because she was raised on a heavy ration so that her udder filled with fat rather than mammary tissue. No mammary tissue, no milk. Sometimes a young bull would stay on a nurse cow – really nurse cows, because the first one dries up in about ten months – until two years of age. This would, of course mean that a bull weighing close to a ton was still a "baby" and would bawl for his momma when he was hungry. Since Holsteins are wonderful milkers, the nurse cow would also raise her own calf which, when sold, would pay for the keep of the cow. So to the breeder it was a good option.

This practice had repercussions in the 4H clubs. It wouldn't be "fair," of course, to use a nurse cow in fattening the club calf. When I was a club leader in the 1940s this possibility was ruled out by a regulation which stated that no calf could be entered in the June sale if it weighed more than 1 000 lb. (450 kg). The assumption here was that a calf that big had either been on a nurse cow, or had been born the previous year. Now, following the modern cattle "revolution" (the narration of which begins in Chapter Eleven) 1000 lb. calves at spring sales are commonplace.

The preparing of an animal for show or sale is called "fitting."[5] The main fitting tool is a feed bucket and the "heavier" the feed, the faster the pounds go on. If the feed is too heavy, the animal's liver and digestive tract will suffer (after all, she is not a monogastric pig, but a four-stomached ruminant), so the art lies in balancing a ration to get near-maximum gains without impairing health.

Among the grains fed to cattle, wheat, corn and barley are the *heavy* feeds and oats is a *lighter* feed.

"Oh, he isn't on real heavy feed, mostly oats," is how a breeder will reassure you if you are wondering if the ration is too "hot." Beet pulp (from sugar beets) is also an excellent light feed. Other feeds like molasses, linseed-oil meal and bran are often used, And, of course there must be adequate protein and calcium (for a mostly-grain ration) as well as the fat-soluble vitamins. More important than anything else is "the eye of the master." A good herdsman watches his cattle with all-seeing vision and solves problems before they develop. Every herdsman has his own secrets which are part of his stock in trade.

Now we can understand what happened to the show ring champions as they encountered hard times on Harry Hays's ranch. From infancy they had been fed grain but under Harry's harsh regime that all stopped and they had to rustle on the range. Their livers were damaged (a common result of high-grain feeding) and their entire gastrointestinal tracts had been modified to handle grain as best they could, not grass or hay, the natural feeds of cows. Livestock men speak of cattle being "burnt out" on heavy feed – the gut[6] stops working partially or entirely and the animals lose weight, to the point of emaciation if the damage is severe. If not too much damage has been done, a summer on good green grass will set them almost right again. But if it's a bad case of burn-out, they will never completely recover.

Fertility is also a casualty of heavy-grain feeding. Fat in itself is a fertility depressor, even when the animal is in good health. And when she also suffers from abscessed liver and ulcerated gut, new little strangers are not likely to appear.

The theory behind heavy-grain feeding of prospective breeding stock is that it will show what the progeny of the animal can do in a feedlot. There are better ways of determining an animal's worth but the fit-and-show way ruled the purebred industry right up to the middle of the twentieth century, and it's by no means dead as we approach the twenty-first.

If the road to hell is paved with good intentions, then surely the show-ring road to cattle improvement can well become a route to perdition. In fact this nearly happened during the 1940s and 1950s.

To understand this, pick up a women's magazine and look at the roasts and steaks in the food section. Then turn the pages of any farm or ranch paper, paying particular attention to the pictures of cattle on the range or in stockyards. How can you tell where the best cuts of meat come from? Which beast yields the best beef? 'Taint easy. Many people have tried. The old-fashioned butcher, who bought a steer from a farmer and then sold him as bits and pieces to housewives was pretty good at it. How imperfect he was he didn't realize till, in supervised tests, he actually weighed all the edible meat and the parts he threw away.

The early cattle improvers worked very closely with butchers and learned what to look for in the live animal. They drew up what became the creed of all breeders, a creed which lasted for 200 years. Here is how we used to describe the ideal beef animal:

> *It is wide, deep and close to the ground.*
> *If its legs and head are cut off, it is close to being an oblong box (for Herefords, Shorthorns and most breeds) and to a barrel, for Angus.*
> *It sits squarely on four strong straight legs at the corners.*
>
> *The top and bottom lines are parallel with each other and are straight. The back is broad and deeply fleshed, with a long flat rump: hook bones are set in smoothly as are pin bones [the bones on either side of the tail]. Fleshing extends deeply over the rib, and well down in both front and rear flanks, and in the twist [the area between the hind legs] – "meat to the hock."*
> *The middle is large but not paunchy – to handle large amounts of roughage.*
> *The chest is deep and wide – to provide space for strong heart and lungs.*

The couple [the space between the last rib and the hook bone] is short,
a "close-coupled" animal.
The point of the shoulder and the withers are "laid neatly in."
The neck is short.
The head is quite short and wide, and may be slightly dished; the muzzle
is wide (to eat lots of grass).
The tail is set "neatly in."
The brisket is trim, not pendulous, and well-carried forward.
The skin is soft and pliable, indicating "mellow" fleshing beneath it.
The quarter – the distance between the hook bones and the pin bones –
is very long, a "long-quartered animal."

In addition to the above, we can also describe how the animal carries himself, how he holds his head, what kind of feet he has, the degree of angle in his hocks ("sickle-hocked" or "posty") and a number of other features. Very important for a breeding animal is whether it looks masculine if a bull or feminine if a female. Both must reveal evidence of reproductive proclivity: will he be able to get over the ground in the pasture? Can he readily service a cow? Has she enough of an udder to raise a calf?

Then there are a number of other characteristics which apply only to that breed, such as color. There are also some breed differences in leg length, overall size, straightness of lines, and so on. A good judge, in addition to looking at the animal, may also use his hands to determine the degree of finish, the mellowness of both fleshing and hide and to unmask the art of the showman in covering "faults." However, modern judges do far less "handling" than was done 30 years ago.

Some cattlemen believe in all of the creed and some in only part of it. The "infidels" refer to those characteristics which obviously have little or nothing to do with beef production as "fancy points." But in judging cattle you have to have a vision of the ideal type clearly in mind.

Judging consists of measuring how close each animal comes to the ideal in type. Commercial cattlemen pay little attention to fancy points but emphasize feet and leg soundness, rugged frames and overall vitality – "good-doing cattle"- pretty much as did Jacob thirty-eight hundred years ago.

For many years, the measure of "goodness" in cattle was the show ring. Reread the creed, you'll find it makes good sense. For instance, the highest-priced cuts, the steaks and good roasts come from the back; therefore a long wide and thick back is what to look for. Also, who is going to argue against strong heart and lungs?

The acid test has always been the butcher's eye – he knows what he can sell – and by and large the ideal type filled his eye. With a few modifications. He didn't really care if the legs were long or short because he cut them off and threw them away; as for the head, that was cut off, too. The tail setting? The laying in of the shoulder? Who cares? One place he differed from the judges was in the length of the couple. Remember the ideal was short in the couple, but the butcher liked a long couple because that is where he cut T-bone steaks. The point about the meat to the hock he found was just fat but he liked that better than the "cat hams" he found on dairy steers. Sometimes he could be fooled, even though it was his money at stake, in determining the real value of a carcass.

Angus Cow
"The Great Mother"

The other pillar of the purebred industry, the nature part, encompasses pedigrees and the herd books. A purebred cow is generally considered special. If she has a rich pedigree filled with the names of show winners and high-sellers, she becomes extra special, for the assumption is that she "will breed on" and that many of her progeny will be like the exalted ones in her pedigree.

The nearer the relationship to a great animal, the higher the value. If your bull is a half brother, or a son or a double grandson of a famous bull, it will help your bank account at sale time.

In the Angus breed, matriarchal worship is part of the pedigree faith. All Angus females trace back on the dam's line to a wonderful founding mother. Her descendents are said to be of her family. Breeders attach certain good traits to families, such as long life and heavy milk production. Sometimes there is a dominant gene that carries forward for generations – like the Hapsburg chin – and this inheritance pattern reinforces the faith in families.

In the Shorthorn breed, adulation of matriarchs was once in fashion. A hundred years ago, the Duchess family became like rare jewels because they had been inbred so much they were infertile! Supply and demand determined their value. If you were a serious Shorthorn breeder, you just had to have a few Duchesses in your herd. And because of infertility, there weren't many around to chose from. So you paid through the nose. That a serious defect in the strain should enhance its value seemed quite normal at the time and only proved the value of a pedigree!

The greatest fault of pedigree worship is that poor- doing animals (like Laban's) are regularly registered and find a market because of their "papers" not because of any intrinsic worth. Also there is the matter of the breeder's honesty in naming the right sire and dam and the correct date of birth. Some years ago I ran into a breeder who used two bulls at the same time in the same herd. He was convinced that he could tell the calf's sire by eye-balling him and felt no compunction about affirming that yes, he was certain that was the correct sire. Fortunately, blood testing for parentage is now routine. But trouble can still arise, as in the case of the American Polled Hereford bull, Perfection.

He was a terrific bull and his semen was sold widely, not only in the U.S. but also in Canada. Then someone suggested he was not a true Hereford – perhaps he had some Red Holstein in him! There were several investigations and finally the American association agreed to recognize his offspring for only a specified three-year period. His progeny in Canada were not recognized. Much money was lost. A few messy lawsuits were the result.

The purebred breeders and all who supported them and their concept of "good cattle" believed what they were doing was right; that they were benefitting the industry and the country by "improving" the breed and, in due course, the commercial cattle throughout the land. Governments and universities believed it, too.

It was a good faith and nearly everyone in the industry was happy with it, happy until they were faced by two challenges: the first from a few people with a strange and sometimes embarrassing curiosity, who said of the creed, "prove it."

The second challenge came from other cattlemen, who found that not only were their cattle getting smaller and less productive, some were actually useless dwarfs: "By following your silly show ring standards and by worshipping your useless pedigrees, you have ruined your breed, I'm going to buy my bulls somewhere else."

The good intentions of the breeders had led them down a garden path, if not to hell, at least to a place where they had to make some real changes in what they were doing.

The proving of fact and the disproving of fiction, the destruction of old myths and the formation of new ones, is the subject of Part III.

By the Way . . .

[1] In Canada the use of the term "4H" did not come into use until 1953, the establishment believing it was "too American." Before that they were called Junior Clubs.

[2] In 1974 the daughter of my ranch foreman showed one of my Maine Anjou-Angus cross calves at a 4H show and won the championship. Previous to the show and sale Cy Hayes, secretary of the Canadian Maine Anjou Association, had instructed me to buy "a Maine Anjou calf, if it's a champion." He wanted it for a big barbecue. "Don't buy it too cheap!" he said. I was happy to fill his order as instructed.

[3] Americans like their Herefords "mellow yellow," while many Canadians prefer a "cherry red."

[4] Dark pigment protects against light; that's why football players smear dark pigment under their eyes.

[5] I bred and raised the Grand Champion Pen of 12 Steers at the Toronto Royal in 1970. However, I did not fit or show them. Those tasks were done by the late Don Dainard of Edmonton who bought the steers as weaned calves at a rural auction market the previous year. They were tan-colored, Charolais-cross calves out of "baldy" dams.

[6] Gut is a perfectly good – not vulgar – word and includes the entire digestive tract from the mouth to the anus.

Chapter Nine

Dick, Henry, Martha
and, of course, Tina
>>>>>>>>>>>>>>>>

Henry got up first. He lit the fire in the kitchen stove. He always had four pieces of kindling and a piece of newspaper right there to get it going. Soon as it was roaring, he pulled on his boots and called to Martha who was still in bed, "Fire's going!" Then he went outside.

Henry, Martha, Tina, Dick, Mouser and Woofer

Dick heard Henry yell and he knew it was time for him to get up too. As he walked by the stove, he put in another stick. Then he went out to the barn. First thing he did was catch Pruney who was standing by the water trough in the little horse pasture. He carried a handful of oats so Pruney would be easy to catch. Pruney always knew he was going to be caught but he just couldn't resist those oats. As soon as Pruney started to eat the oats from Dick's left hand, Dick slipped his right arm, with the bridle rein in his hand, around Pruney's neck. Pruney jumped just a little, pretending to be surprised. But he wasn't, he knew he was caught. Dick put the bridle over Pruney's ears, after pushing the bit into the horse's mouth which was still full of oats. Pruney didn't like it, but that's what happens if you let yourself get caught.

Then Dick jumped on Pruney, bareback, and headed out for the creek pasture where Roanie and Muley were standing around waiting for something. Roanie was milking real good but Muley hadn't had her calf yet, so she was dry. Dick drove them both back to the barn. He left Muley in the corral and tied up Roanie in the cowbarn. Then he sat down on the milk stool with the pail between his legs and milked her. Mouser sat behind the cow waiting. Then Dick pointed a tit at Mouser and squirted some milk at him. He tried to hit Mouser in the eye, but Mouser was smart and got most of the milk in his mouth.

Dick didn't like milking but he had to do it because Martha needed two cups of cream every time she made biscuits for breakfast. When Roanie didn't have any more milk to let down, Dick got up and poured a little milk in Mouser's dish and then put the pail on the bench. He untied Roanie and threw[1] her outside with Muley. The cows stood there for awhile, sort of not talking but liking it, then walked back to the creek pasture. Dick took the milk to the house.

Henry was in the horse barn. He had picked up Pruney where Dick had left him – in the corral with his reins down. He caught Black and Decker, too. He put halters on the three horses and then tied them up in the barn. He was giving them all some oats, not much because they were pretty fat but Henry liked to see horses eat oats after he caught them, today they were going to work pretty hard so they'd need some oats. While Dick was milking, Henry brushed out the horses' backs and withers with the brush he always kept on top of the oat box, then he saddled them up, leaving the cinches loose.

When Dick got to the house, the stove was hot and Martha was putting the biscuits in the oven. She was famous for her biscuits. Two cups of flour, two cups of cream, two spoons of baking powder and a little salt. "You have to be able to count up to two," Martha always said.

Dick poured the milk through the strainer and then took it down to the well to cool it. He brought back the cold milk from the night before and skimmed the cream off it. He saved some milk and added back a little cream for Martha because Tina drank milk, and he put some of the skimmed milk to warm in a pail on the back of the stove for Tina to feed Roanie's calf after breakfast. "You shouldn't feed a young calf cold milk," he always told Tina.

When Muley was milking too, he would put the fresh warm milk from both cows through the separator, but with only one cow, it wasn't worth the trouble of washing the separator, Martha always said. So they skimmed it cold from the well after the cream had risen to the top. There was always some skim milk left over.

"Should get a pig to take that milk," Henry always said. But he never did get a pig.

Sometimes Martha made cottage cheese from the milk left over, but you can't eat cottage cheese every day for dinner. So Dick put it in the chicken trough. The chickens ate some after it curdled a bit and Woofer always took his share; even Mouser would sometimes eat a little of the curds if he'd run out of mice. Anyway, the trough never got full, though it sometimes got pretty sour, and in the winter it froze. Then Dick turned it up-side-down and knocked the ice out.

Tina came into the kitchen just as Martha took out the biscuits. This

was Tina's lucky day. Because instead of going to school, she could help move the cowherd up the Timber Trail to the summer pasture. Tina was excited. She would ride Pruney, Dick would ride Decker and Henry would ride Black. Martha would come along in the old Merc half-ton at noon with the lunch.

At breakfast Henry said, "Tina, first you have to feed Roanie's calf. After that, take Woofer and ride south along the creek to the cut-line and then follow it to the east fence. Then you can gather cows and calves all the way back. Make Woofer chase them out of the brush along the creek."

Tina was glad she'd have Woofer to go after the cows that would hide in the brush. It's awful scratchy to ride your horse through the brush and sometimes it's so thick you can't ride through and have to get off and lead your horse and yell at the cows. But Woofer liked going after cows in the brush. He'd nip at their heels and woof at them and they'd come out a-running.

"Make sure you get all the calves out," Henry said. "Then throw them all into the square section and wait for me. Before I get there, they'll have time to pair up and the calves will have a suck. We sure don't want to have them doubling back to that brush along the creek."

If cows and calves get separated they always find each other by going back to the last place the calves nursed their mothers. So, if that was back in the brush, they'd try to get back there. But if the calves all had a good suck in the open square section, they'd be easy to pick up again if some got away and doubled back.

"Dick, you do a big circle up Half Mountain and push all those yearling heifers down into the coulee and then trail them along to the square section at the north gate," Henry said. "I'll gather everything out of the calving field and push them to Tina's bunch. Tina, you'll be there a half hour ahead of me, so just take it easy and wait till I get there with the bunch from the calving field. Then we'll move our bunch to the north gate. Dick, you'll have yours there by the time we show up."

You've just been reading part of a "Dick and Henry " story, one of many I told to my children when they were little. While I was bathing them and tucking them in, they would be asking what was going to happen in the upcoming episode.

The characters in my tales were a real ranch family. Dick was 25 years old and a bachelor. He lived with his parents, Martha and Henry, who were in their late forties. Tina came later. She was the daughter of the Pretty Young Woman who had moved the summer before into the cabin up the Timber Trail which ran along Half Mountain. During that summer Tina spent most of the time "visiting" Martha and her family and when the Pretty Young Woman had to go away in the fall, well, Tina moved in with Martha, Dick and Henry. They all loved Tina very much and Dick was (as the romantics say) madly in love with the Pretty Young Woman.

Ranch life is very much a family affair. In the story, you saw how everything that anybody did depended on everybody else (including the saddle ponies, the milk cows, the dog and the cat). And everybody felt good when the other members did their part. You also would have noted how much planning was involved in running the ranch. Did you wonder why the cows and heifers going to summer pasture were in three different fields? You saw how Henry had arranged the gather so that the three herds would all be brought together more or less simultaneously and how each rider (and the dog!) would have to do his/her task without mucking things up. You realized how the ranch animals, even the old Merc half-ton, had become personalized and that the ranch people had "feelings" about them.

Henry was obviously a good ranch manager but he had weaknesses, too, like never getting around to buying feeder pigs to use the excess milk. Likely he hated pigs. But he knew all about his pastures and range and his cattle and horses – and his family. He was proud of all of them.

His family recognized his ability and followed his directions, which were very precise, without question. In other episodes you would learn that Henry often included them in the planning and sought their opinions on all kinds of subjects. But when it came to moving cattle, or any major task on the ranch, Henry was the boss. Every successful ranch needs a firm hand at the controls. In the old days, such a man was known as the "ramrod."

Martha was absolute queen of *her* domain, which included everything to do with the house, the meals, the garden, the chickens and the pail-fed calves. She also was the authority – and great love and refuge – in Tina's life. When neighbors called during the day, Martha would be the one to greet them (the men generally were away somewhere) so she also was the main organizer of the family's social life. She went to town more than any of them, bought the groceries and the machine repairs, paid the bills and deposited the cheques. At home, she did all the bookkeeping, including making out the income tax returns. She was thus an effective curb on Henry's occasional urge to buy fancy bulls or unnecessary machinery.

Dick was extremely skilled at ranch work – riding, roping, training horses, handling machinery, checking cattle for sickness and treating them, calving out cows, building sheds and corrals. He respected his dad's abilities, but he knew he was a better horseman than the older man and could handle hand tools such as saws, hammers and wrenches more skillfully. But he was unhappy. He wasn't "running" anything; he had no authority over anybody, not even Tina and he was anxious to "start on his own." (Which, of course, he eventually did after he married the Pretty Young Woman.)

Among cattlemen, there are a number of "bonding" factors: their work and the special skills and knowledge that go with it, where they live, their clothes, speech[2] and figures of speech, topics of conversation, humor, concern about the weather . . . the list is quite long. When a stranger from Toronto, wearing his big-city clothes (especially his hat – or no hat!) appears on the scene, his "strangeness" is palpable; that's why many business, government and professional men with a ranch clientele tend to dress and talk like cattlemen. If not part of the real fraternity, at least they do not flaunt their other-world identity. In a ranch family, this fraternal bond further strengthens the natural family ties, ties that are bound tighter by hardship and by overcoming hardship and by an occasional streak of good luck and good times.

In much of ranch country, the grass grows vigorously for less than two months of the year. The challenge is to manage and conserve that grass over 12 months to sustain a heathy and productive herd. Here's how the work is apportioned through the months on a spring-calving, winter-feed ranch in west-central Alberta (where my ranch was and where Dick and Henry had their adventures).

January and February – Start or continue winter feeding, watching and treating for lice and for bad feet and bad eyes. (Throughout the year, you are always watching for bad feet, bad eyes, snotty noses, diarrhea, "hard" manure, blood and/or mucous in the manure, bloated bellies, labored breathing, loss of hair and loss of condition.) Treat with vitamin A and selenium and vitamin E. Pull out poor-doers and bred heifers for extra feed. Keep water open and salt available. Watch for slipped (aborted) fetuses. Vaccinate replacement heifers (perhaps) for vibriosis and IBR.

March – Move herd to calving area. Put out salt. Prepare for calving, then begin calving. Stock up on pharmaceuticals and

January and February

equipment for calving. Acquire from a dairyman (and freeze) cartons of colostrum – first-calf heifers often don't have enough. Check cows daily for imminence of calving and move springers who may need help to where they can be more closely supervised. Line up dog-house calf shelters. Calve out cows, pairing them up, watching and treating for scours . . . the list of jobs at calving time would fill a book.

April – This is usually the main calving month. Improve your feed – use your best hay. You hope you won't have to pull a few calves, perhaps a C-section or two, maybe replace a prolapsed uterus, treat for milk fever. You better be ready! You'll be busy and you may be up checking cows a few times many nights. This is the main scours month. Move the early-calving cows with their calves to spring pasture, away from the ones still calving. (These were the ones Tina was told to gather.) Line up your bull battery. Put out salt. If you are also farming, you will be starting your spring work, after having got all your machinery in order and seed grain lined up. Visit your banker. Do your income tax.

May – Finish calving, move the pairs (cows with calves) away from the calving area, sort off the drys and the empties, more treatment

of scours, increase and improve the feed (most of the cows are now nursing but summer grass hasn't arrived yet). Move pairs to old-growth pasture. (The main herd which Henry was gathering.) Semen test bulls, ship duds. Put in your crop. Select yearling heifers to go to breeding field. (Dick was rounding these up. Yearlings tend to wander and don't herd or trail as readily as cows.)

June – Buy pharmaceuticals for branding. Move herds to summer pasture. Put out salt. From mid- to late-June brand the calves (dehorn, castrate, vaccinate and apply fly-repellent ear tags). Fix fences. Separate cowherds into breeding pastures. Turn out bulls the last week in June or first week in July – or early in June if you are set up for March calving. Revaccinate and fly-tag all yearlings. Implant (with growth hormone) steers. Cull heifers and move them to summer pasture. Clean corrals and spread manure. Go fishing. Get your haying equipment in order. Start haying – first-cut alfalfa is ready.

July – This is the main haying month; you won't have much time for anything else, unless it rains – then fix fences and corrals and granaries or go fishing. Check bulls often – cows *must* be bred on time. Get ready for silage. Go to a range-management field day.

August – Finish haying. Check your yearling steers and cull heifers; these should be sold from late August through early September. Start creep-feeding calves. Start putting up silage. Pull bulls from cowherd. Ship cull bulls. Finish cleaning corrals; repair as needed. Put out salt. Get harvest machinery and trucks ready.

September – Start grain harvest. Finish silage. Gather and sell yearlings. Check all pumps and pipes for winter watering.

October – Buy pharmaceuticals for fall gather. Finish grain harvest. Gather cowherd. Wean, weigh and revaccinate calves and put in weaning field or sell them. Take off any visible horns on anything. Select and mark (ear tag) replacement heifer calves. Treat everything for lice and warbles. Put out salt. Preg test; sell dry cows and remaining yearlings. Move cows to fall grazing (often grain-stubble fields). Go antelope hunting.

November – Sell balance of for-sale calves and yearlings. Start saved calves on feed, watch them. Check water with colder weather. Pay off the bank. Go big-game hunting.

December – Move cowherd to winter field. Welcome an open winter or start feeding cows. Go to a stock growers' meeting. Watch calves for problems. Check cows daily at feeding. Check water. Put out salt. Avoid selling cull cows in December (price is always low) and *never* sell bulls between Christmas and New Year's when U.S. buyers are taking a holiday. But Canadian cattle buyers have "income tax" orders, so feeders and stockers will have a good December market. (This premium rarely justifies holding them from late August because they won't gain weight unless you have put them on full feed.)

The Dick and Henry stories took the family through all these activities. Lots of opportunity for drama and action in the work of the ranch, and the narrator, of course, added the personal problems of the main characters to make it more exciting.

Quite a few ranchers buy calves in the fall to over-winter and then grass them as yearlings the next summer. This complicates management a bit but is usually a money-maker. We sometimes did this on our ranch, and we also ran a fall-calving herd for a few years as well as the spring-calving herd. In addition, we bred our herd via artificial insemination for six years and operated an on-site feedlot (to fatten for slaughter) for a couple of years. To add to both field and paper work, we also ran an ROP program for several years – weighing calves at birth, at weaning and for those still on the ranch, as yearlings. Finally, many of our cattle were recorded or registered (some imported from Europe) and some of these were sold as "papered" cattle in breed sales. These we usually farmed out to professional herdsmen, "steer jockeys," to fit and show for us.

I mention these activities to show that the cattle business can and will challenge as many skills as you possess in management, accounting, finance, sales and promotion and human relationships, as well as your ability to judge cattle, back up a trailer, ride and rope, diagnose and treat disease, maximize grass production and recognize condition in cattle. It also helps if you are handy with a socket set and a welding torch.

It's more fun if you have some training in genetics, bacteriology, forestry, public speaking, biochemistry, nutrition, meteorology, plant taxonomy, accounting, soils, physiology and anatomy but these aren't necessary by any means. You can get professional advice as you need it, but you should be smart enough to know when you need it and wise enough to not make the same mistake more than twice.

Something else will happen to you as you grow in the cattle business. You will find yourself serving on school, county, municipal and hospital boards. Exhibitions and fairs will rope you in. Stock grower and breed associations will elect you to office. You will be pressed to join a service club. The government will ask you to serve on commissions, boards and committees. To make your grass more productive or because you marvel at God's handiwork, you will join the range management society – and you will become more active in your church! And, of course, you will support 4H, the Boy Scouts, Girl Guides and other youth activities. You may become a politician and run for office. If you aren't careful, you won't have any time left for your ranch or family!

So whatever your talents and aspirations, you can gain fulfillment as a cattleman. If you decide to throw your bedroll in the wagon and sign on the crew, good luck!

By the Way . . .

[1]In cattlese, the verb *throw* is a composite of the transitive verbs *drive, herd*, and *push*. It connotes neither violence nor speed, but rather mastery and control.

[2]When I was a well-schooled seventeen years old, I remember asking my father (a university graduate and sometime professor and editor) when "were we going to move *them* cattle?" As I said it, I knew my grammar was wrong, but it seemed appropriate – we were talking about cattle. Dad, who was a master of words, simply said, "Tomorrow."

[3]The colostrum, or first milk after calving, is tremendously rich in vitamin A and antibodies (to protect against disease) and is sufficiently laxative to move the meconium (solid fecal material which has accumulated in the fetal calf's intestine) along its way. It is absolutely essential for a newborn (of any mammalian species) to get colostrum within the first hour or two of birth. Dairymen discard most of the colostrum from their cows because there is so much of it.

Chapter Ten

Rancher 'Rithmetic

➤➤➤➤➤➤➤➤➤➤➤➤➤➤➤

Cattle are wealth. They always have been. In fact, the words cattle, capital and chattel all have the same Latin root – *capitale*, meaning "head." Hebrew patriarchs were measured by the size and number of their herds and flocks – and so were latter-day patriarchs: In one autobiography a Mormon elder of a hundred years ago complimented a fellow elder on the great size of his herds and flocks, as well as the number of his servants, on his wives and children and, of course, on his buildings and equipment.

In Black Africa, cattle *are* money. To eat your cow on the Dark Continent is like using a hundred-dollar bill to light a cigar in America. A Masai[1] wife may cost an eager groom 10, 20, even 30 cattle as bride price, or *labola*.

Throughout the Great Depression, if you had a few cattle you knew you could always sell one if you absolutely had to get some extra money. It was, of course, like cashing a cheque – when the cow was sold, the balance was depleted to that extent.

It is bad form to ask a rancher how many cows he owns, but all cattlemen assess their neighbors according to that measure. A man need not be ashamed to call himself a rancher if he runs 300 or more cows. If he also owns or leases[2] the land and equipment to handle such a herd, he is running a million-dollar outfit, maybe twice that or more. In the fall of 1990, he could sell his calf crop (if well-bred, good early calves) for $130 000; if he had kept the previous year's calves until they were yearlings, he would have sales of $170 000. By 1993 those figures grew to $170 000 for the calves and $190 000 for the yearlings. If he has only 100 cows (far more common) we can put his gross income at one-third of these figures. The neighbors watch the "liners" – pots[3] or straight-jobs – hauling the cattle to market and say, "There'll be a big cheque in the bank for that bunch!"

And from the late seventies to the early nineties it might have stayed in the bank, depending how much money the operator had borrowed and when. If the bank provided all the money at 12 percent, the income would just pay the interest, leaving nothing for operating costs, replacement of machinery, taxes or profit. At 6 percent interest it's a much brighter picture. If everything were clear – the ranch inherited from parents or bought long ago when land was cheap – then the rancher would be doing very nicely.

Most operators own most of their outfits. If their equity is at least two-thirds, they will be able to hang in there; less than that and they may become one of the families you hear about on the radio – nice people who borrowed money when interest rates were high and now are being forced out by the bad old bank.

Most ranchers are prosperous. Either they or their dads or their grandads or mothers or generous uncles got title to the lands before 1972. Or else they already had money when they went into the cattle business. They own their land and their cowherds and borrow from the bank only to cover operating costs, or perhaps to buy some year-lings for the summer, or pay to have them fed out in a custom lot. Bank "operating" loans (as distinct from capital loans) are absolutely essential to running a successful ranch. A good banker is a must.

But large capital debt will kill you. Here's the hard truth: you aren't ranching to make money but because you have money. Certainly money can, and is, made on ranches – by increases in real estate values and by taking advantage of upswings in the cattle market (like those of 1992 and 1993) and in modest amounts most years if you have lots of equity. All this *if* you have been able to weather the hard times, which means you weren't paying interest on a big pile of borrowed money

"I'm sorry, Suzy, I have to marry the schoolteacher so I can keep my ranch going."

when the market bottomed out.

The most important factor[4] in succeeding in ranching is *the year you started*. What makes your starting year so important are real estate booms, the "cattle cycle" and the cost of long-term money. (The second most important thing statistically is to marry a schoolteacher or nurse. Such a wife provides steady off-ranch income during the tough times.)

Let's look at real estate first. Land should be bought when it is cheap. If you bought your place before the general real estate boom of 1972, you're likely OK. Through the Great Depression and up to the end of World War II, even through the sixties, you could start with little capital if you could somehow get possession of land and borrow money. If you were any kind of operator, the increase in the value of your land soon put you, if not on easy street, at least out of the long lane with no turning. But in those years, who could get any land or borrow any money? Not many.

Returning World War II veterans got government money on easy terms to buy land (but not leases in the early years). The Farm Credit Corporation (the federal government) began to lend money to buy land at between five and six per cent, and by the seventies the chartered banks were lending money and taking land (and later leases) as collateral, something they had not done since before the Depression.

The resulting increase in the "demand" resulting from this vast surge in credit, combined with overall inflation, caused land prices to increase many-fold, with the greatest proportional increase in raw and low-productivity land – typical cattle country. Good farm land increased ten-fold but raw bush quarters went from $1 500 a quarter section (160 acres, or 65 hectares) to $50 000 a quarter – over thirty-fold. If you bought 15 raw quarters in 1960 and sold just one of them 20 years later, you could wipe out your debt and keep the rest – providing you had been able to keep up the interest payments! In effect, you got 2 200 acres free because of your foresight and wisdom in buying land when it was cheap.

Nowadays 'tis much easier to inherit the place or buy if from Dad on the right terms. Truth is there are far more people who want to be ranchers than there are available opportunities. So supply-and-demand will not be denied and the cost of getting started is always higher than can be pencilled out as a business venture.

In a way it is sort of like the road-construction business where "the old iron [big machinery] has to pay for the new iron; the new iron can't pay for itself." If you have substantial equity in either endeavor, you can expand and make more money, but if you start from scratch, you can't make a go of it.

In the construction business, politics is traditionally a friendly help which can compensate for limited capital (lots of scandals here!). But in ranching, politics plays a lesser role for two reasons: the "benefit" is usually readily seen by all the neighbors, who get mad as hell and the *quid pro quo* (dollar support for the party in power) can't be large if earned by cows. Of course we all know of leases being granted to certain people because of party affiliation and of outfits being financed with almost 100 percent government loans. But it's not something you can count on if you are planning to become a rancher.

A few paragraphs back I mentioned the "cattle cycle." Here's how that particular wheel turns: when prices are good, cattlemen expand their herds so as to take advantage of the good times. To do this, they hang onto their old cows and hold back heifers from market to grow them out as cows to have more calves . . . this hold-back of cows and heifers reduces the beef supply and pushes prices even higher, resulting in even more hold-back . . . and so on till, finally, a vast herd of cattle has to be sold, the market is glutted and everybody is losing money. Then we all with one accord dump our "excess" cattle – cows, heifers, young calves, whatever, on the market. Prices collapse, resulting in even more liquidation. This goes on until a shortage develops, prices improve and everybody starts rebuilding herds, pushing prices ever higher. A full turn of this up-and-down wheel usually takes between ten and twelve years. Sometimes the cycle is masked, exaggerated or skewed by drought, a hard winter, depression, tariff changes, inflation or unexpected act or pronouncement of government.[5]

By 1993, cattle prices were high, possibly approaching the top of the cycle? Maybe a good time to buy a cowherd? What made this cycle so hard to read in 1992 was that cattle numbers were not increasing in the U.S. as they should have been, according to historical precedent. Wise men said that U.S. cattlemen were getting old and conservative; that they took such a beating last time round, they were playing it safe. In Canada, however, herds kept expanding and the increased production was exported to the U.S. as feeder cattle, fat cattle and carcass beef.

If you are both clever and lucky, you can figure out the up-coming beef cycle and make your moves to begin or quit ranching, or to expand or contract, ahead of all the other guys – and get rich! Rancher George Ward of Arrowwood, Alberta, says that the way to manage the cycle is to have nothing but steer calves for eight years and then nothing but heifers for two years. (Ward was joking, of course, but a recent breakthrough in semen sexing could enable him to carry out his plan. See Chapter 15, "Bulls in Bottles.")

The amount of "short-life" meat – pork and poultry – that comes to market in North America depends on consumer demand. If people want to eat more chickens, broiler men soon raise more poultry. With pork it takes a couple of years to "gear up" the industry (getting sows bred, farrowed out and the pigs raised). But neither chicken nor pig production is measured in acres or square miles – they can be raised under confinement on a small piece of land. Not so with cattle. The upper limit of beef production depends on grassland availability, as well as consumer demand. "Every piece of beef has to start with a cow and her calf on pasture" was a common quote of R.K. Bennett, a popular government official from the fifties to the seventies.

We North Americans eat *all* the beef produced here (well, not quite all: small amounts are exported to Asia and high-class hotels worldwide.) "If you don't sell it, you smell it." Price depends on whatever is required to "clear the market." Consumption always equals supply. In the short term, the North American society as a whole does not eat less beef because of fat scares, cholesterol, hard times or whatever, it simply pays less for beef. For every meat abstainer, there are many others who willingly buy more steaks if they are cheap enough. It's this reduced price that forces cattlemen to reduce production (some go broke, others plow up their grass and some keep fewer cows). A half dozen years later, with less beef being offered – and hence bought – a superficial economist may be prompted to say: "Consumption of beef is falling off," or he may go further and insist, "demand for beef is down" – even though the price is now much higher! What really has happened is that *available supply* is down now in response to the decrease in *real demand* of six to ten years earlier.

It's a perverse sort of house-that-jack-built sequence. Ten years ago, because of the cholesterol scare, consumers backed away from beef counters, and prices fell. Cutting their losses, cattlemen at first sold more cattle (and consumption went up!) as they culled out extra cattle and so reduced breeding stock; eventually fewer cattle came to market, less beef was available in packers' coolers and by early 1993 beef prices were at an all-time high! They will come down again, of course, as the cattle cycle turns but a real decrease in demand appears to have occurred. Animal fat is a no-no to many. It's unlikely we will ever again see production and consumption reach the high levels of 1965, when the really big sell-down began.

The cost of long-term money is at least as important as the per-acre price of land if you want to make a go of ranching or farming. Most of the foreclosures of the eighties that figured so prominently in the news were the result of borrowing money at interest rates so high that there was no hope of paying both them and operating costs out of current production. When interest rates are high you can't afford to buy a ranch – except for cash!

By 1993, interest rates had sunk drastically. A good time to buy a ranch? Well, cattle prices were near the top of the cycle, so both cows and cow pastures were expensive but grainland was relatively low-priced. A smart operator might find something that would work.

If you do decide to go ranching, you will buy your outfit by the "animal unit" – the amount of land required to provide feed and pasture for a cow and her calf for a year. Often the ad will read:

Nice little ranch. Handles 100 mother cows easily.

If the ad is truthful, the ranch is a 100-animal-unit place. Historically, a cow-unit of land was worth the same as the cow but through

Coming Events

Day Weekend (July 31 – August 2) – SMF Anniver

Musical Ride at the Cochrane Agricultural Grounds

- SMF Casino – Calgary Casino

Annual Dinner & Auction

Frank Jacobs
SFL 40-01-159

the years the price of land has gone up just like Will Rogers said it would ("Buy land, they aren't making any more of it."). In 1992, when a cow was worth about $1 000, a cow unit of land was worth $2 000 for ranches somewhat remote from many people. If on a good road and only a couple of hours' drive from a sizeable town, the price might be as high as $3 000 per unit.

But if the ranch is close to a major city, a cow unit becomes irrelevant in determining price, especially if the city has lots of head offices and a ranching tradition. The country around Dallas[6], as every TV soap-opera addict knows, is *sine qua non* for ranches having value quite apart from their productive capacity. Dallas is the oil capital of Texas and nearby Fort Worth is the state's beef-cattle capital. Calgary is both the oil and cattle capital of Canada, so it, too, is home to many wanna-be ranchers. Only with big bucks will you buy a ranch within commuting distance of these cities. Likely you'll buy it by the acre or, even more likely, you'll pay a stipulated price (we're talking several million dollars now) "for the whole outfit."

Here's how a ranching investment worked out in 1992 (since then prices have gone up and interest rates down). Suppose you start out with 300 cows at $1000 for a good breeding cow – that's $300 000 – and land to run them at $3 000 per animal unit – an additional $900 000. Then get some machinery and horses and odds and ends – for $200 000 more. Why, you've spent $1.4 million. At 12 percent interest, you should be getting a return of $168 000 (at 6 percent $84 000) just to keep the bank happy. Add to that operating expenses of at least $100,000 (if you agree to work for no wages) and you will need to sell your calf crop for $268 000. Fact is, you will be fortunate to have 240 calves to sell, and if you are medium lucky they could average $500 each, to give you gross returns of $120 000. (A few paragraphs back, I said a rancher would get $130 000. But he's established and has his herd "working" for him; you're just starting up.)

Oops, you'll say, better figure that out again. Just $120 000 and my costs are $268 000! Why, I'm losing $148 000 a year and throwing in my work "free." But you're not done yet. If you were planning to pay off the land in 20 years, you would need another $45 000 and of course still another $20 000 to replace your equipment.

The sad truth is you are about $200 000 a year from being in a paying position. You recall the old joke. "Just keep farmin' till it's all gone." At this rate, starting with a credit of almost a million and a half dollars, you could "farm away" another million dollars in five years. Of course, you would have net assets equal to what you started with (if prices stay up!) plus $225 000 in equity from your annual payments. So your net loss is only about $775 000 or $155 000 a year. (A drop of five percent in interest costs, from twelve to seven percent, would cut that loss in half.) A great business!

So, how do those "wealthy" ranchers get that way? First, if they are good managers, they can raise the value of the calf crop from $120 000 to $150 000. And, if they are free and clear at the bank – no borrowed capital to pay interest on – they need only pay operating and depreciation expenses, for about $120 000. And they may be able to shade that by 10 or 20 thousand. That leaves them around $40 000 to live on. Then there are a few years like 1993 – high prices, low interest rates, cheap food. A good time to salt it away.

Most established ranchers don't sell calves but keep them till they're yearlings; this will add another $100 per head net ($300 gross), for an increase in income of $24 000. Of course, the rancher has to have more land to do this but if he already has the land – or cheap lease grazing is available – he will make money with his yearlings. Most successful ranchers do this. And, as I pointed out in an earlier chapter, Pat Burns (the shrewdest of them all) ranched for 30 years without a cowherd – he let the other fellows produce the calves, then he "took the cream" by running yearlings (and older stock).

Why are yearlings much better money makers? Well, to wean a calf from a cow requires six tons[7] of grass and hay, dry weight. For that input, you get between 400 and 600 pounds of calf. But to carry that calf to an 800- or 900-pound yearling takes much less feed, between two and three tons of dry matter. So you get almost as much weight gain for only one-third to one-half the feed.[8] To partly compensate for this difference, you will sell calves for $1.00 a pound when yearlings are selling for 85 cents, or calves for $1.40 when yearlings are $1.00. Moreover, if you buy calves to carry them to yearlings, you will have to pay marketing, trucking and induction[9] costs and take your chances on increased disease problems. Thus, it's more profitable to raise your own yearlings than to buy new cattle – unless you can buy "the other fellow's mistakes" – "compensatory gain" cattle which have been underfed and otherwise mismanaged. In fact, the opportunity for profit in such cattle is often much larger (because they can be bought cheap) than with "pretty" cattle, for which you may have to pay top dollar.

So we see how a good operator with no debt can survive, even thrive, during the hard times and most times are hard. Then when a few good years come back to back at the top of the price cycle he can really sock it away – and buy another ranch later during the recurring hard years when the other fellows are going broke! That's exactly what Pat Burns did. The rancher's aim, after a few good years have made his bank account flush, is not to buy *all* the ranches in the country, just the adjacent one(s)!

Operating expenses? Would you guess $100 000 for a 300-cow herd? I reached into my hat for that one. It depends where you are and how you run the place. If you can graze out all winter, and don't have to put up hay – a "rawhide" outfit – you're operating costs are very low: no hay machinery, no hired men to put up hay all summer and then feed it out all winter.

There aren't many places like that. The late George Ross Jr. used to say, "When I'm looking over a ranch, I always count the haystacks. If there are no haystacks, it's a good ranch." Back in the early sixties he told me that operating costs on his Lost River Ranch in the southeast corner of Alberta were $100 000 – $25 000 for himself and each of his two brothers (neither of whom worked on the ranch) and $25 000 to run the place, a ranch with a 100-mile perimeter fence which enclosed 2 300 cows plus 1 800 yearlings. (To put these dollar figures in 1993 terms, multiply by four.)

Compare Ross's ranch with some places in central western Alberta, where cows through the winter eat three tons of hay for each calf born. To produce that hay, the land has to be first cleared of trees, broken and seeded to grass, at a cost of at least $300 per acre in 1990. There are three successive capitalizations in such a ranch: first, buy the land; second, clear, break and sow it to grass; third, stock it with cattle. And there is no income till several years have passed and all these things have been done and eventually a calf crop is produced.

Such a place looks wonderful in June and July, but the cost of producing a weaned calf there is at least three times a high as on the Lost River, mainly because of the hay cost. Even so, if the land is broken and producing and you don't have to pay for it, you can still make a buck in the cow business there. And if you are not too far from grain farmers, you can buy their straw for very little and use it, with a little grain (and/or molasses) plus some vitamins to winter your cows. You'll need hay only for your calves and a little extra for the cows during and after calving. If you can do this and summer your cows on a community pasture (where the government has paid for breaking and seeding) or on a grazing lease, then you can compete with anybody.

Some of the most profitable outfits combine grain growing on good arable land with cattle on rough land. The cattle summer in coulees, sandy or gravelly land, knob-and-kettle country (round hills with sloughs among them), bushy or rocky sidehills and along creeks, they winter on home-grown straw after having cleaned up the stubble fields in the fall. Meanwhile the machinery to handle the cattle is, in the main, the same outfit that produces the grain crop, so the cows don't have to pay for big expensive trucks and tractors; the grain crop does that. In the prairie provinces, more cattle are raised on places like this than anywhere else.

In much of the interior of British Columbia, cattle are wintered on alfalfa grown under irrigation and stacked as bales, often small square bales. This is very expensive winter feed, but its cost is compensated for by running the cows all summer – from early spring to late fall – on public lands under forestry permits. Even with this cheap summer grazing, such ranching is marginal at best and has been subsidized by the B.C. government since 1974.

An interesting concomitant of this situation is that four big B.C. ranchers have, as a matter of principal, refused to take the government subsidy. They are proud of their independence and even prouder in knowing that whatever they achieve it is by their own efforts. They are the last of the "free men" in our society. Before the subsidy was introduced, these men were recognized as the natural leaders, the movers and shakers, in B.C. ranching. But now they have lost kinship with the much more numerous "stump ranchers," who eagerly have accepted the subsidy and apparently aren't afraid of the yoke of dependence.[10]

This free-enterprising spirit – obviously costly in the short term – combined with the challenges of hard times, hard weather, meddling governments, disease, incompetent labor, rustlers, environmentalists, oil-exploration companies, lumbermen, taxes, hunters – these reveal why the rancher "enjoys" what he is doing and would do nothing else. If he faces and masters all these challenges, then his rewards can't be measured by dollars. Provided, of course, he has enough income to live the appropriate lifestyle (low-keyed and understated, but with lots behind him) of a successful rancher. When he travels abroad, he "visits" ranchers and breeders who show him their cattle and drive him around the country to meet other ranchers and breeders. Such visits are frequently reciprocated. And when he meets with his peers, at a stockmen's convention, at a bull sale, in a foreign country or in his own home they share an unspoken fraternal bond that can be found in no other group.

Everybody envies the successful rancher. Look at it this way: you have $3 million. In the money market this capital will earn you about $300 000 (taxable!) a year. But if you invest it in a ranch – which you manage so as to deal successfully with hard and rewarding challenges – your ranch may provide between nothing and $150 000 "profit" at year's end, as well as a comfortable living. After about 15 years, the capital value of your outfit likely will have doubled, even tripled. Which way would you go? For the real cowman, there's no contest. And he is eager to see his children succeed him on the ranch and in the fraternal community of cattlemen.

What about ranching as an investment, as a means of diversifying a portfolio? It works better in the U.S. than in Canada because of lower interest rates and more generous tax laws. Canadians can write off and defer a few taxes but not on the scale available to the American investor. Moreover, in Canada there are restrictions on provincial lease size. Thus only a few non-cattle corporations own extensive ranches in Canada (mainly in B.C. where foreign capital is welcome) but many American ranches are owned by large corporations.

The manner in which federal legislators are elected in the two countries helps explain why the tax laws are different. In the U.S., people generally elect the candidates who spend the most money during a campaign. And such congressmen are in most cases sitting incumbents who voted and will vote for laws favorable to those providing money for election expenses, viz. corporations or industry groups. At least, such are the hopes and expectations of the investors putting up the money. They maintain active lobbies in Washington to ensure their interests are "represented" in Congress.

So we can expect a number of congressmen from "cattle" states to vote for laws giving tax easement to cattle producers. Their votes really don't have much to do with the general position of either of the political parties but rather with what the congressmen consider will help them get reelected. Since there are elections every two years, a congressman's priorities are plainly spelled out. Thus, representatives from "cattle" states will vote for "good" tax laws for the cattle industry and make deals with other congressmen to support them. They will be rewarded by winning votes from their constituents. Meanwhile, to assist in the garnering of those votes, they have received campaign dollars from "interests" which can and do use "good" tax laws to their advantage – interests which can buy (or already own) big ranches.

Canadian MPs have no such voting freedom or incentive. As W.S. Gilbert wrote in *H.M.S. Pinafore*, they "always vote at the party's call and never think of thinking for themselves at all." If a tax law favorable to the cattle industry is to be passed, it must get the approval of the Cabinet and particularly of the prime minister. It then becomes the policy of the government and is enacted into law. Those who would modify the tax position of cattlemen must work within the party in power; they must gain the support of powerful party members, often including the "bagmen" or fund raisers (who may be senators). And they are well advised to gain the support of senior civil servants whose advice and approval on non-earth-shattering matters the ministers may seek.

In particular, the proposed new law must be attractive to "all Canadians," that is it must appeal to more people than it turns off. Since most Canadians live in Ontario and Quebec, federal laws rarely offend in these jurisdictions. In any event, the Canadian system makes it more difficult for a relatively minor industry like cattle raising, with its headquarters in a "region" rather than in the "centre," to get favorable federal legislation than is the case in the U.S. Not since the days of John A. MacDonald and Matthew Cochrane has big Eastern Canadian business shown much interest in Canada's beef industry.

There is one exception: the usually unheard voice of the Canadian cattle industry became sufficiently resonant in the 1940s to generate the "Basic Herd Provision" of the income tax regulations. The provision was never passed as law but was a "directive" to tax officers involved with cattle producers. It went like this: you are ranching in 1945 with cows worth about $75 each. Now that the war is over, cattle prices will surely rise because meat rationing will soon end and what is more important, the war-time embargo against shipping beef to the U.S. will be lifted.[11] (It was in 1948 and cattle went from 12 cents a pound to 18 cents a pound within one week.) This will double the price of cattle. In a few years your cows will be worth $150, perhaps $200. What can you do in 1945 that will ensure that you will be able to sell your cows – your basic herd – without paying income tax on the huge sum you will receive for them in, say, 1951.

Why, get them enrolled as capital with Revenue Canada as a Basic Herd at $75 each. Then when you come to sell them down the road, you will pay tax *only* on that $75. The rest will be tax-free. In fact, the whole *Someday this will all be yours, son!* amount might be tax free if the cow was *deemed* to have been acquired by inheritance or by tax-paid dollars. A law with such a provision might be a little sticky to get through the House of Commons – interests in Quebec and Ontario might think it would benefit Westerners (which it obviously did) – so rather than going to the trouble of passing the appropriate legislation, let's just make it a directive; tell the tax officers to do it, under advisement.

Success has many fathers (while failure is always an orphan) and almost every agricultural leader of the time took personal credit for both dreaming up the scheme and then convincing the ministers of Agriculture and Finance to go ahead with it. But the great promoter of the idea (and its creator) was a genius named Kenneth Coppock, the then Secretary of the Western Stock Growers' Association and editor of the industry magazine *Canadian Cattlemen*.

Coppock worked with all the prominent cattlemen in the country and with the Dominion government (as it was then known) so that in due course the directive was implemented and was used to great advantage by practically all ranchers.

Coppock was also "close friends" with the P. Burns Company. To provide a home for his various businesses he kept spacious offices in one of the company's buildings. The company further supported him by taking out at least one full-page ad in each issue of his magazine. Pat Burns had influence with the government. He was appointed to the

Senate[11] and when a big new post office was built in Calgary in 1929, it was sited just across the street from the Burns Building in what was becoming an unpopular part of downtown Calgary as it was too far east. By the time the Basic Herd provision was implemented Pat burns had died but the Burns company then owned a great many fully-stocked large ranches along the foothills south of Calgary. They also had a big feedlot and a large and well-regarded herd of purebred Hereford cattle. In addition they seemed to understand the cattle cycle and to have anticipated an inflationary boom following the war. In any event they sold their ranches and herds, including the purebred cattle, when prices were high, after the Basic Herd was well established. Obviously they saved a great deal in tax money.

Later on, to set up a Basic Herd, you were required to pay tax on the value of your herd as of the enrollment date. Then, when you sold all or part of your basic herd, the entire increase in value was recognized by Revenue Canada as capital gain and was free of tax. If your cow was enrolled at $75 and you sold her for $200, you paid no tax on $125. If the tax on the $75 had been paid (or deemed to have been paid) at enrollment, you paid no further tax at all. It was not until the early sixties that capital gains became taxable, at only half the rate of other income. Basic Herd was a wonderful deal – too wonderful – and the government phased it out in the seventies. There were new Pharaohs in Ottawa "who knew not Joseph."

The Basic Herd provision was so valued by cattlemen that they did not seek to get breeding stock declared as depreciating capital – like baseball players! (How else can the owners pay all those big salaries?) This would have enabled a rancher to "write off" a cow during her lifetime but cattlemen feared the government would cancel their basic herds if they sought such a provision.[12] In the end, they lost the basic herd and never did get cows-as-depreciating-capital, a dodge the Americans use to tremendous advantage.

The main pick-up for the Canadian investor is the long-term appreciation in the value of land – capital gain which is taxed at a lower rate. Because there was no capital-gain tax on land in Canada until the early sixties, many modest fortunes were made tax free.

Also many fortunes were lost: by inexperience, mismanagement, hard winters, unrealistic capital debt, price collapses and various combinations of these miseries. The history of Canadian ranching is replete with tales of big-company outfits either going broke or getting out of the business when they saw it was no longer going to be profitable.

So, if a-ranching you would go, chose your father (if he is not already a rancher) from among the wealthy, or marry a rancher's daughter (several such happy stories come to mind) or make a pile in real estate or oil, even construction and have a go. Of course, you may start small: acquire a schoolteacher or nurse for a wife; pick up a small place and then, by luck and good management and working the cattle cycle, expand when your neighbors (in hock to the bank) go broke. Good ranching!

By the Way . . .

[1] In the *Sahel*, a heifer will not calve for the first time until four to six years of age. From then on, she may calve every two years, or even less frequently. Her main impediment to reproduction is nutritional, specifically the lack of digestible protein.

[2] In Alberta, the rancher pays an annual rental to the provincial government for leasehold. But, since leases trade like real property, for cash or credit, he also has a capital interest in his leases and may well be paying off debt incurred in buying them.

[3] A "pot" is a big cattle trailer (18-wheeler), single decked in the front and rear and double-decked in the middle, with the latter hanging down like a 'possum's belly. For hogs or calves, the pot may be double- decked front and rear and triple-decked in the middle. A straight job has no pot.

[4] Second most important thing (statistically) is to marry a school teacher or nurse. Such a wife provides steady off-ranch income during the tough times.

[5] In the early years of the Reagan administration Reagan's chief of his Office of Budget and Management, David Stockton, blew the whistle – said Reagonomics was a fake – and commodity futures plummeted.

[6] Southfork Ranch, the headquarters of the fictitious Ewing clan of TV fame, consists of the buildings with which much of the world is familiar and 40 acres. The place sold in 1984 for $7 million and was auctioned (with one bidder) in a foreclosure sale New Year's Day, 1991, for $3.15 million.

[7] This includes the feed the cow eats and wastes, plus the feed utilized by the "drys" and other non-producers, the bulls and the young replacement heifers. On old-fashioned, traditional ranches, the cost per weaned calf in terms of dry matter was much higher than this because heifers did not calve till three years of age. In the African *Sahel*, where a cow calves no oftener than every two years (four years is commoner) the cost (in natural resources) of weaning a calf is beyond calculation.

[8]In calculating lease rentals, yearlings are rated at two-thirds of an animal unit. But, since the yearling does not have to carry the "unproductives," his net pasture cost is about half that of a cow that weans a calf.

[9]Induction costs include vaccinating, branding and other handling. These are costly in themselves and also cause weight loss. Moreover, the change in environment and the time required for the calf to accept his new home affects his health and his subsequent gains.

[10]One need only travel through the Atlantic provinces of Canada to discover how government paternalism destroys a people. A cattlemen friend of mine, after one such trip, said, "The federal government is making those people dependent on them, just like they did with the Indians." The same sort of assessment is made by prominent American writer Andrew H. Malcolm on page 28 of his book *The Canadians* (Bantam Books).

[11]Appointment to Canada's Senate is at the discretion of the prime minister and in most cases is a reward for "service" to the party in power – the highest, if not best, use of pork-barreling.

[12]In 1957 I introduced a motion in the Agricultural Bureau of the Calgary Chamber of Commerce, recommending that the Income Tax Act be changed to recognize breeding livestock as depreciating capital. My motion was seconded by a prominent rancher and Hereford breeder, Victor Watson. It passed in the Bureau and in the Chamber and later in the Provincial Chamber. But the stock-grower groups turned it down, so the government did nothing.

PART THREE

Revolution
(and the Four Apocalyptic Horsemen)

The revolution was bloodless. Apart from that it was like a lot of other revolutions: it encouraged cheating and lying, was beset by intrigue, pitted friend against friend, involved governments, banks and foreign countries and created a great deal of havoc. The good guys won. But pedigrees, 4H clubs, breed associations, purebred breeders, auctions and competitions – all these antebellum trappings – are still with us and flourishing undiminished, thank you very much! But it really is not the same. There have been profound changes.

Profound changes, yes, but many cattle people lived through the revolution quite untouched by it. They never knew it had happened. Oh, they heard about the new breeds from Europe and also how some of these cattle had sold for sky-high prices. But that wasn't their world. They didn't have much, if anything, to do with purebreds, so they were only dimly aware of the havoc caused by dwarfism or any of the ravages of what I have called the "Four Horsemen of the Apocalypse." They started to crossbreed their cattle, like everybody else, when it paid to do so but that wasn't a big deal. They saw a neighbor "AI-ing" a whole herd of cows to a Limousin bull or perhaps a Chianina and thought he was nuts. They saw strange-looking steers winning prizes at the shows and wondered if somebody else was nuts. But mainly, they kept on with their business.

The people who experienced the revolution were the importers of the Exotics and the Exotics breeders (not necessarily the same people), the developers of performance and progeny testing, the AI companies (including a rash of new ones which subsequently folded), the livestock publishers and auctioneers and sales managers (many of whom are now gone), the universities and research stations, the feedlot operators, federal graders, retailers, livestock shows ("Agribition" in Regina would never have happened without the Exotics) and the few commercial cattlemen who got on top of the developments and made them work for them – or nearly went broke going down the wrong road. To this group we can add a small army of professional men from the cities who invested heavily in the new breeds. Some made money; many later lost it. Meanwhile the old-line breeders painfully watched it all happen.

The four apocalyptic horsemen which heralded the revolution and against whom the breeders and their associations fought doggedly without full victory, did not appear in full armor on the near horizon but rather came surreptitiously in through the back door. They did not at first inspire fear, but were mocked and laughed at or just ignored. When eventually their full visage was seen, it was too late and the damage was done. Or was it damage? The industry changed very much for the better because of them; in fact the horsemen became part of the industry. An industry which thrives now in a new if somewhat imperfect Jerusalem.

During the revolution, it was hard to say who were the good guys and who w ere the bad guys. Since revolutionaries are traditionally the good guys, we could just let it go at that, because, in this revolution, truth and logic were on the side of the rebels. But the opponents – the cattle breeders who fought the revolution – are among the finest people I know. In any rural community, they are leaders. We must not attribute self-serving motives to them. Throughout, they *believed* in what they were doing and saying. On the other hand, many of the apparent good guys were opportunists who came in to make quick bucks out of new developments that others hadn't either recognized or appreciated.

Much of the controversy occurred over a matter of *belief*. We don't mind very much if we are proven wrong on a matter of fact, such as the distance from Calgary to Red Deer. If someone comes along with proof that it's less than we thought, we accept their proof and have little difficulty giving up our original position. But if we *believe* that mellow fleshing is a characteristic of good cattle or that a broad chest[1] is indicative of a strong constitution, we'll stick to that belief no matter what the eggheads tell us. And we'll question their motives if they insist we are wrong – especially if it means that their position is going to cost us money. That is why I talk of the Cattle Religion – it's a matter of faith. We hang on to our faith and we get much more satisfaction out of its fulfillment than we do out of adding up two and two and getting four.

On the other hand, the genuine proponents of the revolution acted from the highest of motives – mostly. They championed unpopular causes, they risked their reputations and in some cases, their positions. They were reviled by much of the cattle establishment. But they knew that truth was on their side and no doubt they experienced personal jollies in fighting the good cause. Their intention was not to harm individuals but to make them see the light – the aim of all evangelists. That they were aided and abetted by persons of lesser moral fibre was not their fault.

When it was happening, over two decades from the fifties to the seventies, it was the most exciting time the cattle industry had seen since the days of the free range. In 1993, the captains and the kings have mostly departed and the scene is peaceful – and rather boring!

In their day, however, the four apocalyptic horsemen rode with fury, striking fear and despair into many hearts.

| By the Way . . . |

[1]Actual measurements of chest cavities revealed that a "wide, deep chest" had no more cubic capacity than an apparently narrow one. Nor has it been shown that chest capacity has anything to do with beef production, even if "it goes to reason . . ."

Chapter Eleven

Dwarfism

>>>>>>>

The first of the four tormentors was an inherited defect called Dwarfism.

Signs of real trouble did not begin to appear until the 1940s. Some of the top breeders, who were forward-looking men and so followed modern trends, had accepted a "small roast" theory as fact. The theory went like this: The new, small families would no longer want (or buy) the big roasts of former days. Therefore we should be breeding small, but meaty, cattle to satisfy this change in consumer demand. With faith in the theory, these breeders were deliberately seeking smaller and more compact bulls to breed to their cows. Prime source for the compact cattle was the U.S., where showring hype had induced a few Canadian breeders to part with much cash in order to get in on the new "improvement."

The first cross to the "compressed" type (as it was then called) produced very attractive cattle – broad, thick, close to the ground – solid meat all the way. The breeder sold these cattle both to other progressive breeders and to ranchers for high prices and cleaned up at the shows with them. So back he went to the same kind for the next bull to make them even broader, thicker, closer to the ground and even more solid in their structure. It looked like the right way to go.

Or was it? Some of the compressed cows when bred to compressed bulls gave birth to what the breeder thought were "throwbacks" – small, compact, potbellied, short-and-crooked-legged animals which, as calves, looked almost mature. "His legs were so short," a young herdsman told me as he described one such bull being raised by one of the most prominent breeders of the day, "that I could never keep any bedding under him. He kept pushing it ahead into the manger." The dwarfs weren't very healthy, never grew much and had a great dishiness of the face which actually impaired breathing so as to make the calf snort. They weren't what the breeder wanted at all. In fact they were a distortion, seen as in a nightmare, of the ideal type. The breeder didn't know it at the time but these were typical "snorter dwarfs," a condition in cattle that had been reported accurately over 100 years earlier:

> On two occasions I met with in this province [Calonia in present-day Uruguay] some oxen of a very curious breed called nàta or niata. They appear externally to hold nearly the same relation to other cattle which bull or pug dogs do to other dogs. Their forehead is very short and broad, with the nasal end turned up, and the upper lip much drawn back; their lower jaws project beyond the upper, and have a corresponding upward curve; hence their teeth are always exposed. Their nostrils are seated high up and are very open; their eyes project outwards. When walking they carry their heads low, on a very short neck; and their hinder legs are rather longer compared with the front legs than is usual. Their bare teeth, short heads, and upturned nostrils give them the most ludicrous self-confident air imaginable. (From Chapter Eight, The Voyage of the Beagle, Charles Darwin, 1832.)

At first, the breeder did not hide his dwarf calves, because he didn't yet know that the first of the four apocalyptic horsemen had struck at him and his breed. One central Alberta breeder proudly displayed one of his first calves from a $30 000[1] bull, imported from the U.S.

"Just like his daddy – only better," was the way he described the month-old dwarf calf to some visiting high- school students. But soon he and his fellow breeders realized they had too many of these throwbacks. Fate was unkind to those who had followed the compressed fad.

The compresses (which Darwin described as "having an intermediate character, but with the niata characteristics strongly displayed") were still winning at the shows but breeders knew something was terribly wrong. Their next move seemed obvious: quietly move out of the compresses as quickly and discretely as possible and buy a bull free of the dwarf taint. This wasn't as easy as they first thought, for when they began to shop around for a "dwarf-free" sire, they found that an ominous silence had fallen over the breed – no breeder was saying anything about dwarfism, in his herd or anywhere else. One rancher-breeder decided to find a bull a long way removed from the dwarf problem. But where could he go? He asked the national secretary of the breed – and got an evasive answer.

Logic suggested that a good source would be some breeder[2] who, to his credit, had resisted the compress fad and still had big, stretchy cattle. Generally this was a good move, but it involved redesigning his ideal type. Now bulls "with some stretch to them – big rugged buggers" were in demand. But the solution was not perfect, even some of the big ones sired dwarf calves. Where to go now?

One safe source for North American breeders seemed to be the British Isles, the original home of the beef breeds. So in the middle and late fifties, English bulls began to make their appearance in North America. They were long-necked, long-headed and a long way off the ground, but they were almost sure to be free of dwarfism. One breeder laughingly described how his son was shocked when they unloaded an English bull from a box car.

"First there was this long ugly head coming out, followed by a long neck – like a snake coming out of his hole – and then came that long, long body!"

After these ugly brutes had tucked away close to a ton of oats and beet pulp to give them some eye-appeal, they were bred to thick and meaty (but perhaps too small and short-legged) cows. They produced very attractive "middle of the road" calves.

Meanwhile, research done for the USDA by a Dr. Scotty Clark at Denver suggested that snorter dwarfism was caused by a simple Mendelian recessive gene. Dr. Clark was invited by the Alberta Cattle Breeders Association to speak to their annual meeting in January, 1954. He told them how dwarfism was inherited: if two animals, each apparently normal but each carrying the bad recessive gene, were mated, a quarter of their calves would be dwarfs, a quarter would be free of the taint, and half of them would be carriers like their parents. Dr. Clark showed pictures and charts to illustrate his talk and his audience groaned as they saw them.

Meanwhile a Dr. Paul Gregory in California had been attempting to identify dwarf carriers by bodily measurements. Surely, Dr. Gregory reasoned, there must be something about the appearance of these carriers that attracted cattle breeders. How else could the population of dwarfs have increased so rapidly? Dr. Gregory surmised that, since the dish in the face of the dwarf is so pronounced, perhaps the carrier's face might be more dished than a non-carrier. (This agreed with

Darwin's observations.) His research bore out his hypothesis: dwarf carriers have a peculiar dish in the face. He then devised an instrument he called a "profilometer" which could be used to determine facial "dishiness" and thus identify carriers of the bad gene.

Dr. Gregory won a number of disciples, who armed themselves with profilometers and then went about the country reading face profiles of breeders' cattle. The solution to the problem seemed simple: sell all the bad-profile cattle, keep the rest and you're free of dwarfs. Before Gregory's profilometer had won general acceptance, a new development occurred which demanded a much more frontal and public attack by the breed associations.

Commercial breeders were getting dwarfs. If you visited a major stockyard in October or November in the mid-sixties, there they would be – poor little dwarf calves, one here and one there among their hundreds of normal siblings. And more of them were showing up every year.

Ranchers were angry. They had put up with over-fat bulls at the major bull sales, convinced that despite the overfeeding of these bulls, they should still buy them because they would "improve" their herds. But, instead of getting improvement, they were getting worthless dwarfs.

It is important to understand that dwarfism appeared in all breeds[3] of beef cattle but the snorter syndrome was mainly a problem of Hereford cattle. Also at that time, Herefords were *the* cattle of the West, constituting over 80 percent of ranch herds. So the rancher's wrath was directed mainly against the breeders of purebred Herefords. And he expressed his wrath by buying a different kind of bull. Not the kind which had been the showring's idol but something which, by his own practical experience would do him some good – those big, long-bodied kind, with enough leg to cover the range, like his father used to raise.

Thus one of the two pillars of the purebred breeder was knocked over. His major customer, the breeder of commercial cattle, no longer believed him when he said a show bull is also a good range bull. Shorthorn breeders listened to the ranchers' complaints but they were too late. Though Shorthorn cattle had not suffered from snorters to the same extent as did Herefords, their breeders had followed the compress fad with even more abandon.

The trend for North America was set by an Edmonton breeder named Claude Gallinger who had imported for his Killearn herd a near-perfect (apart from his small size) Scottish bull named Balmuchie Jasper. Soon, almost every prominent Shorthorn breeder on the continent had a Killearn sire. And the Shorthorn changed from being the biggest of the British beef breeds to being the smallest – perhaps not quite, for Angus breeders were pressing them close in the race to breed little cattle.

So the Shorthorn was hardly an alternative for disillusioned ranchers. Besides, they traditionally used Shorthorn blood only sparingly: the hard winter of 1906-7 had proved the superior survivability of the Hereford in a tough climate. "We use a few Shorthorn bulls once in a while" said the late George Ross of Manyberries, Alberta, who operated a ranch with 100 miles (160 kilometres) of perimeter fence. "They help keep up the size," he explained.

But how can you keep up the size by using bulls of the smallest breed?

Alberta Shorthorn breeders responded to the changing demand by holding a special Range Class at the show held at the time of the Calgary bull sale which boasted it was the biggest in the world.[4] The bulls in this class would be judged on their ability to fill a rancher's needs. A rancher did the judging. They saw no irony or contradiction of belief in this. In fact everyone *knew* there were rancher bulls and breeder bulls. The rancher bulls were bigger, rougher, generally plainer and definitely stretchier than any bull going to head a breeder's herd. But the scheme was not really successful – the breeder bulls still sold for more money than the rancher bulls – and Shorthorns declined to their current status of a minor breed.

Angus breeders solved what problems they had with dwarfs (most of which were "long-heads") by searching out big bulls and breeding to them extensively. The turning point came with a very large bull bred by Jack Stevens of Morrinville, Alberta. Stevens was a good cattleman who had always favored bigger cattle, even when the market was demanding the "ponies." Just when Angus breeders were searching high and low for bigger bulls, he raised a calf that was long and tall, one that 10 years earlier might not have been registered because he was so "off type." Stevens was not a great promoter but the buyer of his bull was a top Angus breeder and showman, Jack McBride of Benalto, Alberta.

McBride teamed up with Dave Canning, an American breeder and promoter. They changed the bull's name to "Canadian Colossal" and advertised him widely as "the million-dollar sire." The trend was set. Ever since then Angus have been getting longer and taller, especially show cattle. They appear to have completely overcome whatever problem they had with dwarfs.

Before taking another look at the Hereford breed to see how Hereford breeders overcame their problem, let's play a little with statistics and probability. Like everything else in mathematics we have to make some assumptions. Let's first assume that our bull and all our cows are carriers for a harmful Mendelian recessive gene. The calves will be duds only if they inherit this gene from *both* the sire and the dam. If they inherent only one bad gene from either parent, then they will be carriers but not dwarfs.

(These cattle are the ones Paul Gregory was looking for with his profilometer and the ones Darwin described as "intermediate in *niata* characteristics.") Since both parents are half good and half bad, a calf may be unlucky and get a bad gene from each parent. He's a dwarf.

To remember what the proportions are, think of this little rhyme:

> *A white pussy cat named Sharkey*
> *Encountered a black tom called Darky*
> *As a result of their sins*
> *She had triplets, not twins,*
> *One black, one white and two karky. (Actually the spelling kakki.)*

In our case we have one dwarf, one free of dwarfism and two carriers – like their parents. That's as bad as the situation can get – 25 percent of the calf crop dwarfs – unless you start breeding the dwarfs themselves.

In the next generation, after eliminating the obvious dwarfs as either sires or dams and again using a carrier bull, you will get 17 percent dwarfs, 50 percent carriers and 33 percent free of the tainted gene. But if you were to use the same cowherd and bred them to a dwarf-free bull (of which there were 25 percent in the first generation) you would have no dwarfs at all, 33 percent carriers and 67 percent "clean" calves. In any event, you would have a much "cleaner" herd in the calves than you had in the parents. So even if you do nothing – select neither for carriers or non-carriers your herd will get progressively cleaner.

In nature bad genes tend to stabilize at a level of five[5] percent or less. That is, five percent can be expected to be carriers and one out of 1600 may get the disease. This means that these bad recessive genes are not normally economic problems in animal production unless there is a deliberate selection for them, as was the case with snorter dwarfism in cattle. The problem can be resolved in one generation by the simple expedient of using only "clean" sires. However, you will never completely get rid of the recessive gene. It will be there at a low level forever, unless you can devise a fool-proof way of identifying the carrier.

Use clean sires, yes, but how do you find them? In the domain of Herefordom, it was a very elusive cat to bell. Not only were ranchers leery of buying purebred bulls, their fellow breeders were shying away, too. Who wants to buy a cow or a heifer if she is a dwarf carrier? To their credit both the American and Canadian Hereford associations took action. The action they took was ill-conceived and condemned a huge number of "clean" cattle but still they did do something. The value of their program was in public relations, not in genetics.

They conducted a pedigree witch-hunt. Every breeder was requested to report on any animal that was a known producer of dwarfs

and all the near relatives of these "unclean" animals. Breed and magazine reps were called to help because of their wide knowledge of the breed. The associations called this witch-hunt, euphemistically, "research." And as such it appeared in the annual reports and budgets.

The search uncovered a vast number of good-looking and performing cattle with "dirty" pedigrees. Most of these were probably free of the faulty gene but nobody in the breeding business wanted to buy them just in case. Also there is no doubt that quite a few carriers escaped the hunt simply because they had never been bred to or bred a carrier. With only one out of four, on average, dwarf calves resulting from the mating of carriers, the process was far from accurate – or fair!

"The Hereford cattle with dirty pedigrees were the best cattle," a prominent Simmental breeder told me." If they weren't really top-notch, the breeder wouldn't have registered them." He used such cattle in grading up his Simmental herd, sure in his own mind these cows were no more defective than any others with "clean" pedigrees that he might buy, and were far better as individuals.

So we had the profilometer and pedigree research doing their thing. But far more important was the deliberate choosing of big stretchy cattle. They combined to combat dwarfism – and they won! So complete was the victory that most young cattlemen have never seen a dwarf and many of them have never heard of the fault.

Fortunately, dwarfism never became a major problem among commercial herds in Canada, even though it was a most devastating problem to purebred breeders. The University of Manitoba acquired a small dwarf herd as a research project. Their dwarfs included both "long-heads" and "snorters" and a few others. The researchers, under the direction of Dr. Elwood Stringham did a survey of the dwarf condition through the pages of *Canadian Cattlemen*, where I was editor for more than two decades. We found that there was a great deal of interest in the defect but that the dwarfism wasn't widespread in commercial herds.

The results of the dwarfism interlude have all been positive in the longer term. First, it convinced the industry that showring standards were not useful – in fact, that they could be harmful in selecting breeding stock; that testing for utility in cattle was far more productive than looking for fancy points. Second, the minds of commercial cattlemen were freed of the purebred myth to the extent that they were willing to meet, even accept and promote, the other three horsemen: Crossbreeding, Performance Testing and Charolais (and other new breeds), all of which had been condemned by the purebred industry. Practically all cattle now, commercial and purebred, grow faster, produce meatier carcasses and generally are superior to our herds of the mid-century.

Caution: are we seeing another fad evolve? Are "long" and "tall" and "extension" the buzz words? If you reread the judging creed, you'll see that many of the sacred words must now be replaced by their opposites. Is the devil getting his due? Is another garden path leading us somewhere? Or nowhere?

The answer is "yes" if these cattle become idolized by the showring to the exclusion of utility considerations. And the answer is "no" if the type is achieved by letting it evolve as animals are selected for their *real* abilities, as measured objectively, to produce quality beef in the most efficient way.

The next chapter describes how this was, is and may be done through Performance Testing.

By the Way . . .

[1]$30,000 in 1950 would be worth $300,000 by 1990.

[2]J.S. Palmer of Marsden, Saskatchewan and his two sons, Cecil and Maurice, got an early start on the problem. They publicly got rid of the "wrong kind" and started over with dwarf-free cattle.

[3]The "oxen" Darwin describes were of Spanish origin.

[4]The Denver sale handled more bulls, many of them sold in multiple lots. The Calgary sale was the largest in which bulls were sold individually.

[5]In humans, cystic fibrosis carriers are estimated at less than five percent of the population and the probability of a person inheriting the disease is 1 in 1600.

Chapter Twelve

Can He Cut the Mustard?

When a rancher goes to a banker to borrow money, he is always asked how many cows he has and how many horses, tractors and other machines are on the place (and are they paid for?). And of course, how much land does he own or lease? Probably the banker will ask for a complete *pro forma* of next year's transactions. He especially wants to know how many and what kind of cattle the rancher is planning to sell. He'll also be curious as to when this is going to happen. The banker wants to be sure he can get his money back with interest, of course.

As well as knowing how many cattle, the banker must know (or guess) what each of these is worth. He doesn't have much trouble with commercial cattle. They're going for slaughter eventually and market prices are broadcast daily. But what about purebred cattle? Is a purebred cow worth $5 000 as his customer insists? Or, as his instincts tell him, $1 000? (Purebred cattle killed by a railroad are always very valuable while those sold in a bank foreclosure rarely seem to be worth much.) Just because she is purebred, is she worth anything more than her value as beef? If she is of productive breeding age, of course she's worth more. But wouldn't a grade cow be just as useful – and just as valuable? Well, maybe, the rancher replies but you see she's a purebred.

Her value as a purebred lies in her ability to produce other purebreds whose value would lie in *their* ability to produce – and so on. Not much here to get a firm hold on. If she can raise purebred bulls which can be sold to commercial breeders for more than beef price, then she has a value above a grade cow – but how much?

The real value of purebreds is all tied up in the mystique of the cattle religion – of blood running out, of a noble ancestry including bloodlines other breeders want, of whether she is of popular type and would do well in the show ring (or has done well), of the reputation of her breeder, of how her close relatives have fared in show rings and sales. In fact about a great number of things that don't have very much to do with the price of beef.

Wrong! will say the breeder. There are certain characteristics that beef cattle must have and she's got them. OK, what are the characteristics and how do we measure them? Does the show ring measure these characteristics? (Remember the discredited creed!) The feed bucket? The nurse cow? Her pedigree? After all, by using these tools, breeders ended up with a bunch of dwarfs and lost the rancher bull market.

While some people were arguing about these standards, a few people with training in the scientific method as well as in animal husbandry saw a real challenge developing. Are there real ways to measure utility in cattle? There should be: we measure race horses by how fast they can run[1], and milk cows by how much milk they give. Let's look at beef production and define what is good: type? pedigree? show-ring winnings? actual pounds of beef produced at least cost? If we can devise an objective method of measuring them, then we should be able to breed superior cattle using the best (by our testing methods) to breed to the best. We'll make progress if we know quite a bit about genetics and the breed we're working with. And if can get some support from ranchers who are looking for useful, rather than pretty cattle, we should be able to make money with our improved cattle. If we can make money at it, the rest will come easy.

And that's what happened. The second apocalyptic horseman was riding. Out on the dry prairie at Miles City, Montana, the United States Dept. of Agriculture (USDA) researchers worked with a group of

Hereford cattle which they called "Line One." First they put numbered tags in the cows' ears so they could tell them apart. Then they put tags in the calves' ears as soon as they were born, so they knew for sure what calf came from what dam. They also weighed the calves at birth and again when they were weaned. Some were fast growers, others slower. The government researchers figured the fast growers probably got more milk (the dams were heavier milkers) and also these calves might have a better propensity to get out there and grow. At weaning the calves were put on feed and weighed again in the spring when they were a year old.

They now had tests which would measure a cow's milk production, by the fall weight of the calf, and the calf's gaining ability by what he weighed at a year of age. All irrespective of show rings or pedigrees.

The next step was to put the yearling on a fattening ration and weigh him again when he was ready for slaughter. At that point, they knew how much feed he took to put on a pound of gain, and how quickly he did it. The final step was to slaughter the steer, weigh his carcass, grade and then portion it into retail cuts. Finally measure what you threw away and what you had left.

This didn't happen only at Miles City and certainly not all at once. Researchers based their selection of the best cattle mainly on yearling weight. Then, breeding within the line they produced a strain of big fast-gaining Herefords. They also developed several other lines but it was the Line One cattle in which ranchers became most interested. Especially intrigued was a Montana rancher at Stanford, in the Judith Basin, a couple of hundred miles west of Miles City. Curt Hughes ran cattle with his brother Gerald on a ranch that their father had started in the 1890s. The Hughes had seen the Hereford breed lose size and were anxious to find bulls a lot bigger and more productive than those they could buy from neighboring Hereford breeders. So they went to Miles City and got some Line One cattle.

Curt Hughes had researched breed development as a student at Boise Idaho, where he was involved in developing a new breed of sheep. So he found a real challenge in the Line One cattle. (A believer in adequate size in meat animals, Hughes used to propose a delightful toast when all present were ready to raise their glasses: "Here's to bigger and better bulls, bucks and boars!"

The Line Ones were great performers and soon Curt Hughes found that other ranchers wanted to buy bulls from him. He had kept records on his cattle; however, none of them were registered. So he began to sell "grade" bulls. Word travelled fast and ranchers in Saskatchewan started to come down to the Hughes ranch to buy bulls. By the early 1960s Curt Hughes was selling more Hereford bulls, all grades, in Saskatchewan than was any purebred breeder in that province.

The ranchers bought his bulls because they knew they were dwarf-free, were fast gainers and the heifers were good enough milkers to raise a heavy calf. And they liked the look of the cattle, too. Though Hughes was selecting mainly by the scale, he culled out anything with bad feet (crooked, or turned in or too small) or with sheep knees (knees knocking together and toes splaying out) and a number of other characteristics which would make the cattle unsound on the range, regardless of how fast they gained.

But Miles City and Curt Hughes were by no means alone in their break from tradition. One of the most remarkable women of this century was busy building a herd of Red Angus based on "performance." Waldo and Sally Forbes had come west to Sheridan, Wyoming and had bought red Angus where they could, in the few existing red herds and also from among the few showing up in black herds. The red gene is a simple Mendelian recessive – as is the snorter dwarf gene – but the red gene is not a bad one. The Forbes wanted to work with the red cattle because the color so distinctly separated them from the blacks. Most breeders of the blacks simply sold their red cattle as commercials, except a few who were breeding their reds under the same rules and procedures as the blacks.

The Forbes' plan was to build a new red breed based not just on pedigree and certainly not on show winnings but on *performance*. Before any cattle could be registered in *their* herdbook, they had to pass their exams – weaning weight, yearling weight and rapidity and efficiency of gain. Waldo died just as the task was well started, leaving Sally with an evolving new strain of cattle and six young children. She accepted the dual challenge magnificently and her Beckton Red Angus became world-renowned as *performing* cattle.

The Forbes' herd did not threaten established breeders to any great extent. Sally was a competitor, yes, but there were not many Red Angus around anyway, so a few more good ones wouldn't do any harm. The Hughes Red Angus bulls, however, did alarm Hereford breeders, for purebred Hereford bulls were then siring 80 percent of all ranch cattle.

At that time both Saskatchewan and Alberta had Purebred Sire Restricted Areas where it was *illegal* to use anything but a purebred bull. The governments had outlawed grade sires in the belief that purebred sires would do farmers and ranchers "good." Purebred breeders, of course, supported these laws, as did all believers in the Cattle Religion. The use of the Hughes' bulls in such large numbers flouted the law. But who would be courageous and foolish enough to lay charges against a rancher for using an unregistered bull demonstratively superior to many purebreds?

Ranchers were learning about performance testing and how it could make them more money. They also had seen how many of the purebred bulls offered in sales would not improve their herds but would actually make them worse.

One such rancher was Neil Harvie of the Glenbow Ranch, just west of Calgary. His herd was all black and Harvie, by weighing his cattle, (at that time the purebred Angus breed was small and compact) became convinced that he could raise far better bulls in his own herd than he could buy from *any* purebred breeder. So he "closed" his herd (with the exception of a few Charolais added later) and selected his best-performing bulls to breed his cows. He also selected the best heifers from his high-performing cows to enter the breeding herd.

Also doing a similar kind of selective breeding, but from a mixed-breed base was rancher Sherm Ewing of Claresholm, Alberta. He called his best cattle "HYTESTERS," – the first and only trademark registered for cattle in the U.S. This was not a breed in the conventional sense by any means. A HYTESTER was just that: he performed well on test and so earned the word HYTESTER tattooed in his ear.[2] His ancestors may have been high testers, but that wasn't the point. The bull himself and later his progeny, by a sophisticated phase of testing, produced beef rapidly at least cost.

A number of other cattlemen in Alberta were thinking the same way as Harvie and Ewing and some of them had programs of their own. Others were contemplating testing but weren't just sure of the best way to begin. So they decided to get together. Thus the first performance-test association was made up of commercial ranchers with not a purebred breeder among them.

The Alberta Beef Cattle Performance Association, often referred to as the "alphabetical outfit," was formed in 1959 (the same year that the Canadian Charolais Association came into being). The ranchers enlisted the advice and support of both the University of Alberta and the Research Branch of what was then (before Trudeau) the Canada Department of Agriculture.[3] The association set up common procedures for testing and recording, and the ranchers went ahead improving their herds. As far as they were concerned the purebred industry was quite irrelevant.

It is unlikely that they would have got going as soon as they did had it not been for a number of key people in responsible positions. I have to be careful in naming them – again that matter of success having many fathers – but the first to speak out boldly and with authority were Harry Hargrave[4] (the ranchers held their first meeting in his kitchen) who headed up Animal Science research at the Lethbridge research station and Roy Berg, professor of animal science at the University of Alberta (later department head and dean) and Howard Fredeen, researcher in animal breeding at the Lacombe research station.

What really got wheels turning was an annual short course jointly sponsored by the Western Stock Growers' Association and the Extension department of the University of Alberta. This was held every December in Banff and the "graduates" of this school became crusaders for realistic cattle improvement, including management, feeding and marketing – and especially breeding.

The "movement" was lucky in that whhat they did and the philosophy and science behind their activities appeared in the pages of *Cattlemen*, a magazine for the industry that had a greater circulation and readership than all the breed publications combined. The magazine lost a tremendous amount of advertising from purebred breeders, especially Hereford breeders, one of whom shook his fist under the editor's nose, accusing him of "ruining the industry." But the editor believed that he was on the side of truth and the angels – despite the loss of revenue – and continued to feature new developments, including the subsequent adoption of performance testing by *all* the breed associations.

Commercial ranchers had started their tests but purebred breeders were still reluctant to accept the principle of *utility* in cattle breeding. In 1959 I talked to the Alberta Livestock Commissioner (now called Director of Animal Industry) and asked him if he were devising a test plan for the purebred breeders.

"I'm not pushing it," Bill Meade told me. "When they're ready for it, we'll give them a program."

Not ready? Why were the breeders dragging their feet? Because they faced two severe obstacles. The first had to do with faith. All their lives they had believed that they knew good cattle when they saw them; now eggheads were coming out with a fancy scheme to show *them* what improving cattle was all about. The second obstacle had a dollar sign attached. If you had developed "reputation" cattle and were selling them for premiums, why change anything? Maybe your cattle, including the progeny of a grand champion bull, wouldn't do well on the test; then how could you sell them? And what would happen to your reputation, your investment and your livelihood? Performance testing threatened the very foundations of the purebred industry: the shows, the sales, all the beliefs about mellow fleshing and meat to the hock and constitution.

Meanwhile purebred breeders were losing business. Some ranchers (like Neil Harvie) were raising their own bulls, some were looking at those tall, ugly, dirty-white cattle imported from the U.S. South called Charolais (the Gilchrists of Maple creek, the Malmbergs of Cardston, Fletcher Bennett of Pincher Creek). These ranchers weren't buying bulls from purebred breeders. So the latter decided to bite the bullet and go for performance testing, too.

The procedure among the established leaders among breeders was to keep the faith and add testing to it. If a bull tested high among his compadres, advertise that; if he didn't gain too well, emphasize his masculinity or his pedigree or his straightness of lines. Sometimes a bull was good to look at and a high performer to boot. He sold for a lot of money.

Before long there were test programs of all kinds. Both the provincial and federal governments got into the act, and every breed association devised special testing procedures for their breed. An international organization was set up in Denver called Performance Registry International (PRI), which co-ordinated many of the existing programs. PRI granted a diploma (Certified Meat Sire) to a bull which sired a goodly number of high-performing steers. That is, the steers underwent the test and the award went to the sire. This was called progeny testing and was a terrific tool when it came to selling semen. Most highly-used AI bulls became Certified Meat Sires just by the laws of average. If they sired thousands of calves, some of them were bound to be outstanding.

The general belief among breeders was that performance testing was just "another tool" to use in improving cattle. You used the tool where it would make you money; where it might cost you money (or reputation) you used something else. In the late sixties I visited a Hereford breeder to get some advertising for a big sale he was planning to have. He was a construction millionaire whom the breeders "had seen coming" and now he wanted to sell some of the progeny of his expensive purchases.

I was accompanied by the publisher of the breed journal and by the breed "selector," Charles Yule, a man of prodigious reputation whom the association used to "select" cattle – actually to weed out the culls – for their major sales. While going through the cattle, we came across a young bull which had achieved an excellent gain record as a yearling.

"Use that in your ads," advised Yule. "That's becoming important now."

The "another tool" syndrome is still the way many breeders look at performance testing but as time has gone by it has become a much more important tool.

Performance testing led to bigger – longer and taller as well as heavier – cattle. So the show-ring standards adapted to the new faith after the faith had adapted to the perceived market. Now judges look for "extension" rather than "compactness." If an animal has extension, is long and tall, and still maintains a marked degree of muscularity, it's a "good" animal. If it is sound in legs and back and shows "breed character" to boot, you've done a good job of breeding. And if, on top of that, you have a good-gaining beast sired by a good gainer, and can prove it with records, you are indeed blessed.

Thus has the new religion evolved. Like the old-time religion, it has all the trimmings: silent and tumultuous worship, holy books, vestments, high and low priests, tenets of faith – the whole ball of wax. The compilation of performance records was a natural for computers and when you added pedigree to record, the computer proved indispensable. This time the commercial industry is largely with the breeders, although many think the trend in type is "too extreme."

At the U.S. Meat Animal Research Center in Nebraska, researchers have measured the change in type and performance as cattle have been selected for growth and gain. Using frozen semen from bulls of the Hereford and Angus breeds that were born in 1968-70, which they called "originals" and semen from contemporary bulls (born 1982-84), called "current," they bred 3- to twelve-year-old Hereford and Angus cows. Birth weights of calves from the current bulls were 12 to 16 percent heavier than those from the old daddies. Weaning weights had increased, too, by 13 to 15 percent. By selective breeding over 16 years, cattlemen had increased both the type size and the rate of gain in their cattle.

Actually a discussion of type is something more than academic. Researchers in Australia have demonstrated that you can't breed for "more meat on the loin," or anywhere else, in order to get more high-priced cuts. The distribution of muscle is in a constant proportion throughout the body *for all types of cattle*. True, some cattle have more muscle than others but you can't change the distribution by selective breeding. At least, up till now it hasn't been done.

Really, all you need to select for is heavy muscling and rapid gain combined with anatomical soundness, plus fecundity. (Remember the old Shorthorn Duchesses which were in high demand because they were infertile and the supply was therefore inadequate!)

So breeders are no longer selecting for "meat to the hock." They still may feel the hide for "fleshing" if they're acting as steer judges but usually they no longer use their hands when judging breeding animals. They're more concerned about "mothering ability" in cows. This means they like to see an adequate udder, well attached, a high degree of "femininity" and a lack of "coarseness" or "steeriness."

In bulls they look for "masculinity," including large testicles in low-hanging scrotums and hind legs that won't "break down" under severe service. Some insist that marbling[5] in the meat is an inherited trait but you can't measure that until the beast becomes a carcass. However, you can measure the back-fat by ultra-sound while the animal is still alive. So judging in a practical sense has become a mix of eyeball and test; and in the ring, the limitations of eyeballing are recognized.

Testing has advanced to the point where the heritability of most traits has been determined by percentages and the traits have been catalogued. For instance, growth rate and milking ability are highly heritable, while fertility and carcass quality are less heritable and therefore more difficult to improve by selection.

The Canadian Charolais Association was the first breed group to devise a complete testing program. They called it "Conception to Consumer." All economic factors were and still are measured under that rubric and the sires rated accordingly. One of the most important traits for Charolais bulls was "ease of calving" because many Charolais calves were so large at birth that cows had difficulty in delivering them. Quite a few, in fact, had to be taken by Caesarean section. By selecting for low birth weight and ease of calving, this problem can be largely eliminated. Charolais breeders today speak of "easy-calving" bulls. Other breeds followed suit and today most associations require birth and weaning weights before registering a calf.

But cattle improvement through performance and progeny testing has not been clear sailing by any means. When cattle are selected for growth – mainly by choosing those which weigh the heaviest at one year of age – they are also likely to be heavy at birth. This can result in difficult calving. Cecil Palmer, a progressive breeder whom I mentioned in the last chapter as one who "went for" big cattle, told me 20 years ago that his program had already produced such growthy Herefords that calving could be a problem, especially if he sold a high-gaining bull to a man with small cows. Thus he had to select for two apparently antagonistic characteristics: rapid growth after birth, limited growth before birth. Recent research, also done in Nebraska, reveals that it is possible to select for both lighter birth weight and heavier yearling weight at the same time, but the increase in yearling weight is not nearly as rapid as when birth weight is ignored.

It's a truism of breeding that the more characteristics you select for, the slower the rate of improvement. And if the traits are antagonistic, you can't get very far. Which perhaps is OK because that's Nature's way. There seems to be a "best" size or range of sizes in every species for carrying out biological functions. When you push beyond those limits, you may be in trouble.

Thus among prize fighters, the optimum size seems to be just over two hundred and ten pounds (90 kg) and six feet tall (183 cm). The same weight and height works very well for a running back in football but in both sports if he is an inch or two shorter (lower centre of gravity) and perhaps ten pounds lighter (better able to "make moves") he may readily outperform taller and heavier men.

Basketball, on the other hand, puts such a premium on height that tall athletes who would be easily outclassed in either football or boxing become stars in the hoop game. Sprinters have different physiques than do distance runners. And to play any position in professional sports, you have to pass the most rigorous of performance tests in every game!

All of which returns us to the matter of type. Again, if we make a comparison with humans, we are better able to understand it. People who make a study of such things have divided us into three general types: mesomorphs (the muscular ones), ectomorphs (the skinny, angular ones) and endomorphs (our fleshier boys – and girls).

The terms are derived from the names of the three types of basic tissue that evolve from the embryo: mesoderm, ectoderm and endoderm. As you have probably guessed, ecto (meaning outside) produces skin and in females, mammary tissue; endo (meaning inside) generates our internal organs and meso (in between) that part of us that is between the outside and the inside, our bones, muscles, nerves and blood vessels.

`Mesamorph`

`Endomorph`

`Ectomorph`

Athletic-looking people – most football players, sprinters, movie actors, livestock auctioneers and modern politicians (because of TV) – are mesomorphs. Among the ectomorphs – who lack heavy bones, bulgy muscles and big bellies – we find fashion models, distance runners, some lightweight boxers (their extra height and reach gives them an advantage over mesomorphs of the same weight), some basketball players and many musicians and artists. As for endomorphs, think of the people you have seen in the movies and on TV: Jackie Gleason, Momma Cass, Oprah Winfrey. Some endomorphic actors have to play comic roles because we (cruelly) think fat is funny, though in cattle it is pretty.

Endomorphs and ectomorphs are survivors. Whereas mesomorphs are killed in battle, suffer heart attacks and die of starvation, the efficient intestines and hearts and lungs of endos and ectos enable them to get by. And their reproductive advantages keeps the race going – especially if they have the wit to outmaneuver more muscular but less intelligent competitors. There are millions of endomorphs and ectomorphs in the Orient, the Middle East and in Central and Eastern Europe.

Of course, most of us are not "pure" in these traits but have a bit of all of them. Most of mankind are neither tall and lanky nor fat and potty nor built like Adonis (he was a meso). Sumo wrestlers combine muscle and fat and basketball players combine skeleton and muscle (both mesomorphic) with ectomorphic physiography. As for a combination of fat and lanky frame, think of the caricatures of the English nobility which appear in magazines. But this type is rare because they are at opposite poles of cell-division development.

Warrior societies honor male mesomorphs, as does our present society which puts its warriors before the TV cameras, in the rink, on the diamond or gridiron or movie screen. In women, America admires ectomorphs ("no woman can be too rich or too *thin*"). In Spain an important man may boast that he "has the biggest house, the fastest horse and the *fattest* wife!" And in a description of the last sexual achievement of an Arab sheik, we are told how "he called for his favorite fat wife" to be his partner in this sort of signature event.

Greek gods were all mesomorphs except for Hermes the messenger (the Roman god Mercury), who was an ecto-meso and Cupid who was an endo.

The goddesses showed less standardization; Aphrodite (Venus) was a plump and soft endomorph as were most of the nymphs who attended her. Athena (Minerva) was a mesomorph-ectomorph as befitted a huntress and Hera (Juno), the mother of all, was a mesomorph gone a little chubby. The ladies painted by Reubens revealed mammary tissue displaced by adipose tissue – they were endomorphs.

In general terms, males tend to be mesos and females are ecto-endo. The greater the difference, generally the "sexier" each is to the other. *Vive la différence! comme on dit en français.*

What has this to do with cattle breeding? A great deal. Dairy cattle are ectomorphs – all skin, fine bone, udder and gut (most of the latter is endomorphic but it has a lining of epithelial tissue akin to skin). Also they are very fertile. The muscle-and-bone plow oxen of Europe, which for a thousand years were used (and selected) for their strength, are mesomorphs and not all that fertile. The familiar British breeds were once mesomorphs. After 150 years' selection for show ring standards – remember fat is pretty – they developed into endomorphs. Since the 1960s breeders have been attempting – with considerable success – to remake them into mesomorphs. Because muscle is meat and that's what we eat.

OK, if muscle is meat, why not just raise mesomorphic cattle and be done with it. Think again of those East European female shotputters. Muscular, all right, but female? Well, maybe. Certainly not feminine. Fertile? Not if they are on steroids. And there's the crux of the matter. It takes male hormones to make muscles grow big and thick but it takes female hormones to conceive, bear young and lactate – everything we ask a cow to do. If we raise a big, heavy-muscled cow, will she be "female" enough to be reproductive?

'*A true ectomorph!*'

She may. But such a cow probably has a small vulva, not much udder and may not "cycle" (that is come into heat) regularly. And her hip structure is so masculine that, despite her great size, she has difficulty in passing a calf through her birth canal. The big European breeds are like this. North American breeders of the European breeds have deliberately selected for femininity (more ectomorphic), which means for less beefiness, in order to improve fertility and calving ease.

The most feminine of cows, the Jersey, is an absolute ectomorph, and tiny as she is, can give birth to a calf with more ease than any other breed. As a beef-maker, of course, she is not with it at all. Unless you breed her to a big-breed beef bull. In which case, she raises a pretty good calf.

Practical cattlemen have dealt with this dilemma by raising "middle of the road" cattle, cows that are female enough – good broody mother-cows, they're called – but still with enough muscle to raise steers which produce acceptable beef in adequate quantity. Some ranchers (specifically the Beef Booster group) have developed specialized: "maternal" lines for their mother cows and then have bred these to a "terminal sire," an all-beef testosterogenic fellow with size and growth and muscle proclaiming his presence. He's called a "terminal" sire because all his progeny, including heifers, go for beef. The heifers aren't kept for breeding because they're too much like their daddy. And just to show how specialized you can get, there are "easy calving" lines, the bulls of which are bred to heifers for their first calves. The calves are small and the heifers have little trouble calving them.

The next time you see a herd of cows in a field, ask yourself if these are maternal cows (loaded with femaleness) or are they general-purpose cows (female enough, but well-muscled, too). Quite frequently you will see some beefy androgenous terminal-sire cows. But you won't find many herds bred specifically to be used on heifers because the industry needs only a few "easy-calving" bulls, the siblings of which aren't the greatest beef producers. The Texas Longhorn is an easy-calving breed. A hundred years ago on the Texas plain any heifer that had trouble calving just died, a cruel but natural selection.

To develop these various lines, each with a different purpose, performance testing was crucial. Each of the traits had to be measured and selected for. Before the advent of performance testing, breeders understood the conflicts involved in producing "useful" cattle but they came to grips with the problem only when it became extreme. Such as when their cows became "too dairy" – read maternal or "too stagy" – read masculine. When I was in France in 1965 at the time of the first importation of French Charolais to Canada I saw great big cows with "zippers," the incision scars following caesarean birth. I took a picture of one of these and published it as a sort of *caveat emptor* to Canadian breeders.

I also saw a number of "double-muscled" cattle. This is a genetic abnormality in which very little fat is deposited in the muscles. In addition, the muscles are huge and bulging which should be an ideal beef type! But the animals are smaller than the breed average, quite infertile and have a lot of zippers among them. I asked the farmer (in my limited French) what he thought of this condition.

His reply: "Pour le boucher, très bon, mais pour l'éleveur, très mal!" [For the butcher, very good, but for the breeder, very bad!]

One North American breed, Sally Forbes' Beckton Red Angus, has been developed entirely by selection, using performance testing. While the Forbes were building up their breed of Red Angus, others were creating new breeds by crossing existing breeds in various combinations and then breeding the progeny together to create a new breed.

The first of these to reach national and international stature was the Santa Gertrudis, a breed developed on the King Ranch in southeastern Texas by combining Shorthorn and Brahman blood. But this was not a "performance breed" in the same sense as Beckton Red Angus. Rather, Santa Gertrudis began much like some other breeds, including the Shorthorn, by finding a "super sire" and then backcrossing to him to fix the type. The founding bull of the Santa Gertrudis breed was called by the inauspicious name of Monkey. While Santa Gertrudis cattle were not tested like either the Line Ones or Beckton Red Angus, they did have to pass a severe test of another sort: they had to produce beef under semi-tropical conditions. The plan was to combine the beef-producing capabilities of the Shorthorn with the Brahman's ability to thrive in a hot climate. This was a success.

An interesting and very productive "synthetic" breed of cattle was developed by the University of Alberta under the direction of Dr. Roy Berg. He combined a number of breeds: Galloway for hardiness and mothering ability, Charolais for growth rate and muscling and Angus for carcass quality plus the qualities also found in the Galloway. Over many years the performance of the synthetics has been compared with a line of straight Herefords that Berg had acquired following the advice of prominent breeders. The synthetics have consistently outperformed the straightbreds by a wide margin. Later Berg introduced dairy "blood" into a synthetic base and further increased productivity. In the next chapter (on Crossbreeding) you will discover why Roy Berg's synthetics proved to be so superior to conventionally bred cattle. Berg, who later became Dean of Agriculture and Forestry at the University, was roundly denounced by many breeders in the 1960s. But time has justified him and he has received many awards and honors through the years.

At the same time that Roy Berg was developing his synthetic lines at the University of Alberta, another colorful cattleman, Harry Hays of Calgary, was breaking all the rules with his "Converters." Hays had already won fame as a breeder of dairy cattle: his "Alcartra Gerben" had set world records for milk production in the 1940s and with his brother Tom, as Hays Farms Ltd., he had exported Holstein cattle worldwide. Hays Farms was the first to ship cattle by air. Hays was also one of the most successful and prominent livestock auctioneers in the country, with a worldwide reputation. He regularly sold beef bulls of all breeds at the prestigious Calgary Bull Sale.

With his financial success (You can't go wrong picking up land close to the smokestacks," he told me in 1962) Hays was able to buy the "Bar U Flats" portion of the historic Bar U Ranch, southwest of Calgary. Here he developed a strain of cattle designed to convert feed to beef as efficiently as possible, the Hays Converters. Hays knew the cattle of his day – both beef and dairy – better than anyone I ever met. His base cowherd were smallish, very tough but fecund "survival" Herefords he acquired from his neighbor on the Bar U Ranch, Allan Baker. To these cows Hays bred sons and grandsons of the Holstein "Fond Hope," a bull of sound conformation but not too "dairy" in appearance. His daughters had closely-attached udders, but were not much in the way of big milk producers. He also used grandsons of the Brown Swiss "Jane of Vernon," a cow which was generally recognized as having "the perfect udder." As a "backcross" to the Hereford breed, Hays bred, by artificial insemination, many of the half-dairy heifers to the big and beefy Silver Prince 7P. Using these four genetic bases, Hays developed a high-performing beef breed which was granted status by Canada Agriculture in 1978.

Just as the Converters were developed to the point of competing with other breeds, the big European breeds appeared on the scene, more or less stealing their thunder. Since Hays was responsible for the importation of the European cattle (see Chapter Fourteen, "Plow Oxen from Europe,") it is somewhat ironic that they limited the success of the Converters, his own creation. The Converters are great performing cattle, but their bulls have enough dairy blood in them to scare off many would-be buyers. They are popular on many Hutterite colonies (Anabaptist peasants, a world removed from the Cattle Religion) where beef production is the prime concern.

Has performance testing been a curse to the breeding fraternity, as it was first seen to be? Not at all.

As we noted earlier, the industry adapted to it and the "New Religion" has acquired many converts as reformed believers from the old faith. All the breed associations now have sophisticated testing programs which give recognition to real superiority in useful traits. Breeders are not just looking for high-performing individuals but are involved in broad programs which will improve the productivity of their entire herd. Bulls are rated according to their EPDs (Expected Progeny Differences) in specific traits like calving ease, yearling weight and so on. Cows short of milk? Since weaning weight depends on the cow's milk production, buy a bull with a better-than-average EPD for weaning weight. And if you are pulling too many calves, get a bull with a low birth-weight E.P.D. So you can now go about herd improvement in a sort of paint-by-numbers way. I expect, however, there will be purebred cattle shows and sales in the sacred cities for many years to come.

If we go back to the banker at the beginning of this chapter who's wondering if he should lend a cattleman money, what shall we tell him? Should he know the rudiments of performance testing of cattle before advancing credit to buy breeding stock? Next time you're in the bank, ask *your* manager what he knows about it. Probably not as much as he should – but he may be learning.

The purebred breeder eventually came to terms with performance testing although his problems were by no means over. He still had to contend with a foe he could not master – crossbreeding.

By the Way . . .

[1]Thoroughbred horse breeding is redolent with myth but the real test is who comes in first!

[2]Ewing says this is "The only production additive that has never caused cancer in rats."

[3]Up till the fifties the name was Dominion Department of Agriculture. "Dominion" was scrubbed, as being too subservient to an English crown, and replaced with "Canada" mainly to appease anglophobes. Thus we had the Canada Department of Agriculture (CDA). But when bilingualism flowered a decade later, and everything had to be readily translated into another tongue, Ottawa put Agriculture in front of Canada (dropping the word Department) so the name read the same way in both official languages.

[4]Hargrave was later demoted for not having any post-graduate degrees. The cattle industry was so publicly and vocally incensed by this act of injustice that the government gave him another responsible position, this time with the PFRA (Prairie Farm Rehabilitation Act) in Regina.

[5]Marbling and its significance in grade standards and international trade is discussed in Chapter Seventeen.

Chapter Thirteen

Outlandish Lusts
(Crossbreeding)

"It's like a football team with only one line and one backfield up against another team with both offensive and defensive teams." Dr. Roy Berg (whom we met in the last chapter as Dean of Agriculture and Forestry at the University of Alberta and developer of synthetic breeds) was talking to a group of cattle-men. "Which team would you bet on?"

Not to be outwitted by the clever geneticist, one rancher replied: "It would depend on how good the players are. Are the players on both teams equally good? If they are, then naturally we'd bet on the squad that had both offensive and defensive teams."

Berg, who was speaking at an annual Feeders' Day at the University, had found the answer he had been hoping for. "That's sort of the way crossbreeding works," he went on. "If you are crossbreeding, you have an advantage over a straight breeder because you have two teams against his one."

Dr. Berg was talking of the leverage that comes from the teamwork of a lipiphobic Jack Spratt and his fat-loving spouse. The platter gets licked clean – and in football so does the other team.

"Of course, if you have good players, it gives you a further advantage," he added.

The message the cattlemen went away with was that crossbreeding pays, and the payoff is bigger if the animals you cross are good to start with.

A tremendous amount of research has been done on crossbreeding of cattle. The results bear out the rancher's wager on the football game: if you crossbreed two straight lines, the calves will be about 10 percent better gainers while nursing their dams and about 12 percent more efficient as feedlot steers. That's for the crossbred calf; the real payoff comes when you use a crossbred cow – she calves easier and oftener, gives more milk and is generally healthier and lives and produces longer. Using crossbred cows to raise crossbred calves will give you as much as a 30 percent boost to production, if you follow through the entire business from breeding cows to eating beef.

If crossbreeding is that great why did it take so long to become a general practice and why isn't more of it done even now? For an answer, remember that until the 1960s, at least 80 percent of the beef cattle in the West were Herefords – Hereford bulls breeding Hereford cows. The system had worked for ranchers since 1906, when "lesser breeds" didn't survive that year of the hard winter. "Herefords for grief and grass!" said it all. If you had grass and hard country and hard winters, Herefords would do the job. And look just great doing it – nothing prettier than a herd of white-faced cattle grazing the green hills of home. And they regularly topped the market!

So it was not surprising that the credo of Hereford breeders and most commercial ranchers for many years, up till the mid- sixties, went like this: "The best cross is one good Hereford on another good Hereford." But, you will say, if you are mating a Hereford with another Hereford, it is not a cross. That's straight breeding. Right. Why, then, were the breeders equating it with crossbreeding? Because other people were "ruining the industry" (read, reducing the demand for Hereford bulls at the sales) by "promoting" absolute nonsense. The eggheads were saying dumb things like: crossbreeding will make you more money; your calves will be faster growing, healthier, will feed out more economically and (what was indisputable *untruth*) a crossbred cow would work better than the straightbred Hereford cow.

If pressed, Hereford breeders might concede that maybe you could use an Angus bull to breed yearling heifers. The Angus calf is smaller and the gestation period may be a day or two shorter, so you may have fewer problems at calving. But why breed yearling heifers? Why not wait till they were two years old and then you'd have no trouble. And you'd have a better-looking cow to boot, not a poor bitch stunted by being bred too soon. Purebred breeders didn't breed yearlings, their association wouldn't even register a calf from a two-year-old dam (bred as a yearling). As for ranchers, the old-time big operators never bred yearlings – too many losses at calving time. Most of those poor young two-year-old mothers had problems at calving and were slow to breed back – or didn't get in calf at all. So you might just as well wait another year till they grew up and then you could do it right.

Sound logic. And sound economics. Or was it?

Well, the economists (and bankers who had lent money to young fellows starting up in the cow business) as well as quite a few ranchers, began to count the unproductive females on a typical ranch. There were just too many heifers on the place which were waiting a full three years before they became productive matrons. The money-wise fellows said, "You can't afford to keep a heifer until she is two years old before you breed her. You have to breed her as a yearling and have her raising a calf as a two-year-old if you want to stay out of bankruptcy."

By breeding yearlings, a rancher can add 10 to 15 percent more cows to the herd. They'll use the grass and feed that formerly carried unproductive heifers from two- to three-year-olds. So not only does he have more total productive units – much like owning more land – he has more overall efficiency in his outfit – more calves to sell for the same inputs. A 10 to 15 percent boost in income is worth grabbing, particularly if the bank is pushing.

Cattlemen don't like keeping books! Those that do breed yearlings. Or, like some of my Ontario friends, they buy bred cows at the sales. (Ontario cattlemen are twice as smart as Alberta cattlemen, as I will point out in a later chapter.)

The breeding of yearlings, and subsequently calving out of two-year-olds, means you have to be a better manager and you can expect to get up in the middle of the night through most of April. And it's going to take more and better feed. (More about all that in a later chapter.)

Cattlemen began to breed yearlings as a regular practice, and sure enough, they found that if they used an Angus bull, they had fewer calving problems because the calves were smaller and the gestation period appeared to be a little shorter. This left them with a number of "baldy" calves – black-bodied with a white (or brockled) face. These were very good calves, even if they came out of first-calf heifers.

They seemed to combine the best characteristics of both the Angus and Hereford breeds. Some of the baldy heifers were kept as replacements to go into the breeding herd. They made wonderful mothers and much better udders and gave more milk than the Herefords. They were attentive to their calves and thrifty rustlers on the range. In fact, they seemed to carry their flesh through the winter even better than their Hereford mothers. Moreover, they had no horns, so didn't have to undergo the unpleasant business of dehorning.

When bred to Hereford bulls, half their calves were baldies, like themselves, and the others were red with white-faces, like Herefords. Moreover, they seemed to have lost the nervous temperament of the Angus.

"It's just like you put an onion in vinegar," one rancher told me. "Takes the bite right out of them."

They had only one strike against them – color. For 70 years,[1] feeder-cattle buyers had discriminated against Angus cattle in Canada,[2] claiming that they did not grow as rapidly nor as large in the feedlot. (They did admit, however, that the Angus had a superior carcass.)

So, when a buyer had an order for white-face calves, he could not fill it with black ones. If you were selling baldy steers, you were never sure whether they'd bring as much as Herefords or whether they would be discounted. In time, of course, they began to command premiums but that took a while. Despite this uncertainty, baldy cows became very popular; some ranchers maintain they "are the perfect mother cow."

The rising popularity for baldies made Angus breeders happy at their bull sales but saddened Hereford breeders. And when ranchers began to buy Angus bulls to breed *mature* cows, not just heifers, that's when it really hurt. And that's when Hereford breeders made a concerted effort against crossbreeding – and came out with their supply "The best cross is a Hereford . . ."

Nor were Angus the only "culprits." This was during the time when dwarfism was making everybody look "for a good big bull" to breed their mature cows. The biggest (and nearest) big bulls happened to belong to a strange dirty-white breed that a few ranchers, whom we mentioned in the last chapter, were using with some success. The cattle, called Charolais, came from the southern United States, where they had been imported illegally from Mexico in limited numbers. Originally they had come from France, where they were purported to be the beef

breed supreme. In this hemisphere they had been crossed with Brahman (Zebu) in varying percentages to better suit a hot climate. They were big and ugly, ringy in temperament, didn't have much hair, nor did they look like beef cattle in the accepted sense: in no way were they "broad, thick, close to the ground and short-coupled."

Bred to domestic cows, these rangy, knobby bulls left remarkably attractive calves, thrifty and growthy and certainly no dwarfs! Buyers did not want them, though and the best return from them could only be achieved by the rancher feeding them out himself and selling them "on the rail," with the packer paying for the carcass, not the live animal. The breeders of British-breed cattle laughed at them.

One person not laughing was Harry Hargrave, the head of Animal Science at the Lethbridge Research Station. Hargrave had been commissioned by the Canadian Government to tour the U.S. and assess the potential of Charolais for Canada. He came home enthusiastic and encouraged his rancher friends to take a look at this new breed. Hargrave, who had tremendous prestige in the ranching community, was the son of a very prominent rancher, had been a ranch manager himself and had been superintendent at the Manyberries station for a dozen years. So he knew what kind of cattle would work on a ranch. His brother Bert, who owned the family ranch at Walsh, Alberta, had already bought a few Charolais bulls.

Interest in the breed grew. The AI units carried Charolais semen. One prominent Saskatchewan rancher, John Minor of Abbey, artificially inseminated some 350 cows to Charolais semen in 1957. (See Chapter Fourteen, "The Exotics.") The steer calves from this program were fed out, slaughtered and their carcasses evaluated. The results were excellent: some of the cut-out was done by a Safeway Stores butcher; he loved the carcasses. The breed was now established and the Canadian Charolais Association was formed in 1959.

It took several years for buyers to accept the crossbred calves, but eventually they came to pay a premium for them. By the mid-sixties many ranchers were using Charolais bulls. And Hereford breeders had long since stopped laughing.[3]

Crossbreeding, of course, was nothing new. Both practical experience and research had shown there were a number of plusses to the practice. But the plus factors had always been perceived in the crossbred calf: not much attention had been paid to the crossbred cow. Except when a rancher used a few Shorthorn[4] bulls to "keep up the size and improve the milk." Their Hereford-Shorthorn daughters were added to the regular herd. Ranchers assessed them like this: "they give you real good calves[5] but the cows are usually thinner by fall, and they don't winter too good."

The cow had put more summer grass into her milk and so into her calf and she had less grease on her back by November. Some ranchers, too, believed the Shorthorn cows tended to get lousy. So, ever since the hard winter of '06, there had been fewer and fewer Shorthorns in ranch herds. There were, however, still plenty of them in farm herds.

"Don't mongrelize!" was a constant admonition. Said another way, it was, "Keep your cowherd straight." The best plan to these purists was to keep a straightbred cowherd and breed a few of these to another-breed bull for a few crossbreds. That's not a practical approach, especially if you use only one bull at a time, which is the rule in a great many farm herds. For these herds, the extension men suggested you use a Hereford bull for two or three years (until his daughters were ready to breed) and then buy a Shorthorn or Angus bull and use him for two or three years. If you had enough cows for two bulls, you could use two breeding pastures, alternating the bulls every two years, thus doubling the useful life of a bull. That way all your calves were crossbreds of some kind and your cows became crossbred, too.

To get even more of a mix, you could go with three breeds of bulls, breeding them in rotation. Geneticists said that was good; breeders and many buyers said it was mongrelizing. It certainly wasn't keeping your cowherd straight. If you go to a fall calf sale, there is nothing more inspiring than a sale ring filled with 50 popping good calves, all marked the same. That uniform color earns dollars. It really shouldn't count but eye-appeal can't be ignored if you want the top price. You can't get uniform color[6] in your calves by rotational crossing. So why bother with crossbreeding at all?

Many cattlemen, not convinced that those percentage increases are real, still ask that question and keep on using one breed of bull. But they are in the minority. If you drive across the country and look at the colors of cattle in the fields, you'll find most of them are mixed: reds with white (and brockled) faces, several kinds of white, various shades of tan and of grey, solid blacks and solid reds, browns, red and white spotted, roans, black baldies, and occasionally a few with a "blanket" or "skunk" rump. The Hereford breed is still much dominant but pushing it hard is the new breed – Charolais. Any one field usually has just a few colors, but in the course of a hundred miles, you can almost fill the spectrum – real mongrelization! In 1950, nearly all those herds would have been red white-faces, with one or two out of 10 black and a few obviously Shorthorns – reds, roans, whites and an occasional spot.[7]

The change has been market-driven. The favorite of the cattle buyers is a "tan Hereford crossbred," a Hereford-Charolais cross. Actually other big European breeds can do what the Charolais does but the tan body color and the white face immediately proclaim the parentage and look uniform in the sale ring or the feedlot pen. Buyers are filling orders for feedlot operators, who in turn will sell to packers. The piper-payer is calling the tune – just listen to the noon broadcast of cattle prices coming from Toronto . . . "heavy exotic cross heifers selling right up with or higher than top steers." And in the previous sentence the broadcaster has told us how "exotic-cross steers sold at a premium." Of course, there is still a good market for well-finished British-bred cattle,[8] especially in the U.S., where carcasses can carry a higher degree of finish (fat) and marbling is a requisite of the top grade. But on the general market, exotic-cross calves weigh heavier and sell for more money per pound, so, many commercial cattlemen ask, why raise anything else?

When it comes to show steers, crossbreds are tops also. Only now the favored cross is with Angus, which is the "prettiest" and "smoothest" of the British breeds and has the most desirable carcass. It "smooths out" the big rough European cattle, adds some "style" to their ungainly forms and movements and puts just the right amount of fat on and in their huge, lean muscles; this makes graders, butchers and housewives smile. All the Exotics "work" in an Angus cross. For judges who are "modern," Angus crosses with the two biggest breeds – Chianina and Maine-Anjou – will get the nod, while more "traditional" judges tend to like Angus with the Limousin, the prettiest of the European breeds. This cross has a terrific record in carcass classes, partly because of the high "yield"- most pounds of edible meat per weight of animal. Charolais-Angus crosses sometimes have "rat tails" – not much hair on them. This spoils them for show, though otherwise they're OK.

My crossbred steers which Don Danard showed in 1970 at the Toronto Royal for the Grand Champion Carlot (actually a group of 12) were tan, white-faced steers out of black baldy dams. The sire was a high-performing domestic purebred Charolais bull. Half of his calves were tan-colored (from the Hereford side of the baldies) and the other half were mouse-grey (from the Angus side). Danard had bought my entire steer calf crop the previous year. He showed the mouse-grey half brothers[9] of the Toronto steers at the Edmonton Spring show in both the Group of Five and the Carlot classes. They didn't do well – stood in the middle of their classes.

The Toronto steers inherited the red body gene from their baldy dams (where, as recessive to the Angus black, it had remained hidden) and this "blended" with the Charolais white to produce the tan. The Hereford white face was, of course, dominant in the baldy cows but had broken down in their calves: some were white-faced, some brockled.

Why crossbreed? The football-team analogy points the way but needs some explanation if you are a mite curious how genes work. Remember our story of the wolves? And how new breeds were started?

How inbreeding and out-crossing work in nature? How outcrosses are strong and healthy and how inbreeding reveals hidden defects? Here's why this happen, in simple terms.

When a sex cell prepares to reproduce, it divides in two, reducing the number of chromosomes (which carry the genes) by half. Then, when the half-cell combines with the also-divided cell of the sex partner, the chromosomes combine to add up to the full number. The undivided chromosomes carry genes in pairs. The Angus carries two color genes for black. The Hereford carries two color genes for a red body. (Let's not worry about the white face just now.) Thus each of the divided sex cells has only *one* gene for color.[10] When these combine the new cell has a full complement – half from the sire and half from the dam. Thus when Hereford is crossed on Angus, each cell of the resultant baldy carries a gene for red and a gene for black. The black is dominant and gives the animal its color. The red is recessive; you wouldn't know it was there. But it is and may show up in the next generation.

In a general population, the recessives (which are often bad genes) stabilize around five percent or less – stay hidden, unless two individuals in that five-percent group mate.This means that between one in 1600 and one in 2500 will show the defect. Often the bad gene is revealed in far fewer individuals than this because it may have to be "associated" with another gene to be expressed. In a closed population (like a breed), especially if you apply selective pressure, the bad genes can appear in 25 percent of the population, as happened with Snorter dwarfism in some herds. Moreover, even if there aren't many bad recessive genes, the ones that are there appear frequently in the close-bred population. Geneticists say it is becoming homozygotic. So animals or people *look* physically more and more alike and *are* genetically more and more alike. When they mate, there are few new genes added to the new individual, so the offspring closely resemble the parents, who are said to breed true. In Dr. Berg's story, it is a one-team football squad.

Every organism faces an environment hostile to a greater or lesser degree. The more and varied its resources, the more strings to its bow. The larger the number of good dominant genes it has the better its chances of survival and the better its performance as a biological entity. (The bad recessive genes will just be carried along at a low level and won't get in the way.) It has a two-team, offense and defense football squad. The way to get this variety of genes is to outcross. The wider the cross, the more opportunity for good dominant genes to appear. (Like replacing a so-so quarterback with a choice of either Joe Montana or Warren Moon.)

An organism with wide diversity of gene origin is said to be heterozygotic and the vim and vigor that comes with these diverse genes is called heterosis. The cattleman calls it hybrid vigor. When you crossbreed, you get hybrid vigor. The wider the cross, the greater the hybrid vigor. And the good properties of the crossbred animal are considerably better than the average of the two parents.

The first agricultural use of what happens with controlled inbreeding and outcrossing occurred not in animals but in seed corn. We go back to the days of Franklin Roosevelt and Henry Wallace when a good crop of corn in Iowa was 40 or 50 bushels to the acre. Scientists who understood genetics, "selfed" (self-pollinated) strains of corn over many generations. This process, as you would expect, revealed many defects (such seeds the researchers cast aside) and the strain became homozygotic – an inbred line. The plants were not big and were relatively unproductive. Then two *unrelated intensely inbred lines* were crossed. Bang! The resultant hybrids were big, extremely high-yielding and healthy plants. Often two such high-producing crossbred lines would in turn be "selfed" over many generations and then these new inbred lines would be crossed for an even bigger bang! That's what the hybrid seed-corn business is all about. The corn in the field does not reproduce itself but comes from specialty seed-corn breeders – and yields well over a hundred bushels per acre.

The same thing was done with chickens. I can remember my father trap-nesting Rhode Island Red hens in the 1920s to select the best layers for breeding, sort of like performance testing of cattle today. Nobody does that any more nor are there any breeds of chickens left – except those raised by fanciers for chicken shows, which are a world removed from the real chicken-and-egg business. High performing "lines" of chickens are developed and inbred for generations (much like the corn) and then these inbred lines are crossed for domestic production, either for layers or broilers, each of a different feather. For turkeys it's the same thing. When did you last see a Broad Breasted Bronze turkey? At one time they were on every farm. Now only a few fanciers keep them. Pity!

There are only a handful of chicken breeders in the *world*. One is Donald McQ. Shaver of Cambridge, Ontario, who supplies chicken producers on all continents. Twenty years ago, Shaver wondered if the same kind of genetic selection and development could be done with cattle. It can, of course, but not in one man's lifetime, because the generation time of cattle is at least three years, whereas chickens can produce two or three generations a year. Shaver searched Europe for the most useful breed overall then in existence. He settled on the Maine-Anjou and imported two bulls in 1970. Since then, using other red breeds, he and his son have developed a line of cattle which they call Shaver Reds.

If we go back to the wolf story we see that Nature works much like the corn or chicken breeder – inbreeding for a period and so revealing recessives (which a harsh environment kills off), then outcrossing – when food is plentiful – to develop stronger and swifter wolves and more of them!

'Santa Gertrudis'

'Brahman'

Just how potent hybrid vigor in cattle can be was revealed 30 years ago at the Range Research Station at Manyberries, Alberta. Hereford cows were bred to Brahman bulls (the U.S. cowboy says bramer or bramma). The heifer calves were raised and then compared with Hereford cows as producers of beef (through their calves). After 10 years, the Brahman-cross cows had produced twice as many pounds of calf as had the Herefords. And the trial was concluded then because most of the Hereford cows had died in a cold winter! This winter hardiness in the crossbreds is amazing because the pure Brahman cannot stand cold – the sires of the crossbreds froze to death at Manyberries. But their daughters could out-winter straight Hereford range cows. When Dr. Hobart Peters wrote up the results of this experiment, practically nobody believed him.

An interesting side note from this experiment is that when the old crossbred cows were shipped to Calgary for slaughter, the stockyards people were afraid to unload them – Brahman crosses make good rodeo stock! They had to get old-time rancher Chay Gilchrist out of retirement to come down and handle the recalcitrant critters. Years earlier, Chay and his brothers had recognized the value of wide crosses and had learned how to "cowboy" Brahmans on their ranches in southern Alberta and Saskatchewan. Lots of vigorish in those hybrids!

The popularity of the Hereford undoubtedly sprang, in part, from its use as a crossbred. Our early range cattle were driven up from Texas after a generation or two in Montana and were mainly Longhorns derived from Spanish cattle. The first "improvement" of these cattle was with Shorthorn bulls. Not only were the Shorthorns much closer to the ideal beef type, they were also a world apart genetically from the Longhorns, so there was much hybrid vigor in these crosses. A little later came the Hereford. White-faced bulls were bred to both Longhorn and Shorthorn-Longhorn cross cows. In both crosses there was another big hybrid boost. In most ranch herds there would not be enough Hereford bulls to handle all the cows, so a substantial number of in-herd bulls would breed many of their female kin. (In Texas, the old ranch practice was to leave each tenth bull entire when castrating the calves.)

So all the white-faced cattle in the herd would be first- or second-cross Herefords, while the mixed colors could be anything else. When the hard winter came, the white-faced cows had, to keep them warm, this extra crossbred vigor, in addition to their heavier hides, heavy woolly coats and fat got from not producing much milk. As the years passed, the ranchers stayed with their white-faces but bemoaned the fact that they weren't the "big old rugged kind we used to raise." Of course they weren't, because now they were essentially purebred.

What really got crossbreeding going was the introduction of cattle from Europe, beginning in 1966. The plan was to "grade up" domestic cows of all breeds to at least 15/16 or 31/32 "pure" and sell the progeny for big bucks. Thus every breeder of the new breeds was also a cross-breeder. All the bull calves along the way up had to go to market somewhere. And they did. Many were sold to ranchers as "percentage" bulls. Others were castrated, fed out as steers and sent to slaughter, first with heavy discounts against them and eventually as premium makers. The next chapter tells all about it.

By the Way . . .

[1]"Legs" Lair, manager of the Matador Ranch in Saskatchewan, in a letter of the 1890s, tells of Hereford steers in Chicago selling for seven cents a pound, with "blacks and Durhams (Shorthorns) a couple of cents less."

[2]In the U.S., where the grading system allows for more carcass fat and gives a bonus for marbling, many Cornbelt feeders favored Angus above other breeds.

[3]In 1957, during the centennial celebration of Herefords in Canada, Clyde McMurchie of Saskatoon, a writer for the Western Producer, composed a little ditty (sung to the tune of "Buffalo Gals") which everybody thought terribly funny: "The Hereford breed has come along way, come along way, come along way. They may catch up to the Charolais in another hundred years!"

[4]I was raised on purebred Shorthorn cattle. Some 40 years later, I picked up a half-dozen purebred Shorthorn cows that were "being given away" at a sale and ran them as commercial cows with the ranch herd. Bred to Charolais bulls, they produced great calves but for various reasons didn't last long. Their crossbred daughters were as productive as any in my herd.

[5]In Britain, a favorite "beast" for both the grazier and the butcher had always been a "blue roan" got by breeding a white Shorthorn bull to either Angus or Galloway cows.

[6]You can get uniformity in color with a three-breed cross of all-red breeds, like Red Angus, Sussex, Salers.

[7]Cattle marked like this are now likely to be Texas Longhorns (easy calvers) – more of them than Shorthorns on ranches today. The wheel has come full circle in a hundred years.

[8]In the fall of 1989, a Calgary-area cattlemen sold his entire crop of big solid-black Angus calves to a feeder in the irrigation country of Southern Alberta for a premium of between 10 and 15 cents per pound – $60 extra per head! Why should he crossbreed?

[9]Charolais-Angus crosses will vary from almost white to a dark grey but generally are mouse-grey.

[10]Inheritance of color patterns is actually more complicated than I've indicated but then this isn't a textbook on genetics.

Chapter Fourteen

Plow Oxen in the Ballroom
(The Exotics and Other New Breeds)

>>>>>>>>>>>>>>>>>>>>>>>

While holidaying in Europe in 1957, John Ballachey of Calgary saw some wonderful red-and-white cattle in the Swiss Alps. The local farmers called them Simmenthalers. Much bigger than any Canadian cattle and also heavily muscled, the cows were used for both meat and milk. In color they somewhat resembled Herefords because they had white faces but their bodies differed, sporting big red-and-white splashes. So impressed was Ballachey that he made arrangements in Switzerland to ship a number of the big cattle to Canada. But when he returned to Calgary he discovered that no cattle had been imported from continental Europe for over 60 years. The reason was aftosa, "foot and mouth disease." Canadian veterinarians were adamant: no European cattle would ever again be imported to Canada.

Simmental

So Ballachey put his ideas about Simmenthalers somewhere on a back burner until a fellow Calgarian, Harry Hays, became Minister of Agriculture under Liberal Prime Minister Lester Pearson. Hays and Ballachey were sitting next to each other on a flight from Calgary to Toronto and the talk turned to cattle.

"Harry, we just have to get some of those big Simmenthaler cattle over here," he said to the minister. Ballachey, a lawyer by training, was the corporate secretary of the newly-formed Alberta Gas Trunk Line company. His father, also a lawyer, had owned a ranch in the High River area and John's heart had always been with cattle and ranching. He owned a small ranch 40 miles (25 km) southwest of Calgary and had been the first secretary of the Canadian Charolais Association. His plea to Hays was not the first that the minister had to deal with.

"As you know, John," Hays said, "The Charolais people have been pushing me to let them bring cattle from France. But we can't do it. Europe has foot and mouth disease. We don't have it, nor do the Americans and we don't dare risk it. Our government would fall if we imported cattle that later proved to be carriers of foot and mouth. The Americans would close the border." He reminded Ballachey of the foot and mouth outbreak of 1952 in Saskatchewan, brought in, it was thought, in some sausage by a German immigrant. This cost Canada millions before it was cleaned up and the American border opened again.

But that was an accident and so forgivable. A deliberate act of the government would never be forgiven. Nevertheless, Hays travelled to Europe, looked around and changed his mind. He was at home in situations like this. Hays Farms – Harry and his brother Tom – had exported Holstein cattle to all the continents. They were the first to ship cattle by air. Harry understood politics as well as international trade in cattle.

There are many stories about what happened next. It is certain that Canada was (and still is) sensitive to positions of the American government. Also there were strong political forces in that country against importation. The breed associations were wealthy and vocal and the veterinary profession, understandably, was against inviting catastrophe. But there were also a number of extremely wealthy and influential

Gelbvieh

Americans who wanted to import Charolais from France. Some had already bought French cattle and were holding them on the island of Eleuthera in the Bahamas, a couple of hundred miles east of Miami. They were leaning heavily on President Lyndon Johnson.

Historically, all cattle entering North America from overseas had arrived at a Canadian port and then were cleared for shipment to the United States if that was their ultimate destination. Horses, on the other hand, landed in the United States first if going either to that country or to Canada. It was a kind of gentlemen's agreement that had worked well for years. So, if cattle were to come to the continent from aftosa-infected Europe, the onus was on Canada to make the shipments safe – or to prohibit them entirely.

In Canada, all the breed associations except the Charolais were lobbying hard to keep out the foreign cattle. So were all the commercial cattle organizations because of the fear of a closed U.S. border. We don't know what (if anything) L.B. Johnson (a Hereford breeder) said to Pearson and Hays but we know that Hays called in his chief veterinarian, Dr. Kenneth Wells, a man of considerable reputation and a able professional. Hays told him to draw up a plan for importing cattle from Europe.

Wells was reluctant to undertake the venture. He had been Canada's veterinary second-in-command in 1952 and it was he who had engineered the clean-up of the Saskatchewan out-break. He knew only too well how hazardous was the task – the testing and quarantine procedures had to be foolproof. If the project failed, the fall-out would be catastrophic, he warned his minister. But Hays was adamant; so Wells put in motion a plan and procedure that *was* foolproof.

Permits were issued in the spring of 1965 and by early summer Canadian Charolais breeders were selecting calves in the Loire valley for export to Canada.[1] The cattle arrived in their new homes a year later after having been examined by veterinarians on French farms, quarantined and re-tested by Canadian veterinarians at the seaport of Brest and then shipped across the Atlantic to a special quarantine stable newly built on Grosse Isle in the St. Lawrence River. There, they spent the winter. When the river was free of ice, they were shipped by boat and rail car to destination centres where their new owners took possession of them. After that, they had to spend three months in on-farm quarantine before they were declared free to go and come as other cattle do. Many of them changed owners as soon as or before the quarantine was over.

Permits for the imports had been issued (upon approval by Dr. Wells) by the federal government to those breeders who had applied.

Every Charolais breeder wanted a French animal but he wasn't sure what he should pay or if he could afford it, so applications for the first importation were manageable. A new factor emerged immediately: every American Charolais breeder wanted a French animal, too – and these breeders had so many bucks that price was no object. If you imported a French bull, which might have cost you five or six thousand dollars FOB to your farm, somebody wanted to pay you 40, 50 – even 80 thousand dollars for him. The first public auction of French Charolais, which was held in Calgary in July, 1967 and "cried" by Harry Hays (who no longer was in the government), saw prices like that. The sale averaged $11 025,[2] with "Amour de Paris," the high-selling bull, going for $58 000. (To convert that figure to 1990 dollars, multiply by four.)

So the great boom was on. Since getting a permit was equivalent to winning a sweepstake, applications for the next importation swamped Dr. Wells's office. Americans lined up to "sponsor" Canadian importers. The "deals" took every form that imagination could concoct. The Canadian government soon forbade the sale and export of the imported cattle, so American sponsors had to make arrangements to keep "their" cattle in Canada for an indefinite period of time. In order to deal with the hundreds of permit applications, Dr. Wells required each request be accompanied by a herd breeding plan. These plans were evaluated by a panel of livestock geneticists. The hope was that the cattle would go to bona fide cattlemen and not to speculators.

Since artificial insemination was the quickest route for spreading the new genes around the country, AI studs were granted permits to import bulls. Result: a mushrooming of AI units across the land, in Alberta, from none to eight within three years. Calgary, which is the *de facto* beef-cattle capital of the country, soon had an AI unit on each of the four sides of the city. If an import permit was like a sweepstake ticket, AI was the way to augment[3] and share this wealth.

Since the Charolais herdbook was "open," you could breed your entire herd of any breed (most were Herefords) to an imported French Charolais bull and "record" all the calves as half-bloods. The half-blood heifers could then be bred to another French bull and their calves recorded as three-quarter-bloods. And so on, right on up to "pure-bred," 31/32.

So dozens of ranches and farms were suddenly using AI. At first the local dairy technician could cope with the business; in fact, to him it was a bonanza. The mushrooming business soon prompted the AI bull studs to put on "schools" where you could learn – for a fee – how to inseminate cattle. Many farmers and ranchers took these courses and inseminated their own herds. Some got provincial licenses and did their neighbors' herds, too. This revolutionary development shook the purebred breeders, because now the "bull was in the bottle," a bottle which could replace hundreds, even thousands, of bulls and no one bought that bottle from a purebred breeder.

Half-blood heifers sold at a premium: an ordinary heifer calf might be worth $100 but would-be Charolais breeders were paying $300 for weaned half-blood calves right at the farm. And when they had kept that calf a year and bred her to another big, heavy French bull (a terrible thing to do to a Heifer) they found they could sell her for as much as $2 000! A boom was on that lasted till 1975.

But the boom wasn't just a Charolais phenomenon. Travis Smith, a sad-faced and determined Mormon rancher from Cardston, Alberta, had seen Simmenthaler cattle and he thought they would be an even better bet than Charolais. In the first place, they were red and white and had white faces; therefore, they could be crossed on Hereford cows without changing the color much. This would appeal to ranchers – feeders, too. Simmenthalers were also better milkers than Charolais, so should raise bouncing big calves. He also reasoned that since they were kept for milk in Europe, they would have "easier" dispositions than Charolais,[4] who were not noted for being tractable. (In this he turned out to be wrong but it didn't matter much as far as profits were concerned.)

Smith, who did not have much money of his own, talked up Simmental cattle (as they became known on the North American continent) at every opportunity and eventually found others who were willing to invest in his new breed. And so Simmental Breeders, Cardston was formed. One of the founders was Ray Woodward, the researcher from Miles City who had been in at the beginning of performance testing and the development of the Line One Herefords. (See Chapter Twelve, "Cut the Mustard.")

The first Simmental bull imported to Canada did not come from Switzerland but from France. There the dual-purpose, red-and-white cattle were called "Pie Rouge." They were related to the Swiss Simmenthaler and probably had a common ancestry. At that time Canada was set up to import Charolais from France but had no arrangements to take cattle out of Switzerland or any other European country. So when Smith and Simmental Breeders, Cardston, got an import permit, they had to settle for a French Pie Rouge rather than a Swiss Simmenthaler.

The settlement didn't hurt a bit; their bull, "Parisien," sired thousands of calves through artificial insemination and made them a great deal of money. Later, when Canada arranged to import cattle from other parts of Europe, the French Pie Rouge were joined by their Swiss cousins, the Simmenthalers and their German cousins, the Fleckvieh. In Canada all were considered one breed and were called "Simmental."

The get-rich-quick-in-the-cattle-business was played just as dramatically with Simmental as it had been with Charolais. But why stop there? Why indeed? There were lots of other breeds in France – and Germany and Italy and ... the only limitation was the size of the quarantine station on Grosse Isle. That problem was dealt with by the Canada Department of Agriculture which built another and much larger facility on the French island of St. Pierre, just off the Newfoundland coast in the gulf of St. Lawrence. Not only was the new station larger but it could handle two importations a year because it was ice free. So, instead of seventy cattle a year, Canada was now in the position of processing close to 300.

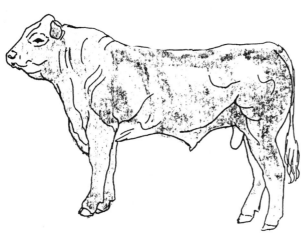

Limousin

Then a new French breed made its appearance. From Limoge, where you get the pretty china, you could also get the bull – a Limousin. Much prettier in appearance and smoother over the bones than the Charolais, the Limousin revealed bulging muscles that suggested a superb carcass – much more meat for pound of animal.

It was true. If you wanted "cut-out" or "yield," the Limousin had it. Moreover, because of its trim bone structure, it was suggested that these would be good cattle to breed to yearling heifers. Some entrepreneurs bought heifer calves in the fall (mostly blacks and baldies), inseminated them in the spring with Limousin semen and, after pregnancy testing them, sold them in the fall as bred heifers. Well .... true enough, the Limousin calves did "come" easier than Charolais or Simmental but they were still big calves. Many an unfortunate heifer gave birth to her first calf via a calf puller or a C-section because her owner had thought it was OK to breed her with Limousin semen.

The Limousin breed was smooth-haired and solid creamy-brown in color and so looked like a good cross with any of the British breeds. The crossbred calves were attractive: with Herefords, brown with white faces; with Angus, solid black; with Shorthorn, mostly solid red, with a bit of white here and there sometimes.[5]

But it was in the showring that Limousin made the biggest noise, especially when crossed with Angus – one carcass breed mated to another carcass breed. They cleaned up in carcass shows because of their high yield and also because of the great size of their "eye of lean," the area of the muscle cross section between front and rear quarters, where the butcher cuts his first club and T-bone steaks. And in the steer shows, they pretty well outclassed the competition for most of a decade. Other things being equal, you were attracted to the Limousin-cross steers because of their "flash" and style. Packers, of course, liked them – "as good as Charolais, maybe better." So the breed took off fast.

Hardly had the Limousin reached Canada when another French breed, the biggest of them all so far, the Maine-Anjou, appeared. They were red with a white star on the forehead and a bit of white on the body. Massive and ungainly, they were the kind of cattle that were hard to get used to, let alone love. They had been chosen by Don McQ Shaver of Cambridge, Ontario, one of the world's few chicken breeders (see Chapter 13, "Outlandish Lusts"). Shaver understood genetics (commercial chickens are produced by the crossing of unrelated intensely inbred lines) and he thought he had found in the Maine-Anjou many genes that would be commercially significant. The animals were growthy, muscular, reported to produce adequate milk and had gentle dispositions – something that could not be said for the other two French breeds we had seen up to that time. Shaver imported two bulls, began to sell semen and a new rush was on.

The Maine-Anjou had evolved in France from crossing English Shorthorns to the large local cattle. Some people thought that by using this new breed they could move back to the "big, good, old Shorthorns we used to have." They hoped to put some size and milk into their Hereford herds.

The first calf crop caused some consternation. The calves were big at birth, many of them well over 100 lb. (45 kg), just too big for some cows to bear. But for cowmen with roomy, feminine cows, there were few problems and the calves gained quickly and efficiently.

Angus crosses were particularly attractive, the smooth tidy Angus smoothing out the big, rough bones of the Maine-Anjou. Those with cows that could bear the big calves stayed with the breed, others went to other easier-calving bulls. Maine-Anjou flourished through the sale boom of the 1970s and for a while was the high-selling breed but it did not reach the popularity enjoyed by the other French breeds.

Simmental enthusiasts could "breed up" with Herefords with no color problems. The first-cross calves looked much like Herefords except they had more dewlap, bigger ears and feet, were knobbier in the joints and had more white on their bodies. They were also bigger.

Herefords also worked well for Charolais breeders. First crosses were usually tan-bodied with white faces and white splotches here and there, mostly on the underline. With each generation the tan got lighter. Somewhere down the line you might get rid of the white Hereford face.[6]

Crossed with Angus,[7] both Charolais and Simmental left grey calves – the Simmental calves having white or brockled faces. This suggests that the Simmental carries genes for at least two kinds of white: the white face is akin to the Hereford and the white in the body (at least some of it) is similar to that of the Charolais.

The Limousin-Angus calves were solid black and thus had the advantage of color uniformity. They were bigger than Angus, more upstanding and more bulging in the rump. The black color was persistent, like the sins of the father, though many three-quarter bloods and up reverted to the Limousin brown. But black at that time had no market advantage. For up-grading, therefore, many Limousin breeders turned to solid red cattle: Red Angus, red Shorthorn and Red Poll! The first-cross and subsequent crosses from these matings were all red. All these breeds provided better-than-average mothering ability; the Red Poll, in fact, is a milking breed. Breeders would contract with the owner of one of these red herds to inseminate all the cows with Limousin semen and to buy back all the heifer calves and sometimes all the calves, for a premium – usually $100 over market for all the calves and $200 over market for just the heifers.

I bought two such Limousin-Red Poll cross bull calves in 1971 to use as "clean-up" bulls on first-calf heifers after the AI season. We sold one after the first year but kept the other for four more years. He, like a modern environmentalist, was in a constant and vocal state of anger, snorting and puffing with his head close to the ground throughout his life. We called him *Snorts*. But he did the job. His calves came easily enough and they were good calves.

With so many new breeds in the country, ordinary cattlemen began to ask the federal government which of these new cattle would be good for *them*. So the Canada Department of Agriculture got into the importing and breeding business, too. Jack Stothart, director of the research station at Lacombe, Alberta, was chosen to head up the new program.

Stothart went to Europe and brought back Limousin, Simmental and from Italy, the Chianina, the biggest of them all. The Limousin were stationed at Brandon, the Chianina at Lethbridge and the Simmental at Lacombe. The rationale for not including Charolais was that they had been around long enough for people to know as much as they needed to know about them.

As well as breeding them "pure" at the stations, the government started a long project in which the large exotic bulls (including Charolais but not Maine-Anjou) were crossed on the three domestic British breeds. Heifer calves from those matings were tested as mother cows. Steer calves from the project were evaluated for rate and efficiency of gain and for carcass acceptance. The project was conducted under farm conditions at Brandon, Manitoba and on dry rangeland at Manyberries, Alberta. The results? There were many pages in the report because so many factors were involved but it became apparent that while use of the big breeds might give you more calving problems, it also produced many more pounds of calf, that crossbred cows out-performed straightbreds, that crossbred calves were money makers in the feedlot, that the half-blood Simmental cows (which had more milk) would wean heavier calves if they had enough feed; that all crossbred cows were more productive than straightbreds; and that the black baldy (Hereford-Angus cross) was an awfully good mother of practically everything.

Another project used farmer and rancher herds to assess big-breed bulls on domestic cows. One interesting result of this project revealed that there were great differences in the performance of the progeny of different bulls[8] of the *same* breed. It was a bull test as well as a breed test and bore out the old maxim that there are good and bad in all breeds.

Remember how Horatius was "given of the corn land that was of public right, as much as two strong oxen could plow from morn till night," (about two acres) because he held the bridge so bravely against Lars Porsena. Well those two strong oxen were probably the forerunners of the Chianina which Jack Stothart brought back from Italy. These cattle are huge – in every way. Moreover, they are long-legged and trim-bellied and can run like a horse and jump like a deer and have a disposition halfway between those two species. Not the dumb, slow-moving, stolid ox by any means. We have seen modern pictures of the Italian farmer using these animals to pull big, two-wheeled carts, as well as drawings of them as the ceremonial cattle of ancient Rome.

By the time the show ring faddists were well into the long-and-tall-is-good stage – first with Charolais and then with Limousin – they discovered Chianina. It was like Balboa gazing at the Pacific. Here was the place on the violin to put your finger! This was "extension" you might dream about. Soon the steer shows were awarding championships to Chianina-Angus crosses. No waste fat, not much visible gut and still a good, heavy muscle cover. "Volume," they called it.

What about the carcass? A bit of a problem there: Chianina crosses fattened up OK but by the time they had enough cover to grade, the carcasses were too big for the established trade – that is if they were fed as yearlings. To make them work, they had to go on feed as a calf right off the cow.

All the big breeds work best this way. It really is an advantage, because you save almost a year – hence feed and therefore money. Moreover, you are feeding the steer when he is biologically younger and so he gains more efficiently. Fed this way, the crossbreds would meet the Canadian grade standards (but had difficulty in the U.S., where more fat and marbling[9] is required to reach top grades). The calves were big at birth but relatively narrow with long, long legs. They did not present more calving problems than the other big breeds. The future looked bright for Chianina.

But you had to be a pretty good cowboy to raise them. Their dispositions were *different*: not really wild; in fact, if you walked out into a field of grazing yearlings, they would all gather around you in a curious ring, raising and lowering their heads as if asking, "Who are you?" and "What do you have for me?" But if they were spooked and one went over a fence, all the rest followed. Moreover, they didn't pay much attention to a man on a saddle horse trying to head them off. They kept going their own way, often at a high rate of speed. The joke at the time was that if you were going to raise Chianina, you'd better put another two strands of wire above your present fences and another rail on the corral. On the other hand, they were easily handled with a feed bucket or a pick-up truck with a few pellets aboard. Once they had followed the truck into the corral, a 12-year-old girl could readily cut them out with a length of Corlon pipe.

In the summer of 1974, I contracted to pasture and AI 130 half-blood Chianina heifers out of dairy cows. My step-granddaughter (mentioned above, with the Corlon pipe) and daughter helped me. We were the first (and maybe only) father-and-daughter team to take a refresher course in AI at the Olds College. I had learned the technique away back in 1953 when I was the AI technician at Salmon Arm, B.C. (I also taught high school there.) Since we also were inseminating about 250 of our own cows in another pasture, we felt we "had a handle" on the job. How all this is done on a ranch scale will be told in the chapter on High

Tech, but I should mention a significant difference in the physiology between Chianina and other cattle: About Step Four in the insemination procedure you remove with your plastic-gloved left hand the manure in the cow's rectum. Such manure in late June and early July, when the cows are on green grass, is, to say the least, quite fluid! But the manure in the Chianina heifers was relatively firm, almost stiff compared with our other cow. Just as the Pharisee felt "he was not as other men," so the Chianina are not as other cattle.

That same year, we AI'd 80 of our own cows to Chianina and another 80 to Maine-Anjou. The next summer I fed out the male calves from these matings as "virgin" bulls, along with an equal number got by our pick-up bulls. They were all "blue tagged." The blue tags supplied by the Canadian government was a signal to the grader to do carcass measurements on them. To my surprise, the government grader ignored almost half of the blue tags (even though I had paid for them and was entitled to a carcass analysis). But I still had enough of a sample to decide that for all practical purposes there were no differences between the Chianina and Maine-Anjou crossbreds. Both breeds had high dressing percentages and big rib eyes. A few of the top Chianina-cross heifers from these matings were introduced to our bull Snorts, joined our cow herd and performed well.

The Exotic boom peaked in the winter of 1974 and 1975. Up till then, prices had just gone straight up. Many cattlemen made money by breeding their cows – any kind of cows – with semen from an Exotic bull and then selling the half-blood calves. A lot of this happened on Quebec dairy farms. These dairy farmers were already using AI so they had no need to change their management. In those years, there was a fair market for dairy heifers but virtually none for dairy bull calves. Many were simply knocked on the head at birth or sold a few days later as "bob calves" for perhaps $10 – or less. A few were fed out locally as veal and many were bought for veal production in New York. The Exotic-cross bull calves, on the other hand, could be sold to be raised as beef and the heifers commanded a fancy premium from western exotic breeders. The Chianina heifers which my daughter and I had so much fun with in the AI chute had such a history.

It took less than two years for the Quebec dairymen to flood the market with Exotic half-bloods, bringing an end to that part of the business. Meanwhile there had been a bit of money made by cattlemen who simply bred any kind of cows and heifers with Exotic semen, got them pregnancy tested and then put them through an auction. This worked until the fall of 1974, when half-bloods ceased to command a premium sufficient to pay for the cost of the AI. Next to plummet were half-bloods, three-quarter bloods and then higher percentages. By 1978 the business had been rationalized and the cattle had to sell on their merits.

Several more new breeds continued to arrive as the market peaked. Coming after the big money had been made on the earlier importations, they never did catch a ride on the high-flying balloon. Some of these were breeds with considerable potential. Among them were the Blonde-d'Aquitaine (a composite of four regional French breeds), which looked a bit like the Limousin, The Gelbvieh, a reddish-yellow German breed and the French Salers. The last two probably would have made a "good rum" if they had had an even start with the leaders.

Gelbvieh (Germans tend to name their breeds by their colors, in this case yellow, is a dual-purpose breed which has been performance-tested in Germany for both meat and milk. Enthusiasts wonder why cattlemen would use any other breed if they want a good "mother cow" that also transmits lots of beef.

The solid-red Salers is a dual-purpose mountain cow from western France. The hair is curly and so appeals to cold-country cattlemen. They have well-muscled long bodies and relatively long legs. Over the past decade, they have continued to increase in popularity and "market share" at the bull sales as ranchers include them in crossbreeding programs.

Also of considerable potential was a late-comer from Bavaria, the Pinzgauer. They are colorful: red-bodied, with a white stripe down the back and a white "blanket" over the rump. Somewhat smaller than the Simmental, these Alpine mountain cattle are used in South Africa[10] in country too rough for Simmental. There is another French breed, the Tarentaise, colored something like the Limousin but of smaller size and finer boned, still a good-sized breed, the Tarentaise caught a foothold in Canada. Two more Italian entries, the Marchigiana and the Romagnola appeared but their numbers never were large. There were also importations of a few others about which not much was heard.

With permits from Europe in short supply, some fellows figured they could make money by importing some of the lesser-known breeds from Britain. No foot-and-mouth disease to cope with there (usually!) and importation is therefore much simpler.

So we had a mini-rush of: South Devons, large dual-purpose cows, reddish brown in color, the "gentle giants," they are called in England; Lincoln Reds, "The Ruby Reds," a sort of bigger, rougher and redder Shorthorn, first introduced by the E.P. Ranch. (remember the Duke of Windsor, formerly Edward Prince of Wales, thus the E.P. name). Welsh Black, dual-purpose black (but horned) cattle from Wales; even a few

Friesians, English Holsteins which are much less "dairy" than ours and more "beefy," came along.

But why stop at Europe? What has Australia to offer? Why the Murray Grey, of course. This breed is colored the same as Angus-Charolais crosses but otherwise is much like the Angus in size and conformation, only with a milder disposition.

The myth of the Murray Grey's genesis involves a unique white Shorthorn bull and black Angus cows. Breeders and developers of the breed in Australia were cousins of Lord and Lady Roderic Gordon, who had immigrated to Canada after World War II and were now raising livestock (at first Yorkshire hogs, then Angus cattle and the advent of Murray Grey, Thoroughbred horses) near Bentley, Alberta. Lord Gordon was a war hero, Lady Gordon (Joan) a beautiful Rumanian noblewoman – a marvelous heroic and romantic story. The Gordons were sure the Murray Grey could contribute a great deal to this country which had embraced with abandon the muscular but graceless plow oxen of Europe.

Lord Gordon flew to Australia in the belly of a 707 freighter and flew right back again with the plane loaded with Murray Grey cattle.

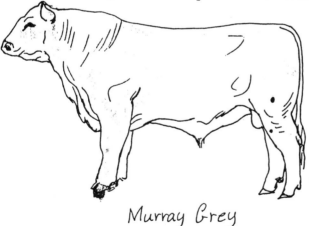

Murray Grey

The inaugural meeting of the new Canadian Association was held in the posh Ranchmen's Club in Calgary.

The great rush to produce crossbreds from Exotic semen and domestic cows had a tremendous effect on the commercial cattle business. All the half-blood male calves resulting from these matings ended up as beef. At first, cattle buyers of all stripes discounted the crossbred calves, as did meat packers, unless the cattle were sold "rail grade" – the price being determined after slaughter, when the carcass was graded and weighed. Now these half-blood calves generally may be sold "on the hoof" for premium prices.

In the early years of Charolais in Canada, buyer resistance to the cattle was so strong that Charolais breeders formed Charcross Feeders Limited, a company that bought Charolais crossbred calves, fed them out in a commercial lot and sold them rail grade to packers. The hope was that the new company would ensure enough money was paid for the then-discounted crossbred calves. Since Charolais breeders were enlisted as feeder-buyers, a new problem arose. These enthusiastic buyers were paying *too much* and the company barely broke even the first year. But the trend was set and eventually auction markets began to hold special, well-publicized sales for the various exotic breeds. The calf sellers were now getting the premiums they deserved.

It was during the heyday of the Exotics that the great ballroom sales were held, new publications appeared and many outgoing entrepreneurs got into the sales management business. When markets cooled down, numerous Arabs folded their tents and silently stole away.

The victors in the wars of the breeds are still marching to tumultuous trumpeters and drummers. The Charnational 90 and its Bull Power Sale introduced a "New Decade of White Magic" in February, 1990, by stalling a famous bull in the lobby of the Saskatoon Inn in Saskatchewan for a couple of days and then selling him from that venue for $80 000.

Agribition, the big all-breeds livestock show and sale held in Regina, Saskatchewan, each November, could never have happened without the Exotics. There is considerable irony in this because the new cattle were brought to this country as part of the revolt against the show ring. In fact, the Simmental Association did not allow their cattle to be shown in the early years. Cattle for utility, not for show, had been the *raison d'etre* for importing the big ugly European plow oxen. Why show them? Because you can make more money as a breeder if you win pretty ribbons.

In the early days of Charolais, before the French importations, the domestic Charolais were so "funny looking" to cattlemen brought up on the British breeds that showing them seemed quite irrelevant. At the 1967 Edmonton Spring Show of Finished Steers, which was then the biggest show of its kind in Canada, a well-known judge was faced with two Charolais steers in a class of 30 Hereford, Angus and Shorthorns. The white steers were several inches taller and obviously heavier than all the rest. It was also apparent that they had a good deal of meat on them. Placing the class was Ed Noad, one of the best steer judges on the continent. He resolved his predicament – he dared not put these strange creatures above the good conventional steers, but they had too much good meat on them to put them at the bottom. but by placing them right in the middle. A Solomon's choice!

"I buried them!" he told me after the show.

Two years later a Charolais-Hereford cross was declared grand champion steer at the Edmonton show, a first for Canada.

And two years after that, an American judge dealt with the problem squarely. Dr. David Ames had come to Edmonton from Kansas State University with a firm picture of a beef steer – abundant red meat, minimum fat and who cares about anything else. He chose as his tops, longer and taller and leaner steers than had ever won a show anywhere in Canada. Charolais crosses won all the top placings in the Singles classes and, just to make sure people were paying attention, Charolais were also awarded championships in the Carcass class and the Group of Five. Ames wasn't run out of town on a rail – Canadians are too civilized for that – but all the old guard were angry. Ames had not judged the carcasses; that job was done by government graders, so other people had begun to think Ames's way, too.

By the time another year had rolled around the trend was established and the "meat-type" steer had been accepted. Eventually (1972) the Canadian grading system was changed to reflect the demand by consumers for less fat. By 1990 the pendulum had swung a back a little because we need a few good, fat steers for the fancy hotel and restaurant trade and if we want to export carcass beef to the U.S., it must meet their standards. The big demand, however, is still for red meat, not fat.

Most of the early importers were not purebred breeders of the British breeds and so were not "true believers" in the Cattle Religion (see Chapter Seven, "The Cattle Religion"). But as soon as the big dollars appeared, many established breeders jumped into the business, bringing their faith with them – the show ring, the feed bucket, fitting for show, selecting for "type" and making use of the publicity tools that had made them money and brought them honor with the British breeds.

Many of the original importers, who were looking primarily for more productive ranch cattle, were left behind as the steer jockeys and promotions took over. Now, all of the exotic breeds are "corrupted." The beasts have become smooth and refined, as well as becoming models of long and tall "extension," and so have entrapped themselves in another myth. At the time of the writing of this book, there is already a reaction to this fad and real cattlemen are increasingly critical of the long and tall.

Every new breed had to have its own *association*, rather *associations*. First, there had to be a national (Canadian) association and also at least a few provincial associations. Since most of the new cattle came to Alberta,[11] there was always an Alberta association. (Eighty percent of the beef cows in Canada are in the western provinces and half of those are in Alberta.) Saskatchewan followed right in line, as did the other provinces as soon as numbers warranted. Because the permits had to be issued "fairly" across the country, new breed associations appeared in Quebec, the Maritimes and of course in Ontario. In many cases, however, most of the Canadian breeders were in Alberta, so an Alberta provincial association was somewhat redundant or would have been had it not been for the Alberta government. It provided a great deal of assistance to *Alberta* associations. Consequently when great international meetings of any breed were held in Canada, they came to Alberta because of the generous grants.

Each new association had to have a constitution and bylaws and had to make arrangements for registering (and recording) members' stock, issuing pedigrees and transfers, holding annual meetings, arranging and promoting field days, shows and sales, perhaps starting a magazine – everything that a competitive breed association could do to assist its members. In August of 1979 the Western Stock Growers Association, which had been formed 80 years earlier in Calgary, sent invitations to all the cattle associations in Alberta inviting them to a meeting to set up a Stockmen's Memorial Foundation. There were 29 invitations! Most sent reps to the meeting.

While the new breeds changed forever the nature of the Canadian cattle industry, they also had a tremendous and positive effect on rural sociology. A Charolais breeder from Manitoba soon found he knew other breeders right across the country – and government men and bankers and press and radio people and breeders of other breeds. They all travelled more, often to other provinces and the U.S. and sometimes to Europe. And, of course, they found their position in their own community was changed, enhanced if they were successful and reduced if they ran into trouble. Usually they had to "sell" their cattle to their neighbors, who at first were skeptical of "what that dumb bugger was up to now!"

As might be expected, a few of the new converts had failed at other endeavors and saw Nirvana or the Golden Mountain in the new breed. Also a large number of professional and business people got into the new-breed business, both to make more money and to obtain a tax dodge. What the early organizations were crying for was "more good cattlemen in this outfit." As soon the profits became apparent, these cattlemen came – bringing the cattle religion with them!

Meanwhile, back at the ranch, almost every commercial herd now contains some percentage of Exotic breeding. More pounds of calf at the ranch, faster feedlot gains and a higher cut-out in the carcass make strong arguments. The British breeds have met the challenge by becoming bigger themselves. At the 1990 Calgary Bull Sale, practically every two-year-old Hereford bull weighed over a ton (900 kg); 20 years ago, the figure would have been 1600 pounds (725 kg). Angus are not only much larger (longer and taller), they are much leaner. When I was ranching in the sixties and seventies, most of my cows were Angus and Angus crosses but certainly of a different "breed" than the Angus of the nineties. Also certain is the fact that you don't have to use exotics to increase the size of your calves – or the amount of meat on them. The Hereford sale bulls just mentioned had sonar rib-eye measurements as large as 19 square inches (122 sq. cm), right up there with the Europeans. The irony is that these days you use Exotics for commercial-buyer appeal, a complete reversal of the market of 30 years ago.

Since the cattle religion has now taken hold of the Exotics breeders, the contemporary subject of interest to serious cattle improvers lies in the development (from whatever breed components) of strains of cattle for specific purposes: maternal lines, carcass (terminal cross) lines, easy-calving lines and a general-purpose line. The next chapters deal with some of these developments.

By the Way . . .

[1] I had arranged with Air France to conduct a tour of Canadian buyers to the Nevers region of France at a special rate. But the cattlement took off as soon as they got their permits; only one waited the few days until the tour was to begin.

[2] One breeder, who could not afford to buy a show halter for his heifer in the sale, asked me (I used to teach calf club members how to make a rope halter in a few minutew) to make him a halter for the sale. He could afford only the rope! (I donated my "labor"). A proper show halter at that time cost about fifteen dollars.

[3] The French bull "Bingo" Belphegor sired more calves than any other Charolais bull – well over 200 000, according to his owner, Tom Eggertson of Pine Lake, Alberta.

[4] The first Charolais in Canada reflected the varying degrees of Brahman blood which had been acquired in Mexico and the southern United States. Cattle like this are still used as rodeo stock. The full French imports were much more docile.

[5] In 1972 we calved out eighty black and baldy heifers that had been bred as yearlings with Limousin semen. An interesting time but it could have been worse!

[6] The white in Herefords and Shorthorns is quite different both genetically and in appearance from the white in Charolais or the Italian breeds. For this reason, eyebrows are raised when breeders of the

Australian Murray Grey say their breed was formed by crossing a white Shorthorn bull on black Angus cows. The "white" in the Murray Grey is indistinguishable from the Charolais white – even to the rat tail!

[7]The grand champion carcass steer at Regina Agribition in 1974 was a Maine Anjou-Angus crossbred which I bred and raised.

[8]I "loaned" 20 Hereford cows to a neighbor to enable him to provide 100 Hereford cows for the test. The government kept half the progeny for their breeding and testing projects and returned half to the cow owners. As my "reward" I ended up with my 20 cows and four Simmental-cross heifer calves which were not much to look at, wild and infertile. But other co-operators in the program were pleased with their half-Simmental heifers. Today, Simmental vie with Charolais for top position among the exotics.

[9]The Canadian grading system did not require marbling, as did the top U.S. grades. Marbling is laid down in older cattle, particularly if they are "long-feds." When the Canadian grading system changed to include marbling in 1992, a Calgary-area feedlot owner told me, "We have to feed them two weeks longer, now."

[10]I saw many Pinzgauer on exhibit at the Rand Easter Show in Johannesburg in 1972. The South Africans told me that Pinzgauer were bred to domestic breeds in high and rough country. The half-blood heifers from these matings were then bred to the solid-red Sussex to produce market "beasts."

Chapter Fifteen

Bulls in Bottle
(Clones in Uteri)

>>>>>>>>>>>>

While students in Animal Breeding were winning their masters' degrees by studying cattle bloodlines and memorizing the names of family matriarchs, their comrades in Animal Nutrition were already deep into the biochemistry of feed-stuffs, the marvels of fermentation in the first stomach of a steer and how to supply enough calcium and phosphorus to get a high-producing dairy cow. Science came easily to animal feeding because there was little mythology in hay, oats and alfalfa. Nobody's faith was challenged if a researcher decreed that there must be more protein in the diet of that milk-cow than in what was fed to her sister who was dry and "in waiting." In fact, such information was eagerly sought by farmers. So the Ag colleges happily obliged by researching and then affable and able extension men spread the good news.

"Always remember, Laddie, the haid is half the bool and the bool is half the haird."

Compare this approach to a lesson taught me by a Scottish stock-man when I was eight. "Always remember, Laddie," he gently reassured me, after having placed my bull calf in first place at the school fair, "the haid is half the bool and the bool is half the haird." He was, to my delight, particularly complimentary of my calf's head. Did I believe him? Did the sun forever shine on the British Empire? Half of his statement was true – the bull is half the herd at the time he is in service there. As for his head? Easy to believe, if first prize (worth a full three dollars or about sixty dollars in today's money) was an integral part of the lesson.

And so the twigs were bent and the faith passed on. Is it surprisiing that for the first thirty of those years I had a strong faith in the cattle religion? Could it have been otherwise when engendered by such intense emotion? And since I won first prize at the school fair three years running with a succession of bull calves, my faith was augmented annually by approbation and real money.

About this time we began to lose a few cattle each year to "shipping fever" (*haemorrhagic scepticemia*). We had been vaccinating against blackleg for years, so we eagerly sought and used a vaccine against this new threat. Also our summer pastures, which we rented in the hills west of us, contained a few patches of "poisonous weed," – larkspur. After losing a few head, we persuaded the landowner to fence off the dangerous area. We also treated for bloat (drenching with linseed or mineral oil or in extreme cases, resorting to the canula and trocar) and we twice had to pump up the udder of our Holstein milk cow when she "came down" with "milk fever."

This technique seems preposterous to the uninitiated. A small tube is inserted into the teat canal and then connected to a tire pump. The assistant pumps quickly until the quarter is inflated. The tube is removed and a tourniquet applied to the teat to keep the air from coming out. The other three quarters are then treated the same way.

The cow, prostrate and near death when the pumping starts, will within minutes lift her head, belch and get to her feet. She will soon defecate and then resume chewing her cud, apparently contented and healthy. The teats usually may be untied within a day or two.

How does it work? Milk fever strikes a heavy-milking cow shortly after calving, just as she begins to make milk in her udder.

The calcium (and other constituents) in the milk come from her blood. All during pregnancy, calcium has been storing in her bones. At parturition, the flow must be reversed immediately and calcium must leave the bones and enter the bloodstream. Just as quickly, large amounts of glycogen must be converted by the liver into glucose and poured into her blood. The calcium and glucose "flows" are controlled by hormones which in heavy milkers may not change direction fast enough. By pumping up the udder, you prevent the formation of milk and induce some milk to be reconverted to blood components. No myth or religion here; this was reality and we did everything that science and practice could teach us to keep our herd healthy. (The modern treatment is to give the cow an intravenous solution which supplies the blood with both calcium and carbohydrate.)

We were just as practical/scientific when it came to feeds and feeding. All cows eat grass. Yes and ground grain, bran and salt and strange-sounding things like shorts, middlings and linseed meal. The last three are "bought" feeds and were not generally fed to our cattle, but to our pigs (hogs, an American term, was never used on our farm) to give them more protein when we were short of skim milk. We also raised our milk cows' calves on skim milk which we fortified with calf meal to help replace the butterfat which paid our grocery bill. The milk cows got "chop" (ground oats) in addition to pasture and hay and greenfeed. The same cows had access to salt and to bonemeal as a source of phosphorus and we added limestone to our pigs' feed to provide them with calcium if we were short of skim milk. There was some faith and mysticism in the feed bucket but mostly what was fed depended on what worked best.

So it was completely natural that we and other farm families appreciated universities, Ag colleges and experimental farms as they did research in animal nutrition. Nor did we fault these same institutions for doing no research into the breeding of beef cattle. Why should they? That nice old Scotsman and my own father already knew what there was to know about breeding cattle.

All the institutions had purebred herds which were kept in fine fit to "show people what good cattle looked like." Since Shorthorns were the breed of the social, political and financial elite, the institutions favored purebred Shorthorn herds. Most universities had all three breeds – Angus and Herefords as well as Shorthorns – while experimental farms would "specialize" in a single breed, usually Shorthorns.

The competitive position of these herds was a little delicate. If institutional cattle became too good, they would be in great demand as breeding stock and so take away business from purebred breeders. On the other hand, they had to be attractive enough to publicize the breed favorably and get non-purebred men into the business. They were expected to appear at the shows but not win too many prizes – with one exception: they could win all they wanted at steer shows. Such winnings brought glory[1] to the institution and the breed but didn't hurt the purebred sales of any particular breeder.

It's not quite fair to say that no research in animal breeding was done by government institutions. Some crossbreeding experiments were carried out and the benefits of "grading-up" (which is a form of crossbreeding) were demonstrated. Grant MacEwan (later Lieutenant-Governor of Alberta and a popular writer) did some interesting work with crossbreds at the University of Saskatchewan. The University was happy to have him carry out these "experiments" – provided they made money! But animal breeding was not treated as a science until two American university men applied the science of genetics to the breeding of livestock. They were Dr. Jay Lush of Iowa and Dr. Laurence Winters of Minnesota.

I did not read Dr. Winters' book, *Animal Breeding*, until I was 30 old. I think we all can think of a few books that gave us a sudden and powerful insight, a great burst of light (what my Estonian friend Heigi Leesment[2] calls a *lutsia intervale*[3]) when we read them. Here was the absolute truth, so real and obvious and we hadn't realized it all this time!

Oppenheimer's *Cowboy Arithmetic* also influenced me the same way (I have bought three volumes of this book, lent them to friends and have never got any of them back).

Simply said, Winters states that the modern breeder must use science and technology to improve his animals. First, forget about the myths of the cattle religion. Then discern and define what you expect of the animal, determine what the animal must do to fulfil this expectation, then provide objective ways of measuring how close it comes to the mark. Everything must be expressed in terms that can be identified, measured and since the animal is a living thing, rated in time taken to get from here to there. (These concepts of cattle improvement were dealt with in the chapter on performance testing. So were some of the breeding techniques which may be used to make improvements in cattle populations once you have devised a system of measuring and rating performance.)

Modern students of animal breeding are so used to doing this that they become impatient with cattlemen who do not fully accept what has been so conclusively proven. They are dismayed that cattle breeders will weigh a bull at two years of age and think his weight is significant without knowing the rate of gain – weight per day of age and average gain during a specific period or the feed efficiency – the feed required to produce a unit of gain. Or that breeders will pay far more attention to how a bull looks than how he and his progeny have performed on standardized tests.

The old ways and old ideas are strong, as we have seen in the rebirth of Russian churches after 70 years of enforced atheism. But what is working to increase rationality in cattle breeding is high-tech.

First came artificial insemination. AI – borrowed from the dairymen and then improved. With AI, because it is possible to "extend" or dilute the semen, one bull can sire hundreds of thousands of calves. So he'd better be an exceptionally good bull and you'd better have a near-perfect way of measuring his worth.

Next came frozen semen. You can "draw"[4] a bull, put most of his extended semen in liquid nitrogen tanks then test him out on a number of cows and if he proves good, sell lots of semen, year after year. If he proves to be a dud, throw the semen away. Do this with lots of bulls and pick the best by what kind of calves they sire.

Then came embryo transplant. This isn't simple by any means, but it enables a single cow to have dozens of offspring, not just eight or ten.

And if you can *transplant* embryos, why not *clone* them? With cloning, the offspring of a single cow can fill a barn, a field, whatever ... and the cloned embryos can go into the liquid nitrogen tank, too; so clones A-through-G can be incubated, grown out and tested and if they are all gee-whiz, the contents of your tank is worth a king's ransom.

Sexing of embryos has passed the experimental stage and is just around the corner from being practical. This technique is causing another revolution. Imagine a whole herd made up of identical cloned females!

Neither cloning nor embryo transplant could happen without first making AI feasible and practical. Fifty years ago, dairymen needed AI for two reasons. One was the bad temper of a dairy bull. While milk cows are the most docile of bovine females, their sex partners are the most dangerous kind to have around the farm. Only Spanish Fighting bulls are worse, for in their breed *both* cows[5] and bulls see man as the common enemy. Many a dairy farmer has been maimed – or killed by dairy bulls. If you don't want to have a bull around, welcome the AI technician.

The other force driving the swing to AI had to do with genetics. Not encumbered much by the cattle religion, dairymen had been measuring the milk production of their cows for as long as anyone could remember. First, unofficially and unscientifically in bucketfuls and then in gallons, eventually in pounds and now in hectolitres. Later (after a man named Babcock devised a quick and simple test for butterfat) official tests supervised by governments and breed associations provided proof of a cow's excellence. ROP (Record of Performance) of both pounds of milk and pounds of butterfat could be recorded on pedigrees. Thus if you wanted to buy a bull to improve your herd, you got a son of a cow with a good R.O.P. record. If the sire of your new purchase also had a high-producing dam, so much the better. If you are breeding AI, the bull you use should have R.O.P. of his daughters to indicate how much milk and butterfat they will produce as part of your herd.

Today, ROP of dairy cattle has been streamlined so that you can measure a bull by the *expected difference* – increased production – be shown by his daughters when compared with their dams, so you can calculate the general improvement he can make in your herd .

ROP soon revealed the most productive cattle; breeders of these cattle asked and got high prices for the bull calves from their best dams. The ordinary dairy farmer could not afford to buy one of these good-record bulls but a group of dairymen could pool their money and buy such a bull for all to use – through the marvel of artificial insemination. In Canada AI co-ops were formed in Quebec, Ontario and British Columbia about the time of World War II. In Alberta, which is not really a dairy province, an AI stud was set up by the provincial government at its agriculture school at Olds.

The only beef breed to endorse and co-operate with the new studs was the Canadian Shorthorn Association. They did this because Shorthorns are also a milking breed and so AI could provide a service to Shorthorn dairymen. The other beef breeds saw AI as the enemy and refused to register any calves got by this new-fangled technique.

Their fear was based on logic: every cow bred by AI is not bred by a bull. And breeders are in the business of raising and selling bulls. Acceptance of AI, they reasoned, would mean the end of the bull business and hence the end of the breed.

That's the way things stood in 1953 when a new player entered the game. It's name was *vibriosis* and it struck in an out-of-the-way place, on the Tobacco Plains Indian Reserve near Grasmere, B.C. The reserve is right against the U.S. border in the southeast corner of the province. The Indians did not use the grass on the reserve but leased grazing rights to the Grasmere Grazing Association, half a dozen B.C. ranchers who operated on either side of the highway running south of Elko down towards Eureka, Montana.

Vibriosis is a venereal disease causing abortion, usually within a few weeks of breeding. Cows that abort once usually get in calf the next month or the month after that or the next year, so the disease becomes a problem mainly with replacement heifers in areas where it is established. But as a new disease in a herd it can cause tremendous losses – late calves, even no calves, the first year among all the cows, and thereafter in the new replacements.

It is spread mainly by a bull breeding an infected cow and then carrying the disease to the rest of his harem. Nor is the disease consistent: it can cause "three week" abortions, so a cow comes in heat, gets bred, has a "silent" abortion and then comes in heat again six weeks after the first time. If rebred at this time, the cow will likely carry to full term but her calf will be six weeks late in coming and not worth nearly as much as an early calf. It is a disease no rancher can afford to live with.

By 1970 there was a vaccine for the disease but in the mid-fifties the only solution was "sexual rest." As was noted in an earlier chapter, a rancher couldn't afford sexual rest for his cows, so he looked for an alternative to a bull: artificial insemination.

The Grasmere association, with 250 Hereford cows, used Hereford semen. This was available from the *dairy* studs, as they kept a few beef bulls for their members who wanted to raise crossbred calves for beef. The AI system had already ruined the market for mediocre dairy bull calves. (This loss of market is what scared the purebred beef breeders.)

The Grasmere program began June 10, 1954 and ran for three years. Then the ranchers reverted to bulls because the disease seemed to be under control and because the AI program was "missing" too many cows. Not enough calves, too many late calves and too many "open" cows in the fall. They weren't so much against AI as they figured they could get more and earlier calves by using bulls.

The procedure was to identify a cow in heat, run her into a corral and then inseminate her. Whereas a dairyman has his cows under close control and rarely misses the signs of heat, a cowboy has to be much more observant. The simplest thing is to watch for cows that are "riding" (mounting) or being ridden by other cows. But riding is not always observed, nor does it always occur. And even if the cow is identified and inseminated, she may not "catch."

Cows cycle every three weeks – with a day or two of variation in some cows. So if AI is carried on for six weeks, or a few days more, theoretically every cow has had two "chances." On a range herd, with good identification and skilled insemination with viable semen, in theory you could expect in the first three weeks to identify and inseminate 80 percent of the cows and get between 60 and 70 percent of *those* in calf, or about half the herd. On the next go-round (of three weeks) you will again do the 60-80 thing for another 25 percent so a total of 75 percent of your cowherd will be in calf to the AI bulls.)

But things rarely work out that way. Some cows are slow to cycle and aren't "eligible." Some have an infection, some are not identified in heat; sometimes the insemination is botched, or the semen isn't up to par or the insemination is done too soon or too late. Or the nutrition is faulty – especially for heavy milkers and first-calf heifers – so conception doesn't occur. Possibilities are for many a slip ... in the AI business. And every heat period missed means the calf, if there is one, will be 40 lb. (18 kg) lighter by fall: $50 less valuable by 1993 prices. So on the surface of it, AI didn't appear to make much sense to commercial ranchers.

But it did to John Minor of the Great Sandhills near Abbey, in southwest Saskatchewan. Minor had seen the good results achieved by some of his rancher friends using Charolais bulls which had come up from Texas, Louisiana and Mexico (this was before the French importations). The really good bulls in this group were either rare or unknown but the AI studs had a few which had been performance tested. Their semen was being used by dairymen to raise calves for beef, just as was Hereford semen. Minor, an entrepreneur and innovator of the first rank,[7] decided to jump boldly into the new-fangled swim. In the summer of 1957, he hired a student from the Guelph Veterinary College, bought Hereford and Charolais semen from a bull stud in Ontario and began his program in June.

To "identify" the cows in heat, he equipped a score of bulls with a stout length of threshing-machine belt around their middles. Riveted to the belts and hanging down almost to the ground beneath the bulls' bellies were gunny sacks.

The bulls hung around the water holes, waiting for the cows to come to drink. A lurking Lothario would quickly spot a cow in estrus, mount her and . . . foiled again! More properly, sacked again! The heavy sacking hanging between penis and vulva was impenetrable. No matter how powerful the thrust, love could not find a way.

Meanwhile the patrolling cowboys cut out the cow under attention and ran her into a chute, where the veterinary student tagged and inseminated her and put a splash of paint on her back to tell the cowboys that this one was done. Each cow was inseminated twice, soon after she was brought in and twelve hours later, after spending the intervening time in a corral. The most inseminations done by the student in one day was 104.

Like all estrus-identification schemes, this one had some imperfections. First, thwarted love was painful to the bull because the sacking was rough and soon became even rougher with encrusted manure, semen, and mud. Pavlov was right: if the experience is painful enough, behavior is modified – some of the bulls quit the game and went away and sulked. Others, obviously slow learners, continued at the unrewarding endeavor till they played out and quit, leaving several cows unattended. Some of the cows didn't come to drink during their standing-heat period and their passion was known only to a few attentive sisters. Sometimes a sack got caught in the bush and was torn off, enabling the lucky bull to not only to identify an estrus cow but to properly serve her.

But many of Minor's 1500 cows were identified, inseminated, and got in calf. In the summer of 1958 in addition to many excellent Hereford calves, there were a goodly number of crossbred Charolais calves (283 cows had been serviced with the Charolais semen) on the ground.

These calves were fed out at Western Feedlots at Strathmore, Alberta. After slaughter a cut-out determination was done by Canada Safeway butchers with Canada Agriculture graders looking over their shoulders and writing all the weights down. A great deal of information came out of these tests, most of it favorable to the Charolais. Minor ran his program a second year and then reverted to bulls for the bulk of his herd.

Meanwhile vibriosis had invaded the LK ranch of Charles McKinnon and his family at Bassano, Alberta. Charlie and his son Neil figured that if they had to go AI in order to beat vibrio, they might as well get as much genetic improvement out of the deal as they could. They decided that the Hereford bulls in the Ontario studs didn't offer them much, so looked closer to home. The hardest and closest look was made on the ranch of Jim Hole, a few miles north of Calgary.

For years Hole had been noted for selling large and meaty Hereford bulls at the Calgary sale but he never showed them. Without benefit of show ribbons, his bulls regularly out-sold most of the bulls in the sale, including the show winners. So, in an agreement with the Ontario AI co-ops, the McKinnons bought Silver Prince 7P from Hole and sent him down to Ontario where his semen was processed and then shipped back to Alberta. It mattered not a whit to them that the Hereford Association would not register any calves got by AI from 7P. The program was a success and from then on, AI was no longer a novelty on the ranch.

A generally accepted practice soon evolved for inseminating a ranch herd. Run a short program, no more than four weeks. Then turn out clean-up bulls. Have your cows in good shape and on a rising plane of nutrition; otherwise they won't cycle and the conception rate will be down among those that you do "catch." Don't start the program before most of your cows are "eligible" – recuperated from calving and cycling again. Run your breeding herd in a small field during the inseminating period so they can be easily seen and gathered. Rest this field the remainder of the summer so it will have abundant grass the next year. Ride your herd early in the morning and just before dusk at night to pick up cycling cows. Corral your pick-ups overnight or through the day so as to inseminate them about 12 hours after detection. Breed twice a day; in the morning after the pick-up ride, breed those gathered the previous evening. After the evening gather,[8] inseminate the cows picked up in the morning. Build good solid workable chutes to avoid stress to man and beast. Make your heat detection as foolproof as possible.

A breeding bull is hard to beat for detecting a cow in heat, so pioneer inseminators tried the next best thing – a bull which can detect but not inseminate. The bull-belt-sack method of Johnny Minor's was soon scrubbed. Instead, there were designed three other systems using bulls. The first involved a veterinary operation that had been devised for steers suffering from urinary calculi (stones accumulating in the urinary tract *above* the sigmoid curve, a peculiarity with which the males of many species are afflicted). An incision was made several inches below the anus; the urinary canal (about the size of your finger) was exposed, severed and then sutured to the skin. This operation had two profound effects on the bull: first, he urinated through this opening (many the ribald and coarse jest about this!) and second, since the canal eventually became the penis, that organ was literally cut off at the root. The testicles continued to secrete testosterone and produce sperm and the bull behaved exactly like a bull, except that his penis forever remained concealed and useless. Turned out with the cows, he would fruitlessly mount every cow in heat that he could find.

Another veterinary operation was the installation of the Penablock – a self-explanatory word. Incisions were made in the sheath just behind the prepuce and a bolt inserted crosswise with a washer on each end to prevent it pulling through the skin. Every time the penis attempted an erection, it would encounter the penablock – this far and no further. Infection occasionally occurred and sometimes the washers would pull out, thus destroying the usefulness of the gizmo but rendering the bull his full capacities once more.

The third operation involved sewing up the prepuce and then making an incision in the side of the sheath a few inches behind it as an alternative path for the protruding penis. This was called a "side winder" for obvious reasons. It was quite effective, the bull never learning[9] how to twist himself to accommodate his now-out-of-alignment penis.

It was also possible to "proud cut" a bull, removing the lower part of the testicle but leaving a portion of the upper part. This "Russian castration" rendered the bull sterile but there was enough testosterone secreted by what testicle was left to inspire him to seek and mount cows in heat.

Since the rider was only checking the herd twice daily, some means of recording the bull's actions had to be devised. The most popular was the chin-ball marker. A leather halter was put on the bull with a ball under his chin in a socket (much like some of the familiar deodorant applicators). A special colored powder was put in the socket. Every time the frustrated bull dismounted, his chin would drag across the cow's rump. The rider then would look for cows bearing the telltale mark. Several colors were available, so by giving each of your *gomers*[10] a different color, you could quickly assess their effectiveness. The chin ball worked well – if the halter stayed on and didn't run out of paint!

An alternative to the chin ball consisted of a hollow plastic tag about three inches long and two wide (8 cm x 5 cm). The tag was filled with dye and covered with a glue on one side. The rancher glued it onto the cow's tail head. When another animal mounted her, the bag broke, releasing the dye. This worked no matter who did the riding – gomer, steer or another cow. Since there are always a few cows who will ride other cows in heat, this system made a gomer unnecessary. Of course you had to run the cows through the chute before beginning the AI program to glue the bags on them and there was always a possibility the bag might come off.

The simplest kind of gomer is a steer or heifer or open cow that you "hype up" with male hormones, so the animal thinks it's a bull. When the hormone wears off, you can feed it out and sell it. The *ultimate* gomer, however, is a cow (often with ovarian cysts) always in intense estrus, which seeks and mounts all other cows in heat. As a detector, "She will beat any bull, hands [hooves] down," says U of A's Dr. Mick Price. But not every farm or ranch just happens to have a "nympho cow" handy at AI time.

Gomers were usually cheap culls, often yearling dairy bulls, that could be picked up for little money and sold in the fall for whatever they would bring. In the six years we ran an AI whole-herd program on the ranch, we used in succession, as well as back tags, two chin balls on "rear-enders" (urinary calculi operations) and two penablocks but no side-winders. Eventually, we gave up on gomers and the last couple of years we simply watched carefully early in the morning and late in the evening.

We also tried heat synchronization – getting all the cows to come in heat at one time and then inseminating them all at once. No gomers or any other kind of identification. Our first trial[11] was in 1969, 23 years before this was written. The technique hasn't improved much in that time. Yes, using hormones, you can get nearly all the herd (if they're eligible and ready to cycle) to come into heat at one time, at least within a few days. But, after it's all over, your breeding success percentage isn't all that great and meanwhile you have had to run your cows as a herd two or three times through the chute. Some people do it but it hasn't taken over the industry by any means.

On small herds under close supervision it's possible to get most of them in calf with AI in six weeks. But on a ranch, you can expect to get just over half your calves by AI in a four-week program and between 60 and 70 percent in a six-week period. Since you have to turn out clean-up bulls in either case and since it's important to keep the calving period as short as possible, the general practice became to run three weeks and then turn out the clean-up bulls.

The best calves are your earliest calves from your best producing cows. During the Exotic boom, there was a great incentive to sell the early heifer calves (which would be "percentage" females by the AI sires) for premium prices and save your replacement females from your later calves got by the clean-up bulls. This practice led to herd deterioration within a few years. On the other hand, if you were keeping your early AI calves for replacements, your herd improved in a spectacular manner. This is the role played by AI today – to add superior genetic material to your herd. Today, AI is rarely used by ranchers but has become the darling of purebred breeders (the same group that had cursed it 20 years earlier). They inseminate a limited number of cows, using semen from a select sire.

And they also use the added marvel of embryo transplant. This allows you to have your cake and eat it, too – add the best heifers from your best cows to your herd while selling their *in-utero* sibling(s) for lots of hard cash.

Considerable experimental work was done on ovum transplantation in the late sixties but the process was not begun on a practical (and large) scale until the early seventies with the boom in high-priced Exotic breeds. The driving genius here was a Calgary dentist named David Deerholm who set up a transplant unit a few miles west of Calgary in 1970. What made the operation feasible was the discovery of how to use substances called prostaglandins which induce heat (estrus) in females upon injection. With prostaglandins, you could get the donor cow in heat at an appropriate time, accompanied by multi-ovulation. When inseminated, the cow thus had many eggs to be fertilized. How do you get those eggs out of her uterus and fallopian tubes and into another cow? – that was the question.

It was done the hard way. Seven days after insemination – usually three inseminations at 12-hour intervals – the *donor* cow was anesthetized, rolled on her back and the embryos removed by surgical operation. Not an easy task, nor easy on the cow. The embryos were then examined microscopically and good ones selected for implant. Meanwhile a group of *recipient* cows had been brought by hormone injection into estrus simultaneously so that they were ready to have the fertilized ova implanted into *their* uteri. Almost any cows could be recipients but Holsteins were favored because they could give birth to and provide adequate milk for, the big Exotic calves. They, too, underwent surgery for the implantation. A lot of cutting and stitching!

There were some spectacular successes with this procedure, like 17 full-blood French Limousin calves produced simultaneously from one cow! And many failures with nothing gained but experience, and a few so-so jobs, with one or two calves surviving. It cost a lot of money: $4 000 for the operation, plus the semen and inseminating fees, plus room and board for the donor and recipients. Plus the cost of the recipients. But with Exotic imports selling from $30 000 and up, it was a relatively cheap procedure. The "success" rate was about 50 percent.

My experience with transplanting was more or less typical. I transplanted four cows over the course of two years and got three living bull calves: absolute zilch from the first operation; the three bulls from the second; four recipients pregnant from the third and fourth cows, none of which produced living calves. The loss of the last group was largely my own fault – or perhaps due to circumstances I couldn't control. I would have done much better to have simply inseminated the cows to a good bull – but cattlemen are gamblers! Within a couple of years the percentages had improved dramatically but I'd had it with transplants!

Some years later, transplanting was done by removing the fertilized ova with a pipette worked through the cervix and then inserting the fertilized ova into the recipient the same way. This is a much simpler and cheaper way to do it, with much less trauma. And now you can get the transplanter to come right to your farm!

The beef breeds all now recognize AI, transplants and high-tech generally. At the 1990 Calgary Bull Sale, 25 percent of the bulls had been got by ET, embryo transplant. In coming full-circle, implanting is now often done surgically but in a much simplified operation involving only local anesthesia and a small incision to expose the horn of the uterus.

You can transplant a cow several – perhaps many – times. If the progeny are going to be worth a great deal, as from high-performing dairy stock or a particularly favored beef cow, you can pretty well "fill the market" from one cow and one or more bulls. The common procedure in beef cattle is to stimulate the cow throughout the year, harvest and freeze the fertilized ova and then transplant them in March and April for January-February calves.[12]

But if you want to do that and have absolute uniformity in the progeny as well, look at *cloning*. Easy to describe; hard to do. Super-ovulate your cow with hormones. Inseminate her. Harvest the ova. Shortly thereafter select the fertilized ova and put them in a petri dish with a nutrient solution. Divide them surgically at the 8-cell or 16-cell stage (you need a microscope). Wait awhile and divide them again if you like. And again! Implant the now-identical twins, quadruplets, whatever, into recipient cows. Wait 280-283 days more or less. Smile with glee as you look at your group of identical clones.

Well, they're not quite identical. Genetically, yes; but *in utero* they were subject to different environments and their color markings may be slightly different, as may be other less evident characteristics.

By 1990, cloning had taken another step forward. Remember how the fertilized ovum had been divided in *two* at the 16-cell stage in conventional clones. Why not divide it into 16? This doesn't work because each new individual needs enough cytoplasm – the life-sup-porting substances which surround the cell nucleus – to nourish it and enable it to grow. Dividing the cytoplasm in two worked OK; there was still enough of it to nourish the two new individual but not much left over.

Then a Cambridge scientist came up with a new idea: save the ovaries of ordinary cows at the slaughter house. Remove the unfertil-ized eggs from these ovaries – the cow's whole lifetime supply is there from birth. Remove the nuclei from these ova and replace them a single cell which you just happen to have to hand because you have just divided an embryo at the 16-cell stage. Actually, you have 16 such cells and can use 16 of the slaughtered cow's ova. Result: 16 clones from your original embryo and these can go into 16 recipients. Well, if you get ten, that's a pretty good harvest. For high-priced breeding stock in great demand, it's a great way to go. Though you just might over-supply the market!

But there's a catch 22 here. The reason for using those de-nucleated cells from packing-house ovaries was to get more cytoplasm to go with the nuclei from the clones. One group of factors in cytoplasm are called mitochondria, tiny, sausage-shaped things which are almost like dif-ferent organisms. These are passed on from generation to generation in the female cytoplasm (the male cytoplasm from the sperm is shed at fertilization). What scientists have been startled to learn is that mitachondria have their own DNA. So part of a female's genetic inheritance is quite independent of the nuclei of ovum and sperm. Thus the female clones begat from packing-house de-nucleated ova are not really identical. The ramifications of this discovery are still largely unknown.

It also is now possible to sex embryos with great accuracy. You do this by matching DNA strands. From your biology you'll remember that a female has two X chromosomes, while a male has one X and one Y. When the chromosomes are matched the two Xs will appear as a band across the pair, while an X and a Y will not match up. So it's possible to select either a female or a male for the original embryo and then clone all one sex from there.

A recent development at Cambridge University (announced in January, 1993) is identifying the sex of sperm chromosomes – either X (female) or Y (male) – and then fertilizing ova with the sex of choice. Want to expand your herd? Raise only heifers. Want to have nothing but bulls or steer calves to sell? Use only male-chromosome semen. When this technique becomes generally practical, both beef and dairy industries will be revolutionized – again!

But we ain't seen nothing yet in the high-tech field. Now they're working on transplanting specific genes into embryos. Not just from other cattle but from other species. You've seen pictures of the "geep," a creature with both sheep and goat genes. Not much practical in that kind of stuff but think how you might transfer disease resistance, growth enhancers (or inhibitors), anti-aging factors.

We've now reached a place where ethics and morality get into the game. Are we playing God? Will we create monsters which will do we know not what? A great deal of wisdom will be needed to rationalize the advances in this area of science for the benefit of all mankind.

| By the Way ... |

[1]Joe Johnson, herdsman at the University of Alberta for many years before World War II, fitted and showed Grand Champion steers at the Toronto Royal and the Chicago International. He was admitted to the Alberta Agriculture Hall of Fame in 1951, the first year the award was given.

[2]Leesment planned and directed the creation of an index of fifty years – from 1938 to 1988 – of the publication *Canadian Cattlemen* (later *Cattlemen*). the index is of inestimable value to students of western Canadian history and of the cattle industry.

[3]*Lutsia intervale,* pronounced *lootsia inter vawlley,* is bastart Latin for "a flash of light" and was a common expression of Heli's mother-in-law.

[4]To "draw" a bull is to collect his semen artificially.The bull is trained to mount another bull or steer or cow or even a dummy. His penis is grasped by a technician and directed into an artificial vagina. The latter is lubricated and has a double wall containing blood-heat water. A small pipette at the distal end collects the ejaculate.

[5]In 1975, while accompanying a veterinarian on his rounds in Ecuador, I helped him run a Black Fighting cow down a chute so he could do a rectal palpation. She did not submit meekly to these indignities. Luckily, the chute was of stout construction!

[6]One ejaculation may be "extended" to 700, even 1500, doses. The Holstein bull "Starbuck" has well over 20 000 progeny and has displaced about 200 natural-serving bulls.

[7]John Minor also became involved in a scheme to buy feral ponies from Newfoundland and then establish a cattle ranch there. The latter scheme failed for a number of reasons, one of them being the number of Newfoundland "moose" hunters. A year later, Minor (with some partners) bought the huge Chilco ranch in the remote interior of B.C. Shortly after, he was killed while flying his small plane from the Chilco to Vancouver. Read the book *Lady Rancher*, by his widow, Gertie Roger.

[8]In herds using an outside inseminator, the technician often would arrive only once a day. He then would inseminate the cows gathered both the night before and that same morning. Most ranchers – or family members – learned the technique at a "school" run by the AI unit and the twice-daily routine was generally adopted.

9Dr. Mick Price of the University of Alberta says he has heard stories (but has no definite proof) of bulls successfully overcoming this handicap.

[10]A gomer is an animal altered bull or steer, or a cow or heifer hopped up with hormones – used to detect heat in cows. The term was coined by the children of Neal and Norma Palmer of Bengough, Saskatchewan, circa 1969. Wayne Clews of Pangman, Sask., a Charolais breeder who was doing semen sales and AI schools at the time, adopted the term and "made it stick" by using it in an address he made to the National Association of Animal Breeders in Denver. Shortly afterwards, the term was used in publications in Texas, Australia and the UK, as well as in Canada. A "first" for Canada and of course, for Saskatchewan!

[11]We had thirty heat-synchronized Charolais heifers penned two heavy-plank fences away from twenty yearling Angus bulls. The day the thirty heifers came into heat, the pheromones started to waft

across the corrals. Yes, love will find a way and no planks of any kind could have resisted the great surge of bull power towards the heifers! Probably a score of the heifers were served in the ensuing orgy before we got everything sorted out and penned again. But we only had two grey calves the next spring. Fertility is higher during the *second* heat after synchronization and that's when you should inseminate.

[12]In the Northern Hemisphere, the most profitable calves are born in January (if you provide adequate shelter) and the least profitable are born in July. In the purebred industry, where cattle are ear-numbered according to the year of birth, the earlier in the year the birth occurs the better.

PART FOUR

Bovines, Humans and Survival

Grass – *by U.S. Senator John J. Ingalls*

Grass is the forgiveness of nature – her constant benediction. Fields trampled with battle, saturated with blood, torn with the ruts of cannon, grow green again with grass and carnage is forgotten. Streets abandoned with traffic become grass grown, like rural lanes, and are obliterated. Forests decay, harvests perish, flowers vanish, but grass is immortal.

Beleaguered by the sullen hosts of winter, it withdraws into the impregnable fortress of its subterranean vitality, and emerges upon the first solicitation of spring. Sown by the winds, by wandering birds, propagated by the subtle horticulture of the elements, which are its ministers and servants, it softens the rude outlines of the world. Its tenacious fibres hold the earth in its place, and prevent its soluble components from washing into the wasting sea. It invades the solitude of deserts, climbs the inaccessible slopes and forbidding pinnacles of mountains, modifies climates, and determines the history, character, and destiny of nations.

Unobtrusive and patient, it has immortal vigor and aggression. Banished from the thoroughfares and the fields, it abides its time to return, and when vigilance is relaxed, or the dynasty has perished, it silently resumes the throne from which it has been expelled, but which never abdicates. It bears no blazonry to charm the senses with fragrance or splendor, but its homely hue is more enchanting than the lily or the rose. It yields no fruit in earth or air, and yet should its harvest fail for a single year, famine would depopulate the earth.

(From a collection of the writings of John James Ingalls: Kansas City, Mo., Hudson Kimberley Publishing Co., 1902. This lovely tribute to grass has appeared several times in publications of the Society for Range Management, Denver, Co.)

Chapter Sixteen

Adding Tenderness

⪢⪢⪢⪢⪢⪢⪢⪢⪢⪢⪢⪢⪢

"And bring hither the fatted calf, and kill it; and let us eat, and be merry."

So spake the father when his prodigal son returned. That story, told 2 000 years ago, made a number of statements. We all see the parable as a lesson in atonement and forgiveness. It is an especially powerful statement of the great joy engendered by the act of forgiving. But there also is one hardly recognized assertion which sort of tags along: if you are going to have a sumptuous and joyous feast, let the main course be beef, fatted beef.

Through two millennia no one questioned the fatness of the beef as being anything but a complete recognition that God's in his heaven and all's right with the world. No one said, "Go and get a few chickens, or bake a cake, or make a pilaf of rice." It was "Kill the fatted calf." And so it has been right up till a few decades ago when our society found itself eating far more food of all kinds than could be used up in physical activity. Too many people were too fat.

The simplest way to reduce caloric intake it to eat less. Especially less fat, for fat has two and a half times as much energy per unit weight as does either pure carbohydrate or protein. So fats of all kinds have become less fashionable even as we have become richer and more able to buy them. Our response to this dilemma is paradoxical: we continue to put fat on our domestic food animals to improve flavor, juiciness, tenderness and ease of cooking, and then we cut the fat off and throw it away. About a quarter of the weight of a traditional carcass of beef is "waste" fat.[1] However, Canada's new "lean beef" is 49 percent leaner.

A century ago when most North Americans lived rural lives, working very hard in the out-of-doors, fat food was a great boon – the fatter the meat the better – a situation which had obtained ever since Biblical times. As children, my sisters and I were enjoined by a stern father who was born in 1875 on a wilderness farm in Ontario, to "eat your fat." Mother, who was gently reared in an upper-class city family, would show how, if you took some lean along with it, the fat on a slice of beef actually tasted pretty nice. So we acquired a taste for fat meat, as did most of our generation. And in due course we passed the habit on to our children, who are now told by their doctors to eat "higher on the hog" (pork chops from the hog's back or ham from its rump rather than cheaper, fattier sow belly).

Yes, the fattening process is costly, but it is still cheaper to add weight by feeding than it is to raise more animals. It costs a cattle feeder less to put a pound of gain on his steer than what he pays for a pound of non-fed feeder cattle by the pound. When I was a boy, there were three forces working to put fat on steers and hogs. First was the appetite for fat meat which had come down through the ages; second was the economics of meat production and third was the great surplus of corn and barley in North America that had to be marketed in some way.

The last two are closely related. If grain is not abundant and cheap, there is no profit in feeding it to cattle. High-cost grain, compared with much cheaper grass, had justified the 300-year-old South American custom of fattening on grass. A similar practice in Britain grew after the repeal of the Corn Laws. When these laws were repealed in 1846, grain could be imported to England without duty. Many corn (grain) fields were converted to "leas" (permanent pastures) because there was no profit in raising grain. The leas were not plowed up till World War II when the country was desperately in need of more grain. Most leas are now in pasture, again mainly for dairy herds and sheep. Some are still used for converting "store" feeder cattle into fat beeves.

Australia and New Zealand have always fattened their cattle on pastures. Recently feedlots have sprung up in Australia to satisfy the Japanese market for grain-fed beef. This is a limited market which both Canada and the U.S. are eager to fill; however the Aussies are about as close to Japan and they can grow grain just as easily as we can. We have already noted that, true to form, the Japanese are buying Aussie stations (ranches) and are building or financing feedlots and meat works (packing houses). When I was in Hong Kong in late 1986 I checked out the beef in a big supermarket in inland Kowloon. There were three kinds of beef available: local, very lean and unattractive and cut in indiscriminate strips; New Zealand, what you would expect, grass-finished and quite lean; and Australian grain-fed, much like what you would find in our own counters. The latter was priced the same as beef in a Calgary store; the New Zealand product was somewhat cheaper and the local beef cost only half that much.

The luxury trade in beef – posh hotels, cruise ships, international resorts – asks for U.S. grain-fed Choice Grade or Prime which is even fatter. On a Greek cruise ship sailing around Southeast Asia in 1989, the chef told me he was provisioned with U.S. beef. Why? Because nearly all the passengers were Americans. The paying customers on board just *knew* that U.S. Choice was the best in the world. That's what they wanted – and that's what they got. (Aussies and Canadians and *les eleveurs des Charolais* in the Loire valley would, of course, dispute this assertion but who would pay them any attention?)

What is good beef? On this continent, we say it is good if it is juicy, tender, flavorful, the right color when you buy it and fat enough – especially "marbled" – so that it is almost impossible to ruin it in the cooking. Beef from grain-fed cattle fills the bill. So the grain fattening of cattle has developed into an important industry in North America.

Carl Sandberg's poem "Prairie" tells of the growth in the livestock industry in the U.S. Cornbelt in wonderfully descriptive language. The American industry was a "natural" given the climate and agricultural production of the Cornbelt. It needed no special government help to thrive.

In Canada, which has a great number of "perverse" economic endeavors based on politics and subsidies and regulations to support them, the industry expanded in typical Canadian fashion – half of it rationally and half of it because of subsidy – in Alberta from settlement onward because of natural advantages and in Ontario during and after World War ll because of subsidized freight rates.

Two driving forces were involved. One, the retail markets were in Montreal and Toronto. Two, prairie grain was almost as cheap in the East as it was in the West, due to freight subsidies which had been introduced (or so Westerners believed) mainly to enable prairie grain producers to sell their product more effectively.

The main effect of this cheap grain (which eastern politicians made sure their rural constituents were kept aware of) was to foster a livestock industry in *Eastern* Canada. (In those years Ontario and Quebec were bot called Central[2] Canada; that tampering with geography occurred with Trudeau Liberalism, Eastern Canada now is what used to be called the Maritimes.)

The cattle-feeding industry in Ontario expanded by importing calves from Alberta and Saskatchewan and feeding them out on grain, also imported from the Prairie Provinces. It was cheaper to ship a calf to Ontario from the West than to ship a fattened steer or its carcass. And since the grain was shipped essentially "free," the business thrived.

However, the great growth in cattle feeding in Ontario with the "corn revolution" of the 1950s. New corn hybrids were developed which would mature and yield heavily as silage *or* grain in Ontario's climate. Within a decade, corn became *the* field crop of southwestern and central Ontario. To eat all that corn silage, more calves were needed, so the West-East[3] shipments grew to keep pace and some Ontario feeders actually imported cattle from states in the U.S. South.

Meanwhile the feeding business also grew in the West, particularly as barley was proving to be a surer and higher yielding crop than wheat in many areas. By 1969 the barley surplus had reached crisis proportions: there were reports of "three for a dollar" sales – three bushels for one dollar – though I was never able to buy any at that price. In desperation, barley growers formed feeding companies to feed out their own grain, resulting in a great number of new and big feedlots across the Canadian prairies.

The new Canadian lots were modelled on the huge "custom" feedyards which have sprung up in Arizona, Colorado, Texas and California. These are quite different from the Iowa farm lots where a "load" (30 to 40 head of cattle) traditionally had been fed corn in bunks with a scoop shovel, "followed" by hogs. The corn would pass through the steers more or less in the whole form and the hogs would pick the partially digested kernels from the manure – along with a goodly amount of B vitamins!

The Iowa farmer – and his bank – owned the cattle and the farmer fed his own grain. The western lots are big, feeding thousands of head

at one time. Most of the cattle are not owned by the feeding company but by ranchers ("first hand" cattle) and by "investors," who can be anybody or any corporation that needed to avoid or delay the paying of income tax. This latter group have always been the big holders of cattle in feedlots. The owners pay for the feed and in the early years they also paid a per diem fee for the feedlot's services. (Ten cents per day per head was common. Today most lots do not charge a per diem but incorporate all charges, apart from "induction" into the feed price.) So the feedlots make a steady, if not spectacular, income, while the investors, using bank money, are the high rollers.[4]

Over the past 25 years, more and more cattle have been fed in custom lots, fewer and fewer in farm feed lots. This development has changed the marketing of cattle: since the manager of a big lot has market "power," he can bargain directly with packers and does not need an agent (the old "commission man") to represent him. The old "terminal" markets in Canada – established 100 years ago at major railroad terminals – have gone with the dodo, except the one at Toronto which continues because most Ontario cattle are still fed on farms. The biggest of the U.S. terminal markets was initially Chicago, (Carl Sandberg wrote a poem about this and Sinclair Lewis a novel) closely followed by the "River" markets, along the Missouri and Mississippi – St. Paul, Sioux City, Omaha, Kansas City, St. Louis. These markets have lost volume as feedlot operators increasingly bypass them and sell direct to packing houses.

What happens in a feedlot? Does the steer go to heaven and then die? Obviously he has enough to eat and other creature comforts, too, for he makes the most money for his owner when he is most comfortable and contented. Because his rumen – the great fermentation vat – generates much heat processing vast quantities of feed, he doesn't suffer from cold weather unless temperatures get close to or below zero Fahrenheit and then only if it's windy or wet. In scientific terms the Lower Critical Temperature for cattle is 10° below F (-32° C) without wind, snow or sleet. Colder than that and the feedlot steer has to use additional feed to keep warm. (For us humans the LCT is 65° F). And the steer likes shade to get out of hot sun.[5] So climate defines the major feeding areas.

Few climates are perfect. In Canada, Southern Alberta has more going for it than any other part of the country. True, there is too much wind (so build wind-breaking perimeter fences or windbreaks within the lot) and sometimes it rains or snows (so "landscape" the lot to provide drainage and hump up the centre of the lot to provide a dry place for ruminating). Also be ready to spread bedding – straw or shavings – in snowy weather.

In Central Alberta the winters are harder. "Don't own any cattle in January, let the other guy do that," was the message given me by Graham Jones, a man who placed thousands of head "on shares" for a major Edmonton packer. The southern B.C. Interior would be a great place to feed cattle but the grain is all grown east of the Rockies. In Saskatchewan and Manitoba they do feed cattle through the winter but have to pay the price of a continental climate. Our prairie provinces are, after all, the Siberia of North America.

In Eastern Canada (oops, Central) cattle have to spend the winter in a barn, which greatly increases the cost of a feedlot. The advantages here are the abundance of corn,[6] the nearby big markets and the government subsidies. These do not equal the good things Alberta[7] has for feeding cattle, so the industry is decreasing in Ontario and expanding in Alberta.

In the U.S. Southwest the climate is dry and warm but there can be occasional rain or snow and the wind blows and the sun is hot. So put up windbreaks and sunscreens made of slatted snowfence. Slope your lots. In very hot weather, you may have sprinklers to drop a cooling mist on animals that otherwise would have to use energy to cool themselves off. More cattle are fed in the U.S. southwest than in any other part of the world. It is here that the modern technology of cattle feeding has largely developed and is best expressed.

But other places are important, too. Kruschev visited the Garst family in Iowa to see their cattle (and corn) operations in the sixties. Gorbachev, when he was Minister of Agriculture, spent some time with rancher Marshall Copithorne[8] near Calgary. Today the whole world goes to the U.S. southwest to learn[9] how to feed cattle in a big way.

There is much to learn. How do you make a monogastric hog out of a ruminant steer? What diseases will he get and how can you prevent and/or treat those diseases? What feed elements should you buy? In what quantities? A Russian – or any other – visitor is not going to learn it all in one visit. The organization, management and financing problems are formidable, even if you are able to cope with the practical and technical aspects. Let's watch a steer as he experiences feedlot life.

He arrives at the lot after a long ride in a crowded "pot" (possum-bellied truck trailer) with 40 to 60 other steers. He's herded down a chute and into a corral, where he's finds water which he may drink if he's not too afraid or riled. There may also be some dry hay in a bunk. Within hours he will be "inducted" – run through a chute and a squeeze, injected and squirted with many things, tagged in one ear, implanted with a pellet in the other ear, branded with a hot iron and then run into a large pen with a hundred or more of his fellows. He is kept moving by shouts, whips and electric prods and by his natural escape instinct to follow along a curved path.

He may have come from another feedlot (where he was being "backgrounded") but more likely he has left a pleasant and unfettered life of eating grass as it grew and drinking water from a stream or pond. An unpleasant stop en route may have been an auction ring – more loading and unloading, shouts, whips and prods – where he was exposed to a host of infectious agents carried by other cattle. He has been under a great deal of stress but that will all change soon.

His owner proceeds to change his lifestyle from that of a bovine "third world" to one of sanitation, nutrition, creature comfort and health. Animal-rights people and their near relatives have painted an erroneous picture of the "free and open" – and by implication, healthy – life of the range steer, and contrasted this with the terrible and unhealthy life of the "imprisoned" feedlot steer. Some entrepreneurs are cashing in on this nonsense by selling what they call "natural" beef. The gullible are buying – at almost double the normal price!

What is "natural"?

Nature in the raw is seldom – if ever – mild. In nature, populations are kept in balance by famine, disease, parasitism and predation. Compare yourself with the wretched African refugees from famine you see on TV. They're "natural." As well as starving, they are riddled with internal and external parasites and are suffering from several chronic diseases and are on the verge of dying from an acute one. *You* have benefitted from vaccination and half a dozen other immunizations given in childhood. Your diet has been fortified by vitamins, proteins and minerals either as regular components of your food (and water if you benefit from fluoridation) or as supplements. You don't have lice, stomach or intestinal worms, liver flukes, fleas, mites, infectious yeasts, molds and fungi, nor are you debilitated by tuberculosis, brucellosis (Malta fever) or malaria, nor blinded by parasites that "sew" your eyes shut.

Nor do you worry much about tetanus, gangrene, blood poisoning, botulism and other clostridial infections. And because your doctor has a vast array of antibiotics to protect you, you're not likely to die of pneumonia or syphilis or pus-forming skin infections[10] (as were your great uncles and aunts). And you have enough to eat. In short, you are part of the First World and you really don't want to live "naturally."

You are alive and well and you like it that way. The farther you are removed from famine, disease, parasitism and predation the better.

'Happy' range cow in a natural 'free and open' environment.

And the good husbandman endeavors to arrange things so that the animals in his care are also protected, comfortable and healthy. That's what you expect of him – you don't want to find trichina worms in your pork or tubercle bacilli in your milk. Left to their own devices, our cattle herds would be "third world" beasts: they would lose many of their calves and yearlings to a clostridial infection called blackleg; many would die of various respiratory diseases; all would be infested with warble flies (the pupae of which form pustules along the back) and with two kinds of lice (biting and sucking) and a goodly number with mites which produce the disease called mange.

Practically all would carry blood titres for tuberculosis and brucellosis. Parts of the country would have anthrax bacilli endemic in the soil with periodic disease outbreaks (always fatal) occurring frequently. (The health or rather lack-of-health situation I have just described pretty well states the condition of the feral bison in Wood Buffalo National Park.)

Several of these disease entities could maim or kill you and me. The last hundred years[11] have seen science identify and overcome these destroyers. To abandon our industry – *and our food supply* – to such devastating foes makes no more sense than to ignore the advances in human hygiene and health which have occurred in the last century.

If someone attempts to sell you some "natural" beef,[12] ask him if the beast was vaccinated for blackleg and other clostridial diseases and for shipping fever. Was it treated for warbles? (In parts of the country the law *requires* this to be done.) Chances are the seller won't know. More than likely, he'll say the calf was vaccinated for this and that but after it went on feed it got no hormones or antibiotics. So, what's natural?

If we did not apply First World hygiene, disease control and nutrition in our food production, our plates would be empty. The important things to know about drugs and cattle are the dose size and the "withdrawal time." Was there sufficient time between the administration of the drug or hormone and the time of slaughter for all traces of the substance to have dissipated? The regulations for dosages and withdrawal times are most specific and the penalties severe. A commercial lot just can't afford to ignore them. Carcasses are continually being tested by the Federal Government for drug residues. They practically never find any. Cattle feeders, as a matter of course, pay strict attention to both dose size and withdrawal time. We can boast that our meat supply is the healthiest and safest in today's world – and in all history.

Terrible, unhealthy life of 'imprisoned' feedlot steer.

So that's what feedlot induction is all about – to rid the animal of pests and parasites, to prevent him from getting sick and to encourage him to make best use of his feed. To transport him from the Third World to the First World.

Just as in the days of the trail herds, easy does it when handling cattle. Nobody tells the steer this but everything that has happened to him, including the shipping, loading, prodding and shouting, has been has been as gentle and quiet as is feasible and practical. TV and the movies delight in showing herds of careening cattle and cowboys racing to "head off the wild stampede." Historical reality was quite different. Herds were moved quietly and slowly; nobody wanted a stampede. So it is with feedlot cattle today. *Rough handling costs money.*

Typically, the induction crew (usually two people, though a single person can get along just fine with the right equipment) are regular feedlot hands but they may be local men or women who work under contract – so much money for so many head – and are not on the regular payroll. In the busy fall season they work long hours every day; in late spring and early summer, they may work only a couple of days a week, even less. The hours and nature of the work suits them just fine.

Don't be surprised then to find women doing the induction. What a few years ago was considered to be men's work is being taken over

by women in some of the big lots. The squeezes are powered by hydraulics, so physical strength isn't what it's all about. More important is to move the cattle through with the least stress. Here the gentler sex can outperform the macho cowboy. *She* handles the needles, the irons and the implanting guns. At Western Feedlots' High River yard, in the summer of 1991, I watched a very competent woman, working alone, process steers faster than one a minute. The feedlot manager told me she could do 700 a day.

The new inductee has to be gradually transformed from a grass eater to a grain eater. This involves changing the "bugs" – bacteria and protozoa – which live in his rumen. If he is suddenly fed a big meal of grain, he will get sick – grain overload it's called. He develops an acidosis condition and he may die. If he survives, he will be a long and expensive time getting better again. So starting with dry hay and perhaps some silage, his diet is gradually changed until he is eating a ration of mostly grain.

In western Canada the grain is barley. In much of the U.S. and Ontario it is corn, in the U.S. Southwest, it may be milo, corn, barley – whatever gives the most calories for the least money. The grain is called the "concentrate" part of the ration. In addition, there is some "roughage" fed – hay, straw, cotton seed hulls, corn stover, orange peels, whatever. The importance of the roughage is to provide bulk to keep the rumen functioning. The most fool-proof kind of roughage is silage, which may be whole-plant corn, ensiled hay (haylage), whole-plant green cereal grains, cull potatoes, whatever will ferment. In the Corn Belt and Ontario corn is supreme. In Western Canada the most popular silage is made from not-ripe barley or a mixture of green oats and barley.

The "balance" of the ration, for both us and our animals, is supremely important. The trick in devising feedlot rations is to provide enough of the more expensive components – proteins, minerals and vitamins – without feeding more than necessary. A tremendous amount of science, research and practical know-how is involved here. Computers are programmed to balance the nutrients and to do it at least cost.

That animal scientists know a great deal more about nutrition than do medical doctors astonishes both the doctors and their patients!

They should not be surprised the amount of information an MD must acquire to get his certificate is so vast, there is little room for facts about food. The animal researcher, on the other hand, may spend years studying the feed requirements of just one kind of animal. In a 1982 talk to farmers in which he was debunking a then-popular (and deceptive) food fad, University of Alberta Professor Dr. Mick Price (later Chairman of the Animal Science Department) said, "Where do the doctors get their information on nutrition? From Readers' Digest!" He was joking but he made his point. Our quarrel with the medical profession is not that they know so little about nutrition, it's that some are unscientific in many pronouncements about foods and diet.[13]

How long does the steer enjoy his First World environment? Long enough to fit the specifications of the supermarkets. Those specs come from a knowledge of what sells from their counters at the best profit margin. Remember Hansel and Gretel? They were being "finished" according to the specs of the old witch! So you, the consumer, determine the bovine's length of sojourn in his happy home.

If he is a big steer when he comes in, weighing over 900 lb. (400 kg) he may take only 60 to 90 days to "finish." If he is a 450-lb.calf, he may be at the feedlot for eight months. If he is fed much grain and little roughage, he will finish faster. But if the steer is fed mainly roughage over a long period (so that he can grow big but not too fat too soon) he may be in the lot for close to 10 months. Generally the system functions so that there is a continuous supply of finished beef, mainly in the form of carcasses weighing between 500 and 700 lb. (225 and 315 kg) arriving every week on the market.

The feedlot operator watches his "conversions" – how many pounds of feed to make a pound of gain. If the conversion is poor – 12 pounds of feed for a pound of gain –, that's costly. However, if it is down around six, that's good and money can be made. Since the steer uses his feed for two purposes, first to keep him alive (maintenance) and second to put on weight (production), the more he gains *each* day, the more money he makes for you. Why? Because his maintenance is a sort of fixed charge, a necessary but no-profit expense, whereas *gain* is what pays off.

So the feedlot manager aims for the highest possible daily gain that can be achieved without impairing the animal's health. A natural corollary to this statement is that the more concentrated the ration, the more efficient the gain and usually the most profitable. Roughages are about 50 percent digestible, whereas concentrates run around 80 percent. That is why grain is used so extensively in feedlots. It is possible to finish a steer entirely on roughage but it takes much longer and is much less efficient in the use of the available resources – unless the roughage is super cheap and the steer can harvest it himself, as he does on the Argentine pampas.

Feedlot operators like to buy steers with lots of frame but no fat. These make the best gains. A few thousand feeder cattle from the Parker Ranch in Hawaii were "grassed" for three months in British Columbia and then fed out at High River, Alberta, during the winter of 1989-90. The next year, 15 000 more Hawaiian steers and heifers were fed there. These had terrific "compensatory gain" – their early life in the tropics[14] had stunted them and when they hit all those good groceries in Canada, they literally took off. Gained almost three pounds (1.4 kg) per day on grass and up to five pounds (2.3 kg.) a day in the feedlot! A "normal" feedlot gain might run from about three pounds (an average) up to four pounds (real good) a day.

Why feed Hawaiian steers in Alberta? Hawaii regularly imports Choice beef from the U.S. mainland; the challenge is how do you convert Hawaiian feeder cattle into Choice grade? Since it is cheaper to ship cattle to feed than feed to cattle, send them to North America where the grain is. But a ship carrying them to any U.S. port would, by law, have to be an uneconomic "American bottom." So ship them to "foreign" Canada in a cheaper "flag of convenience" ship. When they are finished in the High River lot, they will be killed in Canada (most likely right at High River) and the beef may go anywhere the price is right – even to Hawaii!

Cattle feeding is a most capital-intensive business. I can't think of any other endeavor where you have to use so many big bucks with no guarantee of making any back. You pay between $700 and $800 for a feeder steer, spend between $200 and $300 feeding him, trucking him and keeping him healthy; then you sell him for about $1 000. If you feed out a couple of hundred head, you tie up the best part of a quarter of a million dollars. If there is a bad blizzard or a streak of -40 degree weather, you know he's not making you money, or he may get sick and when he does get better, your profit is gone. Or he may die. Or the market may suddenly go all to hell. And the interest on your borrowed money keeps piling up – on hundred-day steers at one percent per month, there goes $30 on every head!

All kinds of hazards and risks; sane people shouldn't be in it but every fall when a new batch of feeder cattle come off the ranges, there is always too much optimism and eager money around for the prudent buyer to buy them at the "right" price.

How can anyone justify cattle feeding to the new wave of environmentalists? First, the pro-cattle people must explain how an animal agriculture is the best way to save our soils. Without animals on our farms we create deserts (see Chapter 18, "Not By Bread Alone"). Next, point out that most of the beef animal's life is spent eating grass (see Chapter 19, "All Cows Eat Grass"). When he becomes a grain-eater he spends as little as two or three months in a feedlot. Third, the integration of grain feeding into the production of beef greatly increases the total production of high-quality protein for human consumption from a given land base – using many non-arable, "worthless" acres and just a few productive ones. More and better food for humans and we save the soil to boot!

By the Way ...

[1]The reference here is to the family which now could afford to eat pork chops (from the hog's back) or ham (from its rump) rather than the much cheaper "sow belly" which was largely fat.

[2]In 1956, the Eastern Farm Writers' Association was formed in Ontario just after similar associations had been formed in the four western provinces. This was quite appropriate and natural, since Ontario was then in Eastern Canada.

[3]Why don't Ontario farmers produce their own calves? The economics of cow-calf operations are negative in Easter Canada: grassland costs are high and snow and mud make wintering of cows difficult and expensive.

[4]A much repeated joke of the 1960s: the three easiest ways to lose money are with women, race horses and cattle feeding. The most fun is with women and the fastest is with horses but the surest way to lose money is to feed cattle.

[5]Fermentation in the rumen of large amounts of feed generates a great deal of heat. This keeps a feedlot steer warm in cold weather but makes hot-weather feeding more costly – the steer has to use energy to dissipate heat.

[6]Where it grows well, corn will produce more food/feed calories per acre than any other crop.

[7]In 1987, the Alberta government introduced the "Crow Rate Benefit," a subsidy for Alberta cattle feeders designed to offset the freight-rate subsidies on feed grains moving from the prairies to eastern Canada which benefit feeders in Eastern Canada. Quite illogical but Canada is hard to govern!

[8]"It will take us fifty years to be able to do this," marvelled Gorbachev when he was shown how the Copithorne family could run several hundred cows and their calves with practically no outside help.

[9]Students of cattle feeding also can learn in southern Alberta. In 1989 Veterinarian Dr. Kee Jim of High River, a feedlot specialist, received recognition as the top veterinary practitioner for bovines in all of North America.

[10]One of the first research "subjects" during the development of penicillin was an English policeman who was heavily infected with a pyogenic staphylococcus – "covered with boils." He responded dramatically to treatment but the researchers ran out of the drug, which they were cultivating in hospital bedpans and he died.

[11]The arrival of American GIs in Britain in 1942 forced that country to begin pasteurizing the general milk supply and cleaning up TB in cattle herds.

[12]The purveyors of "natural" beef claim that the cattle from which it came had no vaccinations, no pharmaceutical injections or oral doses, no antibiotics, no pesticides (internal or external), no hormones, no feed additives – nothing "artificial."

[13]Thomas J. Moore's book *Heart Failure* (Random House Inc.) is a powerful indictment of the medical fraternity's approach to what the author calls "The Cholesterol Myth."

[14]Cattle, practically all ungulates and most mammals, are smallest at the equator and grow bigger bodies as they go north – or south – even though their genetic make-up is the same. Biologists refer to this phenomenon as "Bergmann's Rule," after the scientist who first described it. Breeders of Hereford cattle in Texas are always astonished when they see the great size of the Hereford bulls at the Calgary Bull Sale. To get a really big moose, go to the Yukon!

Chapter Seventeen

Let the Lord Be Thankit

≻≻≻≻≻≻≻≻≻≻≻≻≻≻≻≻≻≻

Some hae meat and canna eat,
And some would eat but lack it.
But we hae meat and we can eat,
So let the Lord be thankit.

"Bring me flesh, and bring me wine." So spake Good King Wencelas[1] to his loyal page as he sought to bring Christmas cheer to a poor man. We don't know what kind of meat was in King W.'s larder but since it was winter-feast time, it would be good. This Bohemian Christmas carol is an example of how meat eating, through the ages, has been synonymous with good living.

Let the Lord be thankit we have meat to eat, not turnips! The newscasts admonish us about the harm we are doing to ourselves by eating meat. Furthermore, children brought up as Bambi lovers aren't into actually *eating* those lovely creatures. So, not only is eating bad for us, we are bad for doing it.

And some meats are "badder" than others. Both dogs and horses were eaten by Lewis and Clark during their journey through the Oregon country but I know only a few North Americans who have eaten horse meat and none who have eaten dog meat. The mere suggestion that a hot dog might derive from Fido was the theme of a successful beer commercial – for Fosters – featuring Down Under Paul Hogan as the not-quite-bright but dog-loving protagonist of good living. Dogs are a regular part of the diet in some Far East countries, and many European butchers sell horsemeat right along with beef and pork.

Whether we retch at or relish certain flesh depends on aculturization of both palate and conscience. How we were brought up, and what tastes and mores we have acquired as we have experienced the good life, determine what's on our plates. If our mothers cooked on coal-and-wood stoves we learned to enjoy well-done meat – beef, pork, lamb, it didn't matter. When Mother put a roast in the oven, she also put enough wood in the stove to ensure the meat would be cooked before the men came in for dinner – the noon meal, which had to be on time. Underdone roast was unpardonable. If it were ready a little ahead of time, no problem, just keep it warm while you make the gravy. Even today, at rural church suppers, the meat will be a brownish-grey, cooked at least an hour past well done. But the gravy, into which has leached all the goodness of the roast has run, will be tasty!

With the advent of gas and electric stoves, accompanied by increased culinary sophistication, we erstwhile farm boys learned to appreciate more delicate cooking: first rare beef, somewhat later rare lamb and game and much later, pork that was "just done." These are acquired tastes. Those who are slow learners or have not yet been schooled in these "rare" sensations are revolted by "all that raw and bloody meat." At the church supper, if there is the slightest tinge of pink in the roast, murmurings arise of "it's not cooked," accompanied by an occasional audible exhortation to "take it out and kill it."

Many of us still turn up our noses at heart and kidney and especially tripe, though we may tolerate liver. (Have you tried *prairie oysters*, the testicles of young bulls, harvested in quantity at a ranch branding?) North America produces far more offals –organ meats rich in cholesterol –than can be consumed here. They are shipped to the Old World and the Far East, where they are prized and relished.

Akin to our squeamishness about eating internal organs is our revulsion at supping upon strange beasts, like small rodents (though rabbits are eaten by many worldwide and guinea pigs are prized in Ecuador), snails and frogs (both delicacies in France), cats, insects, snakes and other "unclean" things. We can justify our revulsions by quoting the Old Testament, which quite clearly defines as edible only those beasts which chew the cud and split the hoof. In the Biblical pastoral society of herds and flocks, this proscription was an easy burden – and good for business!

Modern-day Israel reveals how eating customs can change. In late 1990, a group from Tel Aviv staged a ham sandwich eat-in to protest a recent law restricting the sale of pork. The law had been proclaimed as a sop to ultra-conservative, diet-observant Jews in return for their political support of the ruling party. The sandwich eaters were having none of that. And the butcher supplying pork to the many non-observant Jews maintained he was going to keep right on selling it. Such sales, he said, were a major part of his business.

The original Hebrew proscription of pork was probably a health measure –to avoid infestation by the trichina worm, a parasite of pigs which can complete its devastating two-host life cycle in humans. Hence swine were declared "unclean." For the modern secular Israelis the question becomes, "Now that pigs have been cleaned up, why not eat them?"

Thousands of tests made on the regular meat supply of the developed world, including Israel, assure consumers that they are getting a safe product. Of course, if you have a thing for "natural," you don't believe it. But is natural always good? What about tobacco, marijuana, opium and cocaine? They're natural. Whether they're good depends on your point of view. A number of sudden-death poisons – certain mushrooms, blow-gun curare, the hemlock drunk by Socrates – are natural. The rational approach is to look at the biochemistry of the substance and also what it does to us. It also makes sense to study the research trials that have been run on it.

Nature is both friend and foe to every living organism; that's how she keeps species in balance. She is neither good nor bad but can be wonderfully helpful or extremely dangerous, depending on how we manage her. And this we must do. Every day we defend ourselves against one malevolent nature, just as we take her benevolent sister to our bosoms. In the sweet ear of nature – and to poets – the songs of birds singing to the wide world and to their nests are beautiful, but they spell death to the worms they will eat and poverty to the orchardist whose crops they will destroy.

People tend to worry about the wrong things. For instance, the Great Satan of pollution is the automobile but there are some who will drive their cars five miles to put a few bags of newspapers in a recycling bin. In like vein, some will worry about meat from a steer from a vaccinated steer while blissfully ignoring the salmonella organisms – bacteria which cause severe food poisoning – and lurk in a third of the poultry they buy.

Bacterial infection of food is far more serious in impairing health than are the "unnatural things" man puts into it. I see bread advertised in the store with the label "Contains No Preservatives." This is supposed to indicate it is more healthful, whereas the real danger to the consumer is not from the additives but from what may grow in the food *because* it contains no preservatives. What "No Preservatives" really means is that the bread will get mouldy and rancid sooner. Writing of additives and preservatives in food, Helen MacDonald, a well-known Canadian dietician and nutritionist, says, "Mould and rancidity are a much greater threat to public health." The most lethal of common food poisons[2] is a natural toxin produced by a natural organism, *Clostridium botulinum* which may grow in food. In fact the whole history of man's conquest of disease is a recording of his victories over "natural" enemies.

Nor are our enemies constant in their antagonisms. We all need some dietary salt to stay alive, but your cardiologist may tell you to cut back on salt if your blood pressure is too high. What about another sodium salt with somewhat similar chemical properties: sodium fluoride? A little fluoride strengthens the teeth; too much mottles them. And a great excess may cause arthritis. So, is fluoride good or bad?

The near elimination of cavities in children's teeth which has taken place in your lifetime justifies fluoridization of municipal water supplies; however, an overdose of fluoride can sicken, even kill, you. Cattle in southeastern Alberta may get too much selenium in their feed and lose their hair, tails, ears, perhaps die. Three hundred miles (480 km) away in central-western Alberta, where soil is deficient in selenium, ranchers give their cows and newborn calves selenium injections to prevent "white muscle[3] disease" in the calves.

Everything from sunshine to sexual abstinence to fried eggs can be carcinogenic – it depends on how much. For instance, your oncologist will talk turkey to you in a loud voice about your cigarette habit, but the U.S. Surgeon General, anguished by the enlarged prostrate of a post-climacteric cardinal, is not likely to send a "celibacy is dangerous to your health" letter to the Vatican.

Yes, many foods would be cancer-producing if you could eat enough of them. All the cured meats – including those ham sandwiches the modern Israelis were munching – could do you in, if you had the physical ingesting capacity to swallow several tons of them. Some practical advice: eat a little bacon, ham, smoked sausage, corned beef, whatever but, but if you are worried about nitrosamines, be moderate. Don't eat these meats three times a day, every day.

So far, in surveying good and bad food, I've been walking around the periphery. Now let's get down to the real guts of the controversy – fat meat.

In 1946, my new bride got as a wedding present a Blue Ribbon Cook Book, free (I think) from the Blue Ribbon Flour Co. In addition to recipes, it was filled with good advice to the young homemaker. For example, too much meat is not healthful. Better, the book said, to eat more "plain" foods – such as those made with their flour! This attitude was fairly common at the time; the culprits to be avoided or at least indulged in parsimoniously, were pork (especially if fat and very especially if undercooked), and heavy-brine cured meats and fat meat in general.

Through the next three prosperous decades, beef consumption in North America more than doubled with chicken consumption increasing even faster. More pork was eaten, too, but at not the same accelerated pace as chicken and beef. Chicken increased in popularity as Colonel Sanders made it the fast-food (itself an innovation) of choice. On top of that, it got progressively less costly to produce – the move from the barnyard to the broiler house.

Chicken is now cheaper to raise, buy and eat than is beef. Away back during the Depression it cost three or four times as much. In the fall of 1936, I sold good beef calves at the Calgary stockyards for only four cents a pound, but I was able to peddle "milk-fed cockerels" to butcher shops for sixteen cents a pound. A few years later a California political activist, Rosemary Taylor, touched hearts, pocketbooks and stomachs with her book *Chicken Every Sunday*. At that time, chicken was a great luxury, so the implication was: "How wonderful to be able to eat chicken once a week, not just plain old beef or pork!."

With incomes rising and meats becoming comparatively cheap, North America became a continent of meat-eaters – not just eaters of meat but eaters of fat meat. Grading systems favored fat carcasses. Fancy hotels insisted on fat (Prime grade) beef. American housewives preferred Choice (while not as fat as prime still heavily larded) – and then asked the butcher to "trim off the *waste* fat." True enough, there were many arguments brought forward against fat meat, but they were mainly economic – why spend all that money putting on fat and then throwing it away? A full 25 percent of a Choice carcass was trimmed by the butcher before Mrs. Housewife took it home. What the butcher could not trim off was the fat (much of it invisible) interspersed in the muscle.

The visible interstitial fat – marbling – was (and still is by many) prized as a mark of quality. Tenderness, flavor, juiciness and general "goodness" were attributed to marbling. It was and is an integral part of the U.S. grading system and in 1992 became part of the Canadian system, too. In Canada,[4] taste-panel research in the 1960s pretty well debunked the marbling-is-good myth but to make Canadian beef acceptable in U.S. and Asian markets today, marbling – like Winston Churchill or Douglas MacArthur in earlier wars – is back. Marbling adds more fat to meat and hence is the enemy of the cholesterol warriors, zealots who have targeted beef (and pork and lamb and eggs and cream) as the enemies of mankind.

The great controversy raging today is this: is high consumption of meat good or bad for us?. Nearly everyone says it is bad. Plugged arteries, colon cancer, hypertension, too much cholesterol in the blood, general obesity, death from heart disease – the list gets longer as time passes.

So what's with cholesterol? The answer to this question should be, "Ask your doctor." However, your doctor's knowledge of cholesterol is imperfect. If he is honest, he will say that both high blood levels of cholesterol and surplus fat are dangerous but there is considerable controversy about the subject. How this controversy came about and how the American medical fraternity became compromised by research done by the most prestigious organizations in the public health field and how they drew the wrong conclusions from this research, is told in Thomas Moore's book *Heart Failure* (Random House) A substantial part of *Heart Failure* was published in *The Atlantic* in September, 1989, as "The Cholesterol Myth."

Deaths from heart attacks which have actually decreased by 30 percent in North American since 1978, spurred large and costly research projects were carried out over many years on thousands of people. The aim was to lower blood cholesterol levels, reduce heart attacks and save lives. Moore concludes that lowering your cholesterol is next to impossible with diet. Only a small percentage respond significantly. Using drugs to lower cholesterol is often dangerous. And, he says, it won't make you live any longer.

Professional medical people don't agree with him but concede "the picture has become increasingly complex as the studies have accumulated." Moore does go along with a prominent medical authority who suggests that for most people most of the time:

> *A mixed diet low in calories and saturated fat is recommended along with some physical exercise . . . [but] it is irresponsible to force the public into a costly cholesterol-reducing program without firm scientific evidence of the effectiveness of that intervention. (Eliot Corday, the Journal of the American College of Cardiology, February, 1989).*

Current general recommendations are to keep fat to 30 percent or less of total caloric intake, keep saturated fat to less than 10 percent and cut down on cholesterol.

Also, consider that cholesterol is essential to life; without it, we'd soon be dead. The cholesterol in our blood is manufactured by our livers. How much is produced is thought by many in the medical profession to depend on how much we eat. Moore's analysis of the research on the subject indicates this is not necessarily so.

If you are wondering about beef and cholesterol, here's what the Johns Hopkins Medical Center Letter (February 1993) has to say, "Shrimp are relatively high in cholesterol: one 3.5 ounce serving has 195 mg, as compared to 72 mg for lobster, 83 mg for a skinless chicken breast and 76 mg for lean beef. So lean beef has less cholesterol than either shrimp or skinless chicken. High-density lipoprotein (HDL) is the "good" cholesterol, the letter adds, HDL is a molecular package that circulates through the bloodstream and removes excess cholesterol left by low-density lipoprotein, the 'bad"'cholesterol . . . HDL must be synthesized within your body, so no food can provide it directly.

This is not the place to refute the claims of either the National Heart, Lung and Blood Institute or Thomas Moore. However, this we know for sure: if you are a young or middle-aged man and have high levels of blood cholesterol (especially the LDL or bad cholesterol) you are much more likely to have a heart attack than if your cholesterol level is normal. And the higher the level, the more at risk you are. Especially if you are also fat. This has been proved incontrovertibly.

A logical corollary would go like this: if cholesterol in your blood can be reduced, so will your chances of heart attack. This seems to be a sort of "relative truth" – it all depends.

Medical practitioners use nine interventions to lower heart-attack risk.[5] But the ability of people to follow their advice is generally poor. Two exceptions are the treatment of high blood pressure, where people follow medical advice well, and cholesterol reduction, where response is fair to good. Response to doctors' recommendations for the other seven interventions rank between poor and fair.

So, when a doctor tells his patient to lose weight, quit smoking and quit being a couch potato, he knows that the patient is not going to follow his advice. On the other hand, patients will at least partially co-operate if he puts them on a cholesterol-reducing plan. So that's what happens.

Since most of us eat much more fat than we need, it seems reasonable, even smart, to cut back on all fats.

For beef eaters, that means eat it lean. (Beef in 1992 is much leaner than it was in 1972 and Canadian beef is generally leaner than U.S. beef.) And don't eat too much of *any* high-calorie foods. Exercise and keep slim. We all know meat is an excellent source of high-quality protein, iron and some B vitamins, so enjoy but don't pig out. 'Nuff said!

You may think I'm fibbing when I tell you that not only is our meat supply healthful, it's also cheap! Go back to the middle of the Depression in 1933: steak then cost 20 or 25 cents a pound and a teacher, fireman, or postman, was paid $70 a month. Now these people are paid $3 000 to $4 000 a month, an increase of over forty-fold, even fifty-fold. If meat prices had caught the same ride on the inflationary balloon as did incomes, sirloin would now sell for $8 to $12 per pound.

During the first half of my life, a pound of sirloin cost the same as a haircut. Now I can buy two pounds for the price of one haircut – and that's getting the trim at senior's discount, too! As the years have gone by, we've paid less and less – in real terms – for our food. The people of the last paragraph spent at least a third of their monthly $70 on food; today our food costs only one sixth of what we earn – and we eat much better.

Much better? Yes, far more leafy vegetables and fresh fruit in the contemporary diet. In Canada the per-capita consumption of fresh fruits and vegetables was 34 kilograms in 1967. By 1988 consumption had increased to 57 kilograms. All those fruits and vegetables replaced starchy foods such as bread, pancakes, pasta, porridge and sugar. We're also eating more meat.

What some consider a positive result of an adequate and high-protein diet through childhood is the way we look. It has long been noted in England that the "toffs" and the "working stiffs" are almost of different species. Dress a lower-class Englishman in the clothes of the squire and he looks like – a workman dressed up like "the quality." If he opens his mouth, he immediately reveals his lower status, but his physical appearance speaks almost as loud as his accent. Bangers and mash, without much meat in the bangers, can be seen in his face. No one would have mistaken the Beatles for Oxford undergraduates.

Up until World War II we found it was quite easy to recognize Old World immigrants –they had a "European" look about them. We at first attributed this to genetics; but if they were successful in their new land, their children looked much like us. On the farm where I grew up, about half our neighbors were German-speaking immigrants, peasant families from Saratof on the Volga River in central Russia. In big families, the first-born children tended to look like their parents – European – while those who came later (and had adequate diets) showed few, if any, signs of this aspect of their parentage.

The effect of diet is pronounced among Asians. It is a commonplace that the offspring of Chinese and Japanese immigrants are much taller than their parents and much more "American" in their appearance. They also have more plugged arteries and more heart attacks – and some have less stomach cancer. These differences are apparently associated with diet and life style.

One of the most startling effects of diet on human health concerns the disease diabetes. Dr. Robert Elliott, head of Child Health Research at the University of Auckland Medical School, has discovered that young children, screened for susceptibility to diabetes by a blood test, have been completely protected from developing the disease by treating them with the B vitamin, niacinamide.(Dr. Robert Elliott, "Making Diabetes Obsolete," The Rotarian, May 1992). Dr. Elliott does not expect a continuing 100-per cent success rate –"that would be too good to be true" – but he does think his work "could be the first step toward eradication of diabetes."

Dr. Elliott has been treating his little subjects with the synthesized vitamin. In the outside world, the best dietary source is meats. (Actually pork is a better source than beef – a somewhat difficult admission for a beefman! If you are wondering if you are getting enough niacinamide, here is an alphabetical list of the best natural sources: beef liver, brewers' yeast, chicken, halibut, peanuts, pork, salmon, sunflowers, swordfish, tuna, turkey and veal.)

The same issue of the *Rotarian* that carried Dr. Elliott's report also gave figures for adult diabetes. In the developed world (meat-eating countries) two to four percent of adults are affected by diabetes but in developing countries (low-meat, high-starch diets) the rate is 30 to 40 percent, a shocking 15 to 20 times higher. In light of this, one wonders at the current fad of lots of starch and no meat for a healthy diet.

The way I see it is that moderation is the way to go. The Plains Indians ate buffalo almost exclusively, with some berries and just a few roots and leaves. The squaws worked hard and the braves were physically active. And they were healthy. We don't live like they did but we can be healthy meat-eaters if we are sensible about it.

By the Way . . .

[1]Duke of Bohemia in the tenth century and the patron saint of the Czech Republic. The name is derived from the Greek *Wenzel* and in Czech is written Vàclav. The feast of Stephen (the first Christian martyr) is December 26.

[2]Botulism comes from the Greek word for sausage. In the nineteenth century it was fairly prevalent in central Europe where sausages are

highly prized. In our diets we should be particularly wary of inadequately processed home-grown green beans.

[3]Page While travelling with a veterinarian in the highlands of Ecuador in 1975, I visited a large farm where white-muscle disease had been prevalent. I described to the veterinarian and the farm's *major domo* how we had treated this disease on my ranch in Alberta – injecting selenium in combination with Vitamin E. This was exactly the same treatment that the Ecuadorian veterinarian had used. His reputation on the farm was immensely enhanced by this confirmation of his diagnosis and treatment by "el Doctor Jacobs de Canadá."

[4]The Canadian grading system changed in 1972 to allow much leaner beef to be graded A1. This change was opposed initially by the breeders of British breeds who saw it as a ruse to put the French Charolais (much leaner) beef in the top grade. As of 1992, the grading system measures both marbling and total fat. Beef grading is confusing to most of us. The letter "A" is given to carcasses with a "trace" of marbling; "AA" if there is slight marbling; "AAA" if there is *small* which is a bit more than "slight," more than slight marbling. In addition, numbers are added to the Canadian A grade to show "yield," the percentage of "lean" cuts (those with little total fat) in a carcass. Thus A1 has very little marbling and comes from a lean carcass, whereas AAA3 has considerably more marbling and comes from a fatter carcass. In between are all the other combinations. The U.S. counterpart has no less than 10 categories to represent the various Canadian A grades. Retail customers don't understand all this and ignore it; research trials show we prefer to *buy* lean cuts but once the meat is on our *plates*, we like it fatter.

[5]*Stop smoking* – will lower risk by 50 to 70 percent. *Reduce serum cholesterol* – risk lowered with diet by 10 percent, with drugs 20 percent. *Reduce blood pressure* – often treattment can lower it 20 points. *Exercise* – 45 percent lower risk. *Lose weight* – 30 to 50 percent lower risk. *One (no more than two) ounces of alcohol per day* – 25 to 45 percent lower risk. *Low-dose aspirin* – 33 percent lower risk in users. *Keeping blood sugar normal in diabetics* – insufficient data. *Postmenopausal estrogen treatment in women* – 44 percent reduction. (From Johns Hopkins Medical Letter, February, 1933.)

Chapter Eighteen

Not by Bread Alone

>>>>>>>>>>>>>>>>>

"Eat bread." This was the classic admonition of the immigrant Jewish mother as she directed the life of her favorite son. She didn't say, "Eat grass," or "Eat leaves." Bread would nourish and sustain her child, grass[1] and leaves would not.

But no matter what our mothers say, we cannot fill our bellies with bread day after day. Why? Because there are too many of us and not enough good acres to grow enough bread grains to feed us all, *year after year*. There are huge areas of this planet where food grains will not grow, also large tracts where such grains can be grown only every two, three, four or more years. But grass will grow every year in these places; cattle will eat the grass and we can eat the cattle or drink their milk.

The wondrous thing about the cow is her rumen or first stomach. This organ is a fermentation vat as big as an oil barrel. What's cookin' there, Doc? Mostly grass. There are two reasons why the cow thrives on grass and leaves and woody stems, materials which we can't digest: first, they contain complex carbohydrates that our digestive enzymes can't break down into simple sugars. Second, many carbohydrates, simple and complex, are enclosed in a protective shell made up of impenetrable lignin. None of our digestive juices can touch it. Moreover, many of the carbohydrates inside the lignin are so complex that our digestive juices won't faze them either. Like the midnight express, they pass right through. Eat celery and lose weight!

But in that great fermentation tank in the cow's middle, there are bacteria and protozoa that can split the lignin (some, but not all of it; sawdust isn't good cow feed!) and go right after the complex carbohydrates and smash them into simpler starches and sugars. These, after bossy has chewed her cud, pass on through the next *three* stomachs and are eventually digested and used by the cow much like we digest and use bread and potatoes. The bacteria which had been growing in stomach number-one are also digested along the way and become the cow's "meat," that is they provide her with the essential amino acids. She is a vegetarian basking in all the benefits of a meat-supplemented diet.

This is the genius of the cow. She is the great converter of what is useless to Man into his finest food – almost perfect in the case of milk.

Ecologists, with assists from animal-rights zealots, have badgered stockmen for wasting grain by feeding it to animals. They point out, quite correctly, that it takes almost four pounds (two kg) of grain to produce one pound (0.5 kg) of pork.[2] With cattle (and all ruminants) the conversion is even worse, taking five to nine pounds (two to four kg) of grain to make a pound of live animal. When a big, fat steer is near slaughter weight, the conversion figure may be even more costly. "So quit eating animals!" they shout, furiously frustrated when we apparently don't or won't hear them.

Are we stupid, criminal or what? Well, pigs and chickens are grain eaters all their lives, but because of their good conversion ratios, they are still reasonable sources of animal[3] protein. As for ruminants, they gain most of their weight as grass eaters *before* they eat any grain at all. Whereas both pigs and chickens consume grain all their lives, the typical beef steer dines on grain only for about four months, having spent his first 20 months feeding on grass and/or hay. Throughout the beef cattle in-

" Wal... ya can't farm it, but the cattle thrive on it."

dustry, it is only in the feedlot, nourishing steers from 800 lb. (360 kg) to 1200 lb. (550 kg), that grain becomes a significant part of the diet.[4] Most of the steer's body weight has come from grass. To produce his 1 200 pounds, only 3 000 pounds (1 360 kg) of grain were used, a conversion of about two and one-half to one over the steer's lifetime. A far better use of grain than is made by pigs (4:1) and about as good as that made by poultry.

The question then becomes: what could you have raised on the pastureland that the steer (and his mother) ate as he grew from a fertilized ovum *in utero* to an 800-pound feeder? Well, on some of it you might have grown bread grains for awhile. In some places, like the Amazon, for two or three years; in others for up to 50 years[5] with good management; on the prairie of the Great Plains for perhaps 200 years – but not forever. Other rangelands are quite simply unfarmable. In many areas the ruminant animal is by far the best tool for harvesting food for man from the soil. Best for economics, best for conservation and best for human nutrition.

Man can't live on bread alone because he can't – on a global basis – grow enough bread grains year after year to sustain his species. Where he has tried to do this, he has always produced deserts – in the fertile crescent of Mesopotamia, in Greece, Italy and Spain, all of North Africa and across Asia. No scarcity problem yet in North America; you can find lots of interesting grains to look at, smell and chew in the health-food stores and our conventional bread grains can be bought everywhere. But will they be bought by your great-great-grandchildren?

None of these grains can be grown year after year, running into centuries, except on the ancient lake beds and the deltas of the great rivers, as in southeast Asia. Here the fertile soils are so deep that continuous cropping can go on for a long time and still seed time and harvest do not fail. And even here Man has helped out by adding animal agriculture to his land.[6]

Those who condemn the feeding of grain to chickens, pigs and cattle, rather than letting our species eat it directly and so avoid costly conversion factors, mean well but have not taken a global or holistic approach to the subject. The truth is that a sustainable agriculture cannot be carried out forever on either grassland or woodland soils without animals as part of the system. For centuries European farms always had a large animal component; that's one reason why they can now "out-grain" North America.

We learned in our Ancient History books that the vengeful Romans sowed the farms of defeated Carthage to salt at the end of the Punic

'The Roman soldiers salted the Carthaginian farmlands...? Or...

Wars. Since Carthage had been the "granary" of North Africa, this act of the Romans was devastating, indeed. At least that's what it says in the books. What is more probable is that the land had become salinized because of the way it was farmed, just as is happening in much of Saskatchewan and Montana today. The sowing-to-salt bit made good copy in both Rome and Carthage. The Romans were proud to publicize their great victory and the Carthaginians were happy to have found a whipping boy. So ensuing generations were taught a popular myth. For the Romans, to whom salt was money (literally – we get our word "salary," from the Latin *salus*) the spreading of salt on the vast Carthaginian farmlands would have been a tremendous waste of time, labor and money. In all probability, the guilty hands were those of the profligate Carthaginian farmers, not those of the Roman soldiers.

We know that the Ancients built wonderful irrigation works in Mesopotamia – what they didn't wunderstand was that there had to be ditches to drain the water off the land as well as ditches to bring it on. So their once lush and productive irrigated fields turned into salt marshes. We can hardly blame them; the same mistake has been made across North America, particularly in southern California. Lately you've been learning, from TV and magazines that much of the irrigated land in the western United States is at risk because of falling water tables and increasing salt content.

In Egypt, since the building of the Aswan dam, the lower Nile no longer floods the land to carry off the excess salt. Nor does it bring down fresh loads of silt to re-fertilize Egyptian farms. That silt now piles up behind the dam, year by year decreasing it's holding capacity. About 25 percent of once-irrigated acres (world-wide and even in Alberta) have become salinized and are now unproductive. Irrigation, which in 1991 was producing 35 percent of the world's food supply, is by no means a risk-free or permanent solution to the need for food. As our population grows, the amount of irrigated land per capita decreases. ("Will We Run Low on Food?" *Time*, August 19, 1991.)

We can't indefinitely grow wheat in the continental "bread basket" without destroying its soil. On the northern Great Plains of the U.S. and Canada, salinization is occurring on the millions of acres which are farmed with a wheat-fallow rotation. When Saskatchewan ships a train-load of wheat to China, who benefits? Prairie towns are becoming ghost towns; the farmer is having a hard time of it and his local municipality is no better off; the railways can't haul grain profitably and have to be subsidized; the soil blows in the wind and . . . and meanwhile what we are really doing is shipping Saskatchewan top-soil to China – to be paid for by our own dollars loaned to the Chinese.

Salinization of these dry-land farms became generally noticeable only in the 1980s. One solution, really only an improvement, is to use abundant fertilizer and take a crop every year. In fact, with "adequate" fertilizer (and enough moisture) zero-carbon, even plus-carbon farming is possible if lots of crop residue is returned to the soil. So far, these systems have worked and will work for awhile yet.

All the same, there are cogent reasons for not using large quantities of chemical fertilizer indefinitely, some proposed by the farmer himself, some by agronomists and some by environmentalists. Perhaps a third (in some places much more) of the organic matter in our prairie soils has been "lost" in the past century. Fertilizer and conservation techniques such as "no-till" farming reduce – and hide – this continuing loss but they don't completely eliminate it.

In the next few pages I will describe how loss of soil organic matter has contributed to the "greenhouse effect" and how regrassing our prairies will remove huge amounts of atmospheric CO_2 as the renewed organic soils act as a "carbon sink."

Annual cropping will only be an imperfect solution at best: some work is now being done to develop a perennial wheat. No more plowing or cultivating, just harvest the grain. Great, especially if we consume it where it is grown and return the human excrement produced as a by-product to the soil.

If we ship the grain away, somehow we will have to add to the soil whatever (other than what came from air and water) was shipped out in the wheat. Not a flawless resolution but much better, if it works, than anything we've done to date – esppecially if you can manipulate the wheat genes so wheat plants will fix nitrogen in the soil and you won't have to buy expensive fertilizer, at least not as much . . .

The only way to save our dry-land farms for longer than another 50 to 100 years is to re-introduce grazing animals and a grass sward to a land that once was covered by grass. (Ideally the sward would be permanent, but even several years of perennial forage in a repeating crop rotation would help.) Cattle, sheep, buffalo? Man can eat these animals, he can't eat grass.

Wait a minute, you'll say. What about nuts and fruits and vegetables and tubers? Right, you don't eat just grain. That's begging the question: almost all forms of farming *are* destructive. The growing of nuts and fruits changes the nature of our agriculture but does not eliminate its ravaging force.

Any form of monoculture creates problems. If you have travelled across southern Spain and looked at the base of an olive tree, you will have seen that at least a foot of soil – even three feet (one metre) in ancient groves – has been eroded away during the tree's lifetime. In much of the South Pacific the staple food is taro or cassava – underground tubers rich in starch. Even here the ground has to be cultivated, or it will lose its fertility before long. The classical renewal has been "slash and burn" agriculture.

That is how the rain forests of the Amazon are "farmed" by native Indians. The big problem of slash and burn is that it takes many years

for the land to recuperate after three or four years' cropping. But land recuperation can't keep up with generations of many babies that don't die – a blessing that occurs as soon as doctors and nurses and public health arrive on the scene. And when this new much-enlarged generation reaches maturity and starts having more babies, famine looms. This is happening all around the world.

The blessings of modern medical science, combined with the talents of the engineer, the agricultural scientist and the missionary, have put an unbearable

'Slash and burn!'

load on world resources. We have saved babies in the Third World so that they could grow to maturity, reproduce and then – starve. Meanwhile they inadvertently destroy resources as they desperately search for food – just as we in the First World have done in the last century.

Adage: *Give a man a fish and you feed him for a day; teach him to fish and you feed him for life.*

Corollary: *And then his children and grandchildren, good fishermen all, deplete all the waters of all fish and everyone starves.*

Conclusion: *Third-world development aid destroys resources and engenders starvation unless accompanied by population control.*

This is the real problem of the Amazon where land settlement is taking place much the way it happened a hundred years earlier in North America.

Which leads me to say something about the Amazon jungle as "the lungs of the world." That's a crock. In any *mature* ecosystem, growth equals decay – the huge volumes of carbon dioxide converted by the Amazon canopy to carbohydrates just equal the carbon dioxide (and methane, other hydrocarbons and carbon compounds) given off by the decaying plants and animals, on the ground and in the rivers.[7]

Air "freshening" only occurs when a "carbon sink" is forming, as in the oceans when huge quantities of plankton grow and then sink to the bottom. Carbon sinks also form in the peat bogs of Ireland and Canada's northern forests or when new growth takes place on wasteland, particularly when once-cultivated lands are returned to pasture. Speaking to the annual meeting of the Agricultural Institute of Canada at Fredericton, N.B., July, 1991, Graham Walker, Director of the Surveillance Group of the Canadian Wheat board, said: "Conversion of lands from (feed) grain production to pasture would result in the capture of huge amounts of carbon from the atmosphere. It is estimated that if soil organic matter was increased by 0.1 percent to a depth of 15 cm., 40 megatonnes of additional carbon would be stored in Canada's 33 million hectares of farmland." (*AgriScience*, September, 1991.)

If we use Mr. Walker's figures to estimate how much carbon has been lost from the precious "sink" of Canada's farm soils – guesstimating that a third of the organic matter has disappeared since cultivation began – we come up with a figure of over 13 billion tonnes. Since mankind has added some 160 billion tonnes of CO_2 (about 40 billion tonnes of carbon) to the atmosphere since the industrial revolution (Mac Margolis, "Tomorrow's Trees," *World Monitor*, November, 1991), we can see Canadian farmers have played their part in this ongoing havoc. In the meantime our soils continue to lose organic matter at prodigious rates because of our cereal-grain agriculture.

But to return to the Amazon basin. True enough, burning of the jungle creates vast amounts of excess CO_2 but *new* forests or plantations which replace the burned trees absorb carbon dioxide and release oxygen. Remember the "lung function" occurs under two sets of conditions: first, when new growth exceeds decay and/or burning; second, as a carbon sink develops. If new growth can be converted into soil organic matter, as happens under good pasture management, then there is a true "lung function." If the soils of the Amazon, which are naturally low in organic matter,[8] could be transposed into carbon-rich grassland soils, then millions of tonnes of carbon dioxide would be removed from the atmosphere in the process.

But let's look beyond the Amazon. What has to be said to people *everywhere* is this: if you have two babies (one is better) you will be fed. If you have any more, you and your children may die of famine and pestilence – and war, of course, for necessity knows no law.

In China, evil becomes good and vice versa – the classical yin-yang phenomenon in the land of its creation. There, dictatorial political power combined with a lack of respect for individual dignity and life have implemented a vision of a continuing well-nourished[9] population – one couple, one child. Our Western concept of human rights and freedom limits our advocating this sort of thing world-wide.

In Thailand, population control has been achieved by an education program sponsored by the king, that convinces people they will be better off with fewer children. In India, there has been no general support for population control, mainly due to religious and cultural reasons – sons provide support in old age. The Indian people and their government do not have a universal goal of controlling individuals for the good of the state, such as permeated China's millions for four decades.

Nor do they have the sense of community that exists in Thailand, where every person feels a personal obligation to the king and is anxious to carry out his teachings. No one knows how much moral authority the Chinese government has lost since the Tiananmen Square massacre; we can hope that birth control is maintained and is not thought of as just another of the oppressive measures of an all-powerful state.

In western Europe and North America, we have been seduced by the Pandora's box of material pleasures which money can buy – money that doesn't have to be spent on raising children. We willingly abandon procreation in order to "live better" – to spend our wealth and our energies on "better" things (really destroying resources). Following the ancient admonition to "go and do likewise," some world planners preach raising the standard of living of the Third World up to that of our own. Then, they say, all peoples will be sufficiently well off to practise birth control of their own free will. The trouble with this thesis is that there are not enough accessible (destroyable) resources in the world to carry out such a fantasy. It's Catch 22 all the way. Modern sciences, aided and abetted by do-gooders, have largely destroyed much of Northern Africa and have brought terrifying instability to the rest of the world.

Imagine the increased burden on the planet's resources if Gorbachev's successors were able to bring the lifestyles of their 280 million or so people up to a Golden Arches standard! Think of the greenhouse effect occasioned by an every-family-a-car reality in what used to be the USSR. And look further east. In China right now, a great yellow haze of pollution covers much of the coastal provinces – with people living just above subsistence. If the Chinese become a "modern" society, they – and the rest of us – will sicken, perhaps die, from a polluted atmosphere.

What we seem to be hoping for is that we Europeans and North Americans – can continue to use (waste) resources and that the people of the Third World will somehow live good but primitive lives. That's the way it has been. Let's keep it that way – maybe inoculate the children and drill a few water wells and ship them some of our surplus milk powder . . . Dreaming, dreaming, dreaming. The dream is almost over. Dare we awaken and open our eyes?

Man can live for millions of years as a hunter-gatherer, for tens of thousands of years as a herdsman but for only few millennia as a cultivator. And as "scientific," chemically-based farmer-exploiter, perhaps less than two centuries. Modern sciences, aided and abetted by do-gooders have enabled human and animal populations to explode, and these increased numbers have largely destroyed much of Northern Africa and have brought terrifying instability to the rest of the world.

How much can we do with what we have? And keep on doing it? The Australian Aborigine and the South African Bushmen and our own Plains Indian got along quite nicely without farms or livestock. So they did but there weren't many of them. They ate meat, even if only insects and small animals in Australia and Africa. Every movie-goer knows the Plains Indian lived largely on the meat of the bison.

As somewhat similar hunter-gatherers, a few million of us might get along forever as best we could – with none of the trappings of any civilization, ancient or modern. No doctors or dentists, of course. Not even a blacksmith or a cloth weaver. There might be a specialist arrow maker or spear sharpener. Women would be pregnant as long as food was abundant and the children would be fathered by the dominant, aggressive Type A males. That's the way we lived for thousands of years. It was a "sustainable system."

Our life as herdsmen? We could feed several million more, living in tents and always seeking new pastures with our herds and flocks, like Jacob in the Old Testament. In fact, a nomadic, tribal society – with a population controlled by the food supply continued in the Biblical area until OPEC brought wealth to the Bedouin and Israel "developed" Palestine.

Can we support more people as farmers, rather than as herdsmen? Yes, for awhile. Skip ahead a generation from Jacob to Joseph and the Pharaohs. The trek to Egypt, by Joseph's brethren and his father Jacob, symbolizes man's transformation from herdsmen to farmers to dwellers in cities. And it happened because there was "corn in Egypt." Though the herdsman's life is satisfying and romantic, when he acquires more children and grandchildren (and therefore livestock) than the land can bear, he turns to agriculture. He plows up the range (or migrates to lands he can plow) – to obtain more food. But it can only be a transient phase of his existence on earth. The soil wears out.

It is the need for more food that has driven man to what we consider higher civilizations. Even in Egypt there were crop failures;[10] Moses essentially was leading the Israelites to a land of abundant food – "flowing with milk and honey."

For the three and a half millennia following Moses, the world's population grew slowly, with death and birth almost in balance. The clearing of the forests of Europe off-set the desertification of the Mediterranean countries and the Middle East. European farms had plenty of animals, if we are to believe the woodcuts we see of the times and read about the great banquets. The fertility of these woodland soils, initially leached of many nutrients, increased *because* of cultivation, not *in spite* of it, since animal manure was a concomitant of the plough and grass was planted for pasture where trees had once stood. By grazing and manuring these paddocks, cattle and sheep – to a lesser extent mules and horses – ensured a sustained and permanent agriculture.

Everything went kaboom during the Industrial Revolution that followed the discovery of the New World. As fast as colonists to the Americas produced food, they found markets for it, if they could get it there. So steamships and railways were built. No sooner had the rails reached Abilene, Kansas, than the trail herds of beef came up from Texas to be hauled away to the East. The great prairies were broken and planted to corn and wheat to sell to an industrializing Europe. There came a time when the world (at least that part of it that functioned in an economic sense) had more food than it needed, even though populations had exploded. So we had the Great Recession and World War II.

After the War, science, technology and human compassion invaded the Third World. This prompted the Green Revolution, which meant that vastly more food could be produced from the same acreages by using new methods, new varieties, pesticides, herbicides and fertilizers. The earth responded bountifully – but at what cost?[11] We are just now beginning to find out. Twenty five years ago, pesticides, herbicides and fertilizers were *good things*; now we know they can destroy us.

It is not enough to say: stop farming or stop polluting or feed the hungry, or do it all naturally. Rethinking will have to occur on many fronts. But this we do know: to maintain and increase productivity on woodland and grassland soils – and that's nearly all our soils – we must include animals that chew the cud. Moses was right in his preference for ruminants and his rejection of monogastrics. (Though for entirely different reasons than those given in the Book of Deuteronomy!) We need cud chewers to eat the grass and legumes that we must grow to save our soils – and ourselves.

But do not cud chewers belch forth methane which then ascends to the heavens and depletes the ozone layer? Good question. Consider this: if the cow did not eat that biomass (grass, hay, vegetable, grains) it would rot or burn or be eaten by some other creature. In any event, carbon dioxide would be produced and in the rotting process so would methane. Another name for methane is marsh gas, produced from rotting biomass (the stuff which cows did *not* consume). And if other animals (this including you and me) partake of biomass, we and they have a proclivity to get rid of the gas, one way or the other. But let's not quibble, the methane production from cattle is less than one percent of the world's total. A cow's yearly methane production is equivalent, in ozone depletion, to the carbon dioxide produced by driving your car 3.2 km, according to researchers Thomas Drennan and Duane Chapman of Cornell University.

However, we must not make the mistake of thinking that these cud chewers can save us themselves. In fact, uncontrolled grazing creates deserts as inevitably as any other soil mismanagement. The U.S. West and southwest was grazed out in 20 years following the Civil War. Much of that damaged land has partially recovered, but some of it has become a desert.

Even greater denudation is caused by the goats of the Mediterranean countries. These "last-chance" ruminants are destroyers *par excellence* of vegetation both above and below the ground. In fact, all grazers and browsers – from gophers to elephants – if left unmanaged and uncontrolled will become too numerous and inevitably destroy the vegetation which supports them. This leads to desert formation unless and until other forces (disease, pestilence, predation and man in various ways) reduce their numbers.

This throttling of fecundity is referred to as the "balance of nature." In the wild, it is not a balance but rather consists of great swings from abundance to scarcity. In pre-history, man's numbers, along with those of other natural beings, soared and plummeted in response to starvation, predation and disease. Later, war, monasticism, exposing infants to die and other social customs helped limit numbers. Today, with so many population controls removed, we pretend that there will be no crash. But there will be. It has already begun.

Somehow we will have to find a balance among farm chemicals, increased yields, soil degradation (or improvement!), changes in wild life, corrupt (and honest) governments, water, air and animal pollution, human health, economics of supply and demand, religious taboos, hungry people, war ... It's a very long list if you include all the relevant components. The successful reconciliation of all these factors will require the wisdom of many Solomons.

By the Way ...

[1] At one time, perhaps a million years before Abraham, her child might have eaten grass. Your appendix (if you still have it) is a vestigial portion of a much larger *cecum*, a fermentation vat where bacteria broke down grass and leaves into sugars. Rabbits and horses still have theirs.

[2]Modern pork production may have a conversion rate of less than 3:1, a pound of pig for less than three pounds of feed.

[3]In certain parts of Africa, where the diet is mainly "mealies" (maize), people develop protein deficiencies which are generally grouped together as "meat hunger disease." Poaching of animals in game preserves is one way of "treating" this wretched ailment.

[4]Dairy cows eat a great deal of grain in North America but even vegetarians don't quarrel too much with this because milk is such a valuable food in so many ways.

[5]In the 1900s, Alberta accepted a number of U.S. Mid-West immigrants who had "already wore out two farms in North Dakota." In 1879, my grandfather moved from Ottawa to a farm at Thamesville, near London, Ont., only to find that the soil was already "worn out" from continuous wheat cropping.

[6]In southeastern China, the "animal" in animal agriculture is often man. What is euphemistically called "night soil" sustains rice crops year after year. In "advanced" societies, flush toilets deplete our fields and pollute our waterways with our "night soil."

[7]Page Famed writer and photographer Loren McIntyre stated (in a lecture given aboard the *Stella Solaris* on the Amazon river, February, 1991) that the silt and debris carried to the sea by the Amazon is equivalent to a continuous stream of 30 lanes of ten-ton trucks moving at three miles per hour. Instead of forming a delta (and carbon sink), this organic matter and eroded soil is swept away by ocean currents to join the Gulf Stream. As it decays, it reduces the oxygen supply in the ocean.

[8]Soils deteriorate in fertility under tree cover and improve under grass cover. The poorest soils are found in the tropical rain forests and the best (other than transported soils, as in deltas) on the grass-covered plains of the temperate zones. Some "conservationists" don't understand this and think they are saving the soil by planting trees.

[9]The fat, happy and well-loved children I have encountered in China starkly contrast with the ill-nourished urchins of the Andean countries who have shined my shoes.

[10]Where food is abundant and the living is easy, man does not become "civilized," but sits idly by his mud hut doing nothing much at all, according to the historian Arnold Toynbee.

[11]In Indonesia today, consumers pay three times more for "old" rice (the kind their fathers grew) than they are willing to pay for "new" rice (the high-yielding varieties requiring chemical agriculture,

foisted upon them by do-gooders). Does this preference reveal foolish stubbornness or a deeper and more basic wisdom?

Chapter Nineteen

All Cows Eat Grass

▷▷▷▷▷▷▷▷▷▷▷▷▷▷

In a western movie, what do the horses eat? There's our hero, riding full gallop into the sunset – or dawn or swirling-dust storm – on an obviously well-fed and eager horse. If this were for real, he would soon have to slow the pace – his mount couldn't keep that up for very long. Before the sun set, his trusty steed would need to be fed. But what do we see after the hard ride? The horse standing loyally near the campfire, maintaining his flesh and stamina on pine-freshened air and clear, cool water.

Where are the oats?

Since most of the audience know little or nothing of an animal's nutritional requirements, the drama is not impaired by a visible lack of horse feed.

Horses, cats and puppy dogs all have to be fed regularly – a hard but good lesson for a child when he gets his first pet. So do cattle.

If the feeding can be done on pasture, so much the better. And that's what ranching is all about. In fact without grass there can be no cattle industry. But with too many cattle the grass disappears. Between 1866, after the Civil War, and 1890, the grazing of cattle on "free" grass on the unfenced western plains and inter-mountain country of the United States resulted in the denuding of the whole area. It wasn't until the Taylor Grazing Act was passed in the thirties that control was achieved over the number of cows that a rancher could turn out on the U.S. public domain.

In the western ranch states, other than Texas, most grazing land is owned by the federal government. Some states also own a great deal of public land. Indian reservations cover a lot of cowboy country, too. The reservations, as well as running cattle belonging to the tribes or to individual Indians, often lease land to ranchers. A rancher's spread may include some deeded or patented land – often homesteaded by a grandfather or great grandfather – augmented by a BLM (Bureau of Land Management) permit or lease and perhaps by some U.S. Forest and Indian Reservation grazing permits. In Texas, which has had a special heroic and violent history "under six flags," most ranches are owned privately. The ranchers stock their ranges according to what they perceive is best for them. This partially explains the Texan character.

In Canada, where John A. Macdonald sent out a mounted police force[1] in 1874 before the land was leased2 to ranchers (1881-82), overgrazing was far less severe. Canadian leases were generally rated too high in carrying capacity but this was nowhere as bad as letting hired guns determine the number of cows on any range.

In 1930, Prime Minister McKenzie King turned over natural resources, including crown lands, to the prairie provinces (to prevent them from voting for R.B. Bennett – it didn't work and Bennett was elected). Over time, Alberta and Saskatchewan worked out reasonable stocking rates which could be maintained even in drought years. British Columbia, which had been a province since 1870, controlled most of its grazing lands by issuing annual (but renewable) grazing permits, as well as a few long-term leases. Even so, much of the good grasslands in the western provinces were overgrazed until the thirties. The great drought forced rationalization after much damage had been done.

Most of "occupied" Manitoba is farmland and was taken up by homesteaders. The sandhills around Carberry are not suited to farming and so are used for grazing. Overgrazing need not be a severe problem there because of the relatively high rainfall and the high water table under the sand. However, where "she was et to the ground," the sand took over and pastures turned into dunes. Farming attempts in this dune area were disastrous, leading to it's return to grass – where possible.

The major difference between the sandhills of Carberry in Manitoba and the Great Sandhills of Saskatchewan is about eight inches (20 cm) of rain. In Manitoba you can conduct "humid-area agriculture," but southwestern Saskatchewan is dry-dry. Not only does the lack of rainfall demand different farming techniques, it also requires a different approach to weather, banks, machine companies, land tenure, education, capitalization, the roles of government and women and the philosophy of the operator.

A person steeped in humid-area agriculture does not understand the Great Plains of North America or the people who live and work there. And one of the things he doesn't understand is what happens to grass in a dry country when animals eat it or people drive over it. It's not the same at all as what happens in Simcoe County or along the banks of the Wabash.

The first thing to learn about a dry-land range is its fragility. You shouldn't play golf or tennis on it. The passing of a wheel[3] is harmful and too many feet soon make a trail where the grass does not grow – this year or 20 years from now. When we look for "a nice grassy place" for a picnic or to pitch a tent, we rarely realize what harm we do. In humid areas the damage is minimal – the grass soon grows back. But not on dry range, where it may take years to repair the damage done by an afternoon softball game. As for motor bikes and "quads," they are prime desert-makers.

The science of range management and years of rancher experience teach us that grazing must be carefully controlled. Take half, leave half is a common rule. That is you only use half of a year's growth. In arid and semi-arid country take only a third. To an Easterner, that's "wasting" half to two-thirds of your production. Another rule is to "rest" a pasture at least one year out of three – better two of three – during the "grand period of growth," the few weeks when the grass is growing vigorously and increasing the size of its roots, as well as its stems.

This is when the grass is greenest and most lush and the temptation to use it is irresistible to most cattlemen. Of course, the grass should not be grazed between the time it starts to grow and the grand period of growth, for then it is "living" off the carbohydrate reserves in its roots. When ranchers are told this by range managers, they say, "What do you expect me to do with my cows? Put them in cold storage? They've got to eat every day."

That's the rub. But if you have cows and grass, you can keep your cattle grazing and your grass growing – if you know how and plan ahead.

Not every one knows how. Many are like me who as a boy learned "all there was to know" about cattle breeding from a nice old Scotsman and my own father; and about grass that you couldn't use it too hard and if it rained that sure helped. Stockmen have been eager students of cattle diseases and nutrition but they have resisted new knowledge of cattle genetics and they have been just as slow to concern themselves with the science of range management.

When I say to some of my cattlemen friends that I am going to a range-management meeting, they aren't quite sure what I mean. And other people who should be vitally interested in the subject – fish and game associations, wilderness advocates, environmental consultants, outdoor recreationists and ecologists of all kinds and many politicians – equate range managers with ranchers. This is much like equating hospitals and funeral parlors – they both deal with people who have died, don't they?

There are two main reasons why many stockmen aren't interested in grass management. First, in the short term they can't afford it. If you overstock your grass by 50 percent, you will harvest between 30 and 40 percent more pounds of beef (and income), for awhile, perhaps a long while. You need the income and it would be foolish to cut back and "waste" the grass. Then, one year, you're out of grass. And you, like our bankrupt Federal government, can't afford to do much planning or renewal. (In the last two decades this has happened all over the Sahel, in Africa, where most of the grazing now comes from annual grasses.)

On the Canadian farm or small ranch, herd numbers have to be sharply cut and, more often than not, beef production then continues for years at a sub-optimal level under poor management. On big ranches a common approach to grass use is to simply reduce numbers so that the grass handles the herd easily without much management. Rest-rotation? Grand period of growth? Why worry about all this newfangled stuff? We keep our range productive and make a nice living doing what we're doing.

Drive from Calgary to Banff in June, 1989. Forty miles (65 km) out, you pass through the Indian Reserve at Morley. On either side of the road you see bands of mares with young foals. The grass is green and there is still enough of it to keep the mares and little foals happy and contented. It is a delightful pastoral scene.

But if you are a range manager you are appalled. First, this level pasture is a thin-soiled gravel flat. The kind of grasses that naturally grow here are deep-rooted (therefore tall – remember in biology, as much above ground as below!). These grasses should be allowed to grow in the summer and then used in the winter after the above-ground parts have died. By grazing the tall grasses short in the summer, you weaken or kill them and they are replaced by short-stem unproductive plants which can better withstand the horses' teeth. If they are short-stemmed, they are also shallow-rooted and their short roots find precious little water in the gravel. The net result is scant summer grazing and zilch winter grazing – and this on a field which, with its long grasses, if used wisely would be a wonderful place for stock in the winter. This field[4] should never be grazed in the summer. But the horseman says, "I want to keep a close eye on my young colts, where else can I run my mares?"

The other reason for bad grass management by so many is that the subject appears neither simple nor easily mastered – egg-head stuff. You don't become qualified by reading the last six paragraphs – though that might help! It's the kind of subject where you have to get a grasp of the basic principles first and then apply them to your place. And after you understand these principles, there is much detailed learning to be done, such as the identification of the grasses and other plants on the range, and being able to tell if the "good" grasses are increasing or decreasing. Can I tell what less desirable grasses and other plants are invading my land? How do I plan a year's grazing on my various pastures? Five years' grazing? Provision for a dry year? How do I measure the "condition" of my grass?

The artificial-insemination programs on ranches in the seventies, responding to the Exotics boom, had an unexpected bonus: ranchers learned a lot about grass management. To have a small field with enough grass to hold the herd during the three to six weeks of the program required that it be rested the balance of the year. And keeping the herd in these small quarters for that short time meant that a main pasture was being rested during the grand period of growth – for several years in a row.

The results could be startling. In my little field where 220 cows ran for two weeks, from mid-June to July 1, and then were never let back till the next year and there was a great increase in the number of alfalfa plants. When we first started, I hadn't realized there was any alfalfa there at all. Five years later, I had begun to wonder if it were safe (for fear of bloat) to put the cows out into so much alfalfa. There was, of course, a great amount of dry old growth that they had to eat along with the new plants and that seemed to balance things out.

Also the weed yarrow almost disappeared. On the other hand, in the big field, which was rested during the grand period of growth, the grass became more vigorous and productive, and the yarrow increased, too! Apparently the cattle tended to graze it more or less preferentially in June and ignore it later on. To control yarrow, I would have had to reverse my time of use of the two fields perhaps every third year.

Why did the alfalfa increase? It was protected all summer and fall and so went into the winter in strong condition. The standing plants trapped the snow which provided a blanket to shield the crowns from frost.

Also the plants matured and went to seed each fall and the heavy concentration of hooves in the spring pushed the seeds into the soft ground. When these seeds germinated, there were no cattle to eat off the young shoots – the cows were all in another field – and so the new plants survived.

A new and positive force in grass management in North America came in the eighties from southern Africa in the person of a charismatic protagonist, Allan Savory. Savory introduced two concepts: first, high-intensity, short-term grazing (often referred to as "cell grazing"); second, an holistic approach to grazing, ranching and in fact, living.

In this approach one considers ranch management and work in terms of your goals in three important areas: your personal aspirations (family, lifestyle, personal fulfillment), your economic goals and your hopes for the geography/ecology of the ranch. All decision making and each activity must be measured against these goals. They are all of prime significance; if what you are doing negates or does not carry you forward to your goal, you shouldn't be doing it.

My AI field is an example of high-intensity, short-term grazing. The original theory was to graze everything off a field in a short time and then give the field adequate time to recuperate. There were so many cattle on a small space that the unpalatable grasses and forbs, as well as the cows' favorites, all got chewed off. Compare this with conventional pasturage where daily the cow selects the "good" grasses in a big field and thus depletes them, while the undesirables are ignored and so thrive and increase.

Some practical Alberta ranchers, who must provide a year's grazing in the few short weeks the grass is growing, have modified this system. They leave the herd in a field until regrowth just begins on the few favorite plants grazed when the cattle were first turned in; the remaining wolfy "rough" will be chewed off during the dormant season.

The second advantage to the cell system is that every field is rested, at least for a while, during the grand period of growth. So, total production increases. If you are giving your best grasses a break and are also raising more grass, you should have it made.

Another benefit of crowding many cattle onto a limited area for a short period results from the trampling into the ground of many grass seeds – seeds produced through the years and lying dormant.[5] After the next good rains, new grass shoots spring up all over. Savory has recommended this procedure to the state of Montana to combat knapweed, a noxious and vicious weed which has taken over huge areas. After the initial heavy grazing, the ranges will have to be protected to allow the new grass to compete with the knapweed. The knapweed will not be eliminated but will be sharply reduced. It then will probably take a vast army of "controlled" insects to beat (eat) the knapweed into the ground (biological control). So far, attempts at chemical control have been ineffective and expensive.

Savory's cell systems initially didn't come cheap or easy. The rancher had to fence his fields into small paddocks, each of which had to be provided with water. In addition, he had to move his herd every few days – in some instances hours. This required more capital and labor. In the summer of 1983 I visited some range pastures belonging to the University of Montana, just west of Bozeman. The research fellows were instituting a short-term, high-intensity program as a field trial. They got about half the fencing done – and then ran out of money and had to wait for the next appropriation. The same thing can happen to private ranchers – who might not have a next appropriation!

Professional range managers weren't exactly happy with Savory when they first heard of his systems. They knew about high-intensity grazing; in fact, such a system had been used by researchers at the University of Alberta to kill out aspen poplar trees by "forcing" steers to eat them when the sap was young and flowing. Most of the pros felt Savory had oversimplified the problem, that each situation required specific analysis and then management according to what had to be done to improve and sustain production. They were particularly concerned about very dry areas, where high intensity of any duration might be disastrous.

In the past decade much research has been done on grazing intensity and duration of grazing periods. What is the way to go? From what

I read, as with all complicated problems, it all depends. But Savory is gaining a wider and wider discipleship.

He does this by introducing holistic concepts. You gain these concepts by both revelation and reason. The good news is imparted to you at schools and seminars that Savory and his group conduct. You enroll, pay your fees, take the course, embrace the holistic philosophy and neither you nor your ranch are ever the same again. There is, enthusiasts say, much more to it than just short-term, high-intensity grazing. And I'm sure there is.

A few paragraphs ago we were passing Morley on the way to Banff National Park. Now let's keep going, past Canmore and through the park gates. Note the high mesh fence on your right. It was put there in 1988 so game – mainly elk – would be kept off the road. Now look at the grass on either side of the fence, grass that was planted by man to restore the wastage of the bulldozers. Beyond the fence, there is little grass; the elk have grazed it close. But on the road side, it is lush, tall and thick, improving every year.

Two lessons here. Grass grows best when protected from grazing animals – at least for a few years. There are too many elk in Banff Park or at least along the fence.

How many elk should there be? And where? Thirty-five years ago (before there was a four-lane highway or a fence) I visited this area with a group of professional range managers and we looked at what the elk were doing to the grass. Guess what? Overgrazing. The park wardens knew it and were quietly carrying out a "depopulation" program, hoping that those nice animal lovers in Toronto wouldn't hear about it.

The idea back then among wildlife enthusiasts was to leave all the plants and animals alone in the park; let Nature manage things. Of course, we should put out the fires and "do something" about the bears but the elk were sacred. The plan now seems to be to keep animal populations high enough for people to see them but not so high as to damage the environment.

Adjusting an elk population to a pasturage is not simple. Some government administrators have thought it was. Perhaps the strangest hiatus of mixed forces throbs away in and around the National Elk Refuge near Jackson, Wyoming. The number of elk here is many times more than the natural carrying capacity. The government grows grass and buys hay for them all. Years ago the Refuge raised its own hay: recently it's cheaper to buy it. And the former hay lands can now grow grass to pasture even more elk!

The elk summer in high country all around the area, many on nearby ranches and then "go on welfare" through the winter. The main costs are shared: the feds provide the hay[6] and the ranchers provide summer grazing. Meanwhile, the state of Wyoming can sell a great number of elk licenses, which are highly prized because it's not too hard to "get your elk" in this kind of situation.

To supply elk for hunters and to take the pressure off complaining ranchers, state governments have bought out some cattle outfits and set up elk ranches. British Columbia has an elk ranch, too. With no cattle to compete against them, the elk should thrive in their new homes and

" Time to move in on the rancher's haystacks."

leave the ranchers in peace. Surprise! At first quite a few elk did as they were instructed but as time went by more and more of them preferred the ranchers' summer range. They all found the ranchers' hay meadows and stacks irresistible in the winter.

How to explain this ingratitude and perverseness? First we must think of summer grazing and winter grazing as two distinct entities. In almost all big-game areas the limiting factor – what "we need more of" – is winter grazing. In other words, the number of elk in a given range is largely determined by the amount of winter feed. Elk are both grazers (they eat grass) and browsers (they eat barbs, twigs, leaves, young stems) and will adjust their diet according to what is available. Given their druthers, they eat grass. In fact, before settlement they grazed the prairie along with the buffalo. On the other hand deer, especially mule deer, are browsers by nature and when fed just hay in a zoo, look scruffy.) Cows are mainly grazers and browse a limited amount.

So, elk and cattle can be prime competitors, while deer compete little with cattle. On a high summer range, untouched during the winter's deep snow, both cattle and elk eat grass, with elk competing with deer for browse. The cattle are browsing to some degree, but are competing mainly with elk, very little with deer.

During high summer there usually is enough feed for everybody. The most palatable grass is the regrowth after light grazing or the grass moderately used the previous year. So both elk and cattle congregate in such areas, often overusing them.

They all love alfalfa! Especially in the spring and summer while it's growing and in the fall and winter when it's stacked.

On the specialized elk ranch where cattle are excluded, the summer use is not heavy enough to keep the grazing fresh; the grass matures and after a few years is neither as palatable nor nutritious as it used to be, so the elk migrate to the cattle ranches. There, both cattle and elk keep the grass down, often overgrazing (and damaging) it,[7] while the elks' special domain remains underutilized. The rancher is not happy, for the damage to his summer range is worse than before the government bought the elk their own ranch.

In the winter, things get worse. The old valley hay-lands on the elk ranch grow rank and unharvested all summer. So when the snows push the elk down to lower elevations, where do they go? No contest: to the aftermath of the cattle-ranch hay meadows, green with the protein-rich regrowth stimulated by fall rains and naturally to the hay stacks. When everything is eaten up, the elk are forced back to their own farm, to have a go at the coarse (high in lignin and not nutritious) but abundant feed in the former hay fields.

Ungrazed grass, like the elks' winter field, tends to grow toward *climax* condition, with only one or two species dominating. If lightly or moderately grazed, the climax species will yield a bit to other species, resulting in more variation in the cover. Both biologists and environmentalists (as well as ranchers!) consider such species diversity a *good thing* because a variable population is more resistant to stress. This diversity (and improved range condition) is often best achieved by completely resting the area one year out of three and grazing it at different times during the other two.

Elk go over fences with the greatest of ease, so they cannot be managed like cattle. The best elk management comes from moving cattle in and among them during their summer grazing and by using cattle to "freshen up" their rank lowland winter feed by limited and controlled grazing. This encourages the elk to "camp" where they should be in the winter. If cattle are allowed to do this, then the rancher must be willing to reduce the stocking rate on his own place and share his grass with the elk. I saw this occurring in the summer of 1987 near the little village of Glen in southwest Montana. In a remarkable arrangement, rancher Maynard Smith and a nearby state elk ranch, together with the administrator of federal lands, have worked out a management program that provides more feed for both the elk and Smith's cattle – while benefitting the range!

" It took humans a long time to realize that we animals complement each other on the range."

There's a lesson in the Smith elk story – actually several lessons. The prime one is that there are usually more than one (obvious) use for a piece of rangeland; here we have game animals and livestock, each with a valid claim for its use. The rival users benefit if they co-operate to manage and share the resource. In this case both the rancher and the hunters are happier. Without working together everybody would be worse off; with a co-operative agreement, the sum adds up to much more than zero.

The biggest concession was made by the wildlife people. They recognized that the game wasn't free for the taking and that they had to make a contribution. So their agency bought a ranch. Then they found they could benefit themselves in several ways by working with the rancher, rather than opposing him. The difficult concept for them to accept was that cattle actually improved the elk range and provided more and healthier game. But it was so.

And I hope they tell the Smith elk story to fish-and-game people everywhere. Too many hunters and naturalists believe that the elimination of cattle from public lands will automatically improve and increase the game. I hope they will learn to think about range holistically and about cattle positively.

The cattle industry had to make concessions, too. There are now fewer total cattle using the same area in that part of Montana. Somebody, in this case the State Fish and Wildlife Department, had to buy out a ranch. So the cattle that used to run on that ranch are now gone – fewer total cattle in the area. The important lesson is that the remaining cattle can help make the elk range better. The sharing of a managed resource – or the managing of a shared resource – is a much better solution than excluding one or the other of the users.

Let's look at the Banff Park fence again – one that no elk can jump! I'm certainly not advocating any cattle be grazed in the park. But let's do a few what-ifs.

If a few cattle were grazed every third[8] summer in the high areas, where feed is abundant, this would improve the grazing for the elk and entice them away from the fence. Then, in the winter, the feed available to the elk along the fence would be more abundant. As compensation, the ranchers would be expected to provide winter grazing[9] – perhaps even some hay – for elk. (Near Waterton Park, they are already doing this free – in spades!)

Following this plan, the elk are better fed winter and summer and grass along the highway has a better chance to grow and become more productive. The rancher's benefit is more summer grazing for his herd.

Unfortunately, when considering conventional ranches outside the park, sportsmen and environmentalists, who don't understand the principles of range management, have shown little interest in discussing rational game-l;ivestock management proposals.

The eventual solution must be to rationalize game as a resource, with users paying the costs of maintaining the resource as well as harvesting it. This is the way it works in all mature societies but we are too close to frontier times for this method to be politically acceptable yet. So discord and injustice will prevail for quite a few more years, at the expense of the environment and those who raise cattle. In North America food is so abundant and so cheap (taking less than 15 percent of our income) that its production is near the bottom of the priority ladder. Much more important to use the great outdoors to have fun. Or perhaps not even use it at all – just sit quietly at home, knowing it (like the Queen) is out there, somewhere.

Which brings up the question: why raise beef cattle at all? In most parts of the world, the answer is: don't do it. Use your better land, where rainfall is adequate, to grow cereal crops. If you must use cattle to keep up the land's fertility level, raise dairy cattle because milk is such a wonderful food. Or at least raise dual-purpose cattle as they do in much of Europe. When you look at the globe, you find that only in the Americas, Africa and Australasia are there real beef-cattle spreads. And here they are on land that is too infertile, too dry, too hilly, too stony, too subject to frost for cereal production.

True enough, in France and Italy and parts of Germany there are true beef breeds and specialized beef production. But these activities are vestigial: until the end of World War II, the forerunners of these cattle were plow oxen. Since then, they have remained only because of huge subsidies paid to farmers. Raising beef in France or Ireland or Italy makes no economic sense (except as a soil-conservation technique!) unless governments keep out South American and Oceanic imports and subsidize local farmers at twice the going world rate, as well as also subsidizing the export of surplus production to North America. Of course they are awash in a sea of subsidized milk as well, so they figure if they're going to raise cattle, they can help the milk surplus by staying with Charolais rather than Friesians.

In Chapter 18, "Not By Bread Alone," we saw how much of the world's agricultural land will disappear – or already has disappeared – unless ruminant animals become part of the productive mix. But short-term economics don't like beef production, especially the cow-and-calf part. Ruminant grazing in the short term is just not the "highest and best use" of productive land. It takes about six tons of dry feed – grass, hay, straw – to produce a weaned calf. It takes less than three tons of dry grain to raise that calf to a big slaughter-weight steer two and a half times the size of the weaned calf.

In North America the rule is for cows and calves to be found where there is cheap grass and finishing steers where there is cheap grain. The cattle from the American range states tend to be fed out on irrigated crops in Colorado, Arizona and Texas[10] and in the corn states along the Mississippi and Missouri Rivers.

The grazing of range by cattle justifies grain feeding later. By using the two resources together, we obtain more high-protein food more cheaply and at less strain to the environment than by "going it alone" – on all high priced land, as in the Loire valley of France, or on all low-capacity out-back, as in Australia.

In Chapter Sixteen, "Adding Tenderness," we saw that the fattening cattle with grain is a uniquely North American industry. It grew up as a means of selling Iowa corn. With grain feeding came a high degree of fattening, for it was cheaper to put a pound of gain on a corn-fed steer in a pen than it was to buy another pound of feeder calf or yearling raised on grass. The U.S. grades of Prime and Choice could never have evolved without this unique method of marketing corn from the mid-west states. But before there can be a great cattle-feeding industry, there must be grass-covered hills and plains where cows can raise their calves.

In Britain there always had been a few head fattened on "meal" but there, and most everywhere else, cattle reached market weight and market finish on pastures – on grass and legumes. The "grazier" bought "store" (stocker) cattle and grazed them until they were ready for slaughter.

Grain feeding in Australia, essentially a pastoral land, developed recently in response to demand from Japan for limited amounts of fat beef. The Japanese have bought or financed "stations" (ranches) and packing houses in Australia. Now they're doing it in the U.S. They produce a special product at home near the city of Kobe (often called Kobe beef but more properly Wagyu beef, after the name of the breed which produces it). The animal, preferably a heifer, is fat, mature, slow-fed over a long time (with grains, even beer!) and massaged by the handler, supposedly to improve the marbling and texture. The meat is served in extremely thin slices and costs a fortune. As you might expect, the Japanese don't allow any foreigners to buy Wagyu cattle or their semen or embryos. They consider the breed a national treasure. However, they haven't quite been able to keep it all to themselves: Wagyu semen from "percentage" bulls (with some Wagyu in them) is available in North America and the pure stuff can be bought in Oceania.

New Zealand raises grass-fat beef on steep, hilly pastures. New Zealanders make more money with sheep, by selling wool as well as meat but they need cattle to "eat off the rough." The cattle improve the pasture for sheep grazing.

In Argentina the big *estancias* produce two-year-old cattle on grass, which are fattened on alfalfa pastures in the more humid areas near the east coast. For years the natural market for Argentinean beef was in England; since the advent of the Common Market, Britain no longer takes southern hemisphere beef in quantity.

Both Australia and New Zealand, formerly dependent on the British market, now export to North America, the highest-priced accessible market in the world (apart from Japan which is not yet a free market).

The U.S. has a restrictive meat import law which keeps Australian imports in check but poor old helpful Canada lets too much of the stuff pour in (mainly manufacturing beef not suitable for roasts or steaks). And then we ship beef and many of our young cattle (both feeders and fats) as well as cull cows to the U.S. Meanwhile our packers lose business and employ fewer people.

Canada occupies a sad, silly and unique position in the world beef trade: in 1992 we imported more beef per capita than any other country but we still exported 30 percent of our domestic product. As recently as December, 1992, the Western Stock Growers' Association requested the federal government to enact a "Meat Import Act similar to the United States Act" to deal with this problem. Don't hold your breath: Canada is known for being a sucker on the world scene and we are applauded for our generosity.

Is the writing on the wall? The open range has long since gone; how long will the modern ranch last? If the wilderness enthusiasts have their way, ranching is doomed. Tree huggers have a potential for much larger political leverage than the handful of ranchers operating on government land. Consider the seal hunt in Newfoundland which was shut down by emotional appeal. Now the seals have become so numerous that the fish stocks are disappearing. So the Newfoundlanders have received a double whammy. In cases like this, reason and rationality don't count for much.

If you look at the world holistically, keeping our soils in mind, you come to realize that a beef-eater is a far better environmentalist than is a vegetarian. Somehow, someone must figure out a way of telling people that food doesn't come from the grocery store, that a resource must be used if we are to make a living and eat. That all consumption may be harmful to a degree and that the best choices are those which minimize damage to the environment or, better still, improve it. Such a choice is the raising of ruminant animals on wooded and grassland agricultural soils as an adjunct to cereal production and on rangelands under carefully managed regimes in conjunction with other regulated activities such as forestry, mining and recreation.

If we handle our cows right, they can provide us with meat and milk from lands too poor or too dry or too rocky or too cold or too steep to farm. On our better lands they can ensure soil productivity – so that grains can be grown there – for a thousand more years.

By the Way . . .

[1]Though it isn't part of the heroic history of the North West Mounted Police, an important function of the police patrols was to evict "squatters" and "nesters" from ranchers' leases.

[2]Politics and leases have strong mutual affinity. John A. gave the first 100 000-acre lease to his good Conservative friend and neighbor Matthew Cochrane. And when the provinces took over public lands, politics were not ignored. In Saskatchewan during the CCF heyday it helped to be a friend. I was told by a former employee of the CCF government who dealt with grazing lease allocations that he always used to check the application to see if a CCF membership card were attached. In Alberta tradition was also maintained: when a Social Credit scandal in the Lethbridge area was in full bloom during the late fifties, I asked a rancher in southern Alberta (a loyal Social Crediter, of course) if the scandal offended him. His reply: "Yeah, sure. But what's a bit of scandal when you know who to talk to if you need a little extra lease?"

[3]Just east of the little village of DeWinton are the wheel tracks of the Macleod Trail, where the bull trains first passed 120 years ago on the long haul from Fort Benton on the Missouri River to Fort Calgary. This old trail became obsolete in 1890 when the Calgary-Macleod railway was built and has not been used for a hundred years.

[4]In the summer of 1991, good range management in this area meant that he rested field was producing a good hay crop. Chalk up a plus for the Stoney Indians.

[5]Research done by the Lethbridge Research Station at Stavely, Alberta, indicates that such concentration and the resulting trampling is actually harmful if the field is not also rested.

[6]Excess buffalo from nearby Yellowstone Park appear at – and break up – the elk feedracks in the winter. The Refuge managers are upset by this because they "have no budget for bison." Nor do area ranchers, whose haystacks are just as appealing to the elk and bison as are the government hand-outs.

[7]Botany lesson: young grass shoot has a growing point or meristem. If clipped or grazed *above* this point it simply keeps on growing, producing palatable forage. But if clipped or grazed *below* the meristem, the grass' new growth must then restart from the root, thus depleting the plant's resources and reducing its vigor; of course, slowing down and reducing new production. This explains why wild

horses, which graze much closer than cattle, do so much damage to a range. So do sheep with their slit upper lips and so do hares.

[8]Good range management usually requires two years' rest for each year's use in critical areas.

[9]Canada Parks estimates that 3 200 elk summer in Banff Park but only 1 600 head winter there. Half the herd leaves the park to winter on provincial forestry lands and on adjacent ranches.

[10]The Cactus Lake feedlot in the Texas Panhandle has a capacity of 800 000 head.

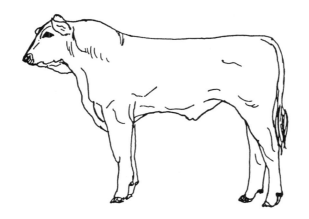

Chianina

Blonde d'Aquitaine

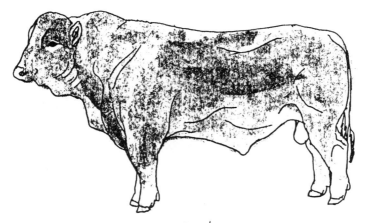

Salers

Pinzgauer

Maine-Anjou

Hay's Converter